The Consequences
of Confederate
Citizenship

Jeff,

Thanks for your friendship and support for the last half-century (almost). I will always be deeply grateful.

Mel

P.S.: The handwriting is not so great these days

Conflicting Worlds

NEW DIMENSIONS OF
THE AMERICAN CIVIL WAR

T. Michael Parrish, Series Editor

The Consequences of Confederate Citizenship

THE CIVIL WAR
CORRESPONDENCE
OF ALABAMA'S
PICKENS FAMILY

EDITED, WITH COMMENTARY AND
NOTES, BY *Henry M. McKiven Jr.*

Louisiana State University Press

BATON ROUGE

Published by Louisiana State University Press
lsupress.org

Designer: Kaelin Chappell Broaddus
Typefaces: Adobe Caslon Pro, text; Bonhomme Richard, display

Letters within the Pickens Family Papers are reproduced with the permission of the Doy
Leale McCall Rare Book and Manuscript Library, University of South Alabama.

Cover photograph: Umbria, the Pickens family home. Prints
and Photographs Division, Library of Congress.

Library of Congress Cataloging-in-Publication Data

Names: Pickens (Family : 1817– : Greene County, Ala.), author. | McKiven,
    Henry M., editor, writer of added commentary.
Title: The consequences of Confederate citizenship : the Civil War
    correspondence of Alabama's Pickens family / edited, with commentary and
    notes, by Henry M. McKiven Jr.
Other titles: Conflicting worlds.
Description: Baton Rouge : Louisiana State University Press, [2025] |
    Series: Conflicting worlds: new dimensions of the American Civil War |
    Includes bibliographical references and index.
Identifiers: LCCN 2024048447 (print) | LCCN 2024048448 (ebook) | ISBN
    978-0-8071-8367-0 (cloth) | ISBN 978-0-8071-8429-5 (epub) | ISBN 978-0-8071-8430-1
    (pdf)
Subjects: LCSH: Pickens family—Correspondence. | Confederate States of
    America. Army. Alabama Infantry Regiment, 5th. Company D—Military life.
    | Group identity—Confederate States of America. | Plantation
    owners—Alabama—Greene County—Correspondence. | Rich
    people—Alabama—Greene County—Correspondence. | United
    States—History—Civil War, 1861–1865—Personal narratives, Confederate.
    | LCGFT: Personal correspondence. | Biographies.
Classification: LCC E467 .P5833 2025 (print) | LCC E467 (ebook) | DDC
    973.7/82—dc23/eng/20250203
LC record available at https://lccn.loc.gov/2024048447
LC ebook record available at https://lccn.loc.gov/2024048448

CONTENTS

CONTENTS

Photographs follow page 138.

The Consequences of Confederate Citizenship

Introduction

The Pickens correspondence includes the letters James and Samuel Pickens wrote home while serving in the Army of Northern Virginia, and the letters their mother and siblings wrote to them. Most collections of Civil War letters, whether published or unpublished, are limited to the letters soldiers sent home. Letters soldiers received from home were often lost in battle or were not recovered when a soldier died. Those collections that do include letters to and from home tend to be between husbands and wives.[1] There is a relative dearth of correspondence between soldiers and their parents and siblings.[2] The Pickens family correspondence is exceptional in that it opens a window through which the reader may observe a well-educated and articulate mother, her daughter, and her sons in the army as they expressed the fears, anxiety, and depression that the war imposed on them all, while seeking to reassure each other that they would soon be reunited and resume the privileged lives that the labor of over two hundred enslaved people provided. Through their letters, the Pickenses bore witness to each other's experience as they sought reassurance that their sacrifices for the Confederate nation would not be in vain. All struggled to transcend what many historians have argued was an "unbridgeable" gap between home front and battlefront.[3]

1. A recent example is Davis and Bell, eds., *The Whartons' War*.
2. See, for example, Pate, ed., *When This Evil War Is Over*.
3. Martha Hanna, "A Republic of Letters"; Bonner, *The Soldier's Pen*, 6–8.

The Pickenses in January of 1861 regarded the possibility of a war over secession as unlikely. They left their home, Umbria, in Greene County and traveled to Raleigh, North Carolina, where four of Mary Gaillard Pickens's children would continue their education. Mary Gaillard's sons, Sam and James, traveled on from Raleigh to Charlottesville, Virginia, where they had attended school since 1859. After arriving in Raleigh, Mary Gaillard grew increasingly anxious about the possibility of war. Her fear when reading Sam's and James's dispatches from school was that one or both might join their classmates who were volunteering for the Confederate Army. Sam and James excitedly wrote in defense of secession and of their hope that Virginia would join Alabama in leaving the Union. Worried that her sons' zealous defense of secession might lead them to volunteer for the army, Mary Gaillard advised them to stay in school and let others do the fighting, while they supported the Confederacy in other ways. She was relieved when Sam and James wrote to assure her that they had no plans to join the Confederate Army. Kenneth Noe has identified men like Sam and James as "reluctant rebels." Unlike the majority of the men in Noe's database, the Pickens brothers' correspondence with their mother in 1861 reveals the tension between devotion to Confederate independence and loyalty to family. Their letters were those of eager rebels but reluctant soldiers. Although they were fully committed to Confederate nationhood, they well understood the emotional toll service in the army would inflict upon their mother.[4] Thus, when the family returned to Alabama in the summer of 1861, neither Sam nor James volunteered. Instead, they did as their mother wanted and defended the Confederacy in the fall of 1861 by supervising two hundred enslaved people on three plantations as they reduced cotton production in order to expand the production of food crops to help meet the demands of the Confederate armies and of the families of soldiers.

As the military situation deteriorated in the spring of 1862, the demands of the Confederate state forced a redefinition of the obligations of Confederate citizenship. With the passage of the Conscription Act of 1862, the government mandated that male citizens serve in the army if they were not exempt for medical or other reasons or could provide a substitute. At the

4. Noe, *Reluctant Rebels*, 8–10.

time, Sam was serving as a ninety-day volunteer, having responded to Governor John Gill Shorter's call for men to defend Mobile after the city's garrison had been sent to defend Corinth, Mississippi, from advancing Union troops. With passage of the act, Shorter transferred the volunteers to the Confederate Army for the duration of the war. Under the Conscription Act, men already in the army could not hire a substitute. Sam had the option of joining his hometown unit, Company D, Fifth Alabama Infantry Regiment, Rodes's division, Stonewall Jackson's corps, Army of Northern Virginia, or going wherever the army sent him as a conscript. He objected to the circumstances that landed him in the army, as did his mother, but he had no legal way out and would leave Umbria Plantation in November to join Company D in the Shenandoah Valley. Beginning with the Battle of Fredericksburg, Sam would fight in every major engagement of the Army of Northern Virginia until his capture at Petersburg in April 1865.

Unable to keep Sam out of the army, Mary Gaillard feared that James would also be drafted. In letters to Sam while he was in Mobile at a camp of instruction in the spring of 1862, she emphasized the need to keep James out of the army. Her concern was not that she was unable to manage the family and the plantations without his assistance—she had been doing that for years. Her fear, and Sam's, was that James, whose health was fragile, would not be able to endure the rigors of life in the army, emotionally or physically. After initially suggesting that he wanted to accompany Sam to the Virginia front, James agreed with his mother and Sam that he could better serve the cause and help the family by staying at home. With the assistance of Sam and family connections, James secured a substitute. He remained at home until 1864, when the Confederate Congress passed another conscription act requiring those who had hired substitutes to enter the army.

Mary Gaillard had devoted her life to protecting her family and had always suffered anxiety and depression when separated from any of her children, but under Confederate conscription laws her sons were required to serve in the army. As her letters reveal, this "redefinition of women's sacrifice," as historian Drew Faust has written, was emotionally wrenching for Mary Gaillard.[5] But, as a believer in providential Christianity, Mary Gaillard could

5. Faust, "Altars of Sacrifice," 1209.

3

only accept what she saw as part of an unknowable divine plan. Through-out the war she looked to her faith in God to comprehend the emotional suffering the war inflicted on her and her children and to protect her sons from death. As she reminded Sam and James often in her letters, although God's intent was only known to him, it was to God that they must look as they faced the existential threat of combat. If she ever read Confederate propaganda that urged families to write soldiers "encouraging and cheerful letters," Mary Gaillard and the rest of the family generally ignored it.[6] Mary, for example, never concealed the emotional turmoil she suffered each day as she imagined the possibility that Sam's name might one day appear on a list of the dead. Such honest expression of her emotional distress was intended to reassure her son that the bonds of family remained strong and that she and his siblings supported him and the cause for which he fought. Mary's grudging acceptance of Sam's departure never evolved into disillusion with the Confederate struggle. Rather, her commitment to the success of the war grew stronger. Most letters included some expression of hope that God would favor the Confederacy with a victory over its enemies that would secure Confederate independence.[7] In her view, only Confederate victory would restore her family and the life she had enjoyed before the war.

James's letters to Sam also tried to reassure him that the family supported him and the Confederate cause. While he included accounts of the family's social lives and news of friends, James devoted more attention to business, political, and military affairs than his mother did. His letters reveal how closely civilians followed the opposition in the North to the Lincoln admin-istration, hoping that Confederate military success would so erode support for the Union war effort that the United States would be forced to end the war on Confederate terms. As the correspondence reveals, the Pickenses loyally accepted Confederate policies intended to provide for the army even before Sam's enlistment. With Sam's departure for the Virginia front, that commitment deepened and became personal; support for the Confederacy was support for Sam and, later, James.

6. *Southern Republic,* July 20, 1861.

7. On religion and Confederate identity, see Rable, *God's Almost Chosen Peoples;* Ott, *Confederate Daughters,* 2; Quigley, *Shifting Grounds,* 10–11.

Sam's sister Mary's letters between 1862 and the summer of 1864 kept Sam informed about the family's social life. She filled them with news about friends whom the family visited and who visited Umbria, all intended to lift Sam's spirits and do her part for the war effort.[8] Judging from her correspondence, she assumed most responsibility for gathering clothing and other items to be sent to Sam and her fiancé, Captain Tom Biscoe of the Fifth Louisiana Infantry Regiment.[9] Mary's early letters always reassured Sam that that she and the family intended to preserve the life he had left and was defending in the army, in anticipation of his eventual, and triumphal, return. Mary's generally lighthearted tone changed, however, in 1864, when Biscoe was killed at the Battle of Spotsylvania. Her letters describing her depression and struggle to find meaning in Tom's death offer insight into the devastating emotional toll the war exacted.

Sam tailored his letters in response to what each correspondent had written to him. When he wrote his mother, he always sought to allay her anxiety and to assure her of his devotion, before offering his advice about business issues she had raised. His conversation with James addressed problems managing the plantations as well. But James was the correspondent in the family who wanted to discuss military and political affairs, and Sam obliged, to a limited extent. With Mary he engaged in conversations about literature and the social life of the family. Then, with the death of Mary's fiancé, Sam struggled through his letters to help her manage her debilitating grief. Although the letters to each correspondent differed in content and tone, there was a common theme that ran through the narrative of the war Sam constructed for his family. His mother insisted that he write as honestly about his experience as she did, assuring him that only by knowing everything could she be relieved of the emotional strain that not knowing inflicted, but Sam's descriptions of combat and his life in camp were sanitized versions of the bloody scenes he witnessed and the miserable conditions he experienced in camp.

8. On the ways young women such as Mary sought to support the Confederate cause, see Rable, *Civil Wars*, 137–39, and Ott, *Confederate Daughters*.

9. Biscoe commanded Company K of the Fifth Louisiana Infantry Regiment. See Compiled Service Records of Confederate Soldiers, National Archives (CMSR), Louisiana, RG 109, rolls 0155 and 0148.

His few descriptions of battle imposed an order on the chaos he experienced, allowing his correspondents to imagine a level of control over his fate that he knew did not exist.[10] Knowing that all, especially his mother, feared for his well-being and his survival, Sam devoted attention to the routines of camp life, the rigors of long marches, his constant longing for the war to be over so he could return home, and his confidence that the Confederate armies would ultimately prevail. Although the Pickenses kept up with the war in the newspapers, their understanding of the Confederate struggle was largely shaped by Sam's reassuring correspondence.[11]

After reform of Confederate conscription policy in late 1863 and early 1864, James could no longer avoid military service. The exemption for one man on plantations with twenty or more enslaved people did not apply to James because the family had already used that provision for an overseer. James reluctantly left Alabama in March 1864 to join Company D in Virginia.[12] While in Alabama assisting his mother, James had written Sam letters in which he expressed his wish to serve the Confederacy as a soldier as Sam was doing. He was aware of the increasing marginalization of men who remained at home as "shirkers" and deadbeats who took advantage of the crisis to advance their own selfish ends. As James watched his brother and friends march off to war, he struggled to reconcile his status with the ideals of southern manhood. In letters to Sam, he justified his decision to avoid military service as essential to the defense of the Pickens family, a justification his family and, for the most part, the community accepted. Yet James could never escape the nagging fear that he could not measure up to the men in the Confederate Army, whom he admired. And then, when he entered the army, he found the physical and emotional demands too much to bear. When he first faced the enemy at the Battle of the Wilderness, in early May 1864, he suffered a complete emotional collapse. In James's letters to his mother while being treated in military hospitals in Virginia, he expressed

10. Roper, "Nostalgia," 445–48.

11. On the importance of soldiers' letters in shaping the civilian understanding of the war and reinforcing civilian commitment to the Confederate nation, see Gallagher, *The Confederate War*, 74–76.

12. Sacher, *Confederate Conscription*, 217–21. The overseer was William Lawless. See Mary Gaillard Pickens to Sam Pickens, August 22, 1863, in chapter 6, below.

little shame over his performance as a soldier that he and the family had predicted.[13] Rather, the letters were long confessions of guilt over his failure to find a way to remain at home to take care of the family.

The story the Pickens correspondence tells is not one of material deprivation. The family never suffered from lack of food or other shortages as did their poorer countrymen. In the army, Samuel and James were shielded from the worst conditions in camp by their enslaved "body servant," John. Yet, as the letters attest, all families of soldiers in both the Confederate and the Union armies shared the daily fear that a loved one might never return home. In the Confederacy, commitment to defending a way of life dependent upon enslaved people and the shared sacrifice of sons, husbands, and brothers to achieve that goal brought emotional strains that bound all families of soldiers together despite their place on the social scale; sacrifice became more a source of national identity and cohesion rather than of corrosive class conflict that would have made Confederate defeat inevitable. But in 1865, those bonds rapidly broke as those with the most to lose, like the Pickenses, continued to grasp flickering hopes for victory, while their less well-off comrades increasingly gave up and went home to their struggling families.[14] Until the bitter end, the Pickenses believed that somehow the Confederacy, and the world they had known before the war, would survive and ultimately flourish.

The Pickenses were well educated, and their letters usually followed the rules of standard grammar and usage the modern reader will recognize. A few words that might appear misspelled to the modern reader were considered standard in the nineteenth century. For example, the spelling of "connection" as "connexion" was still common at the time. Likewise, abbreviations such as "thro" (through), "tho," and "altho" (although) have been left as written without the insertion of [*sic*]. At times, a correspondent omitted punctuation. I have silently added punctuation when necessary to clarify meaning. Where words and/or phrases were unclear because of damage or quality of handwriting, I have noted the omission in brackets. The Pickenses mention

13. By 1864, breaking in battle was no longer necessarily viewed as a moral failing. See Walsh, "Cowardice Weakness or Infirmity," 492–526; Linderman, *Embattled Courage*, 166–67; McPherson, *For Cause and Comrades*, 76–81.

14. The experience of Sam and James supports Joseph Glatthaar's argument in "Everyman's War," 229–26, and *Soldiering in the Army of Northern Virginia*, chap. 11.

many acquaintances and relatives in their letters and usually describe who they are. When it is unclear who the correspondent was writing about, I have identified in notes those for whom there was enough information in the letters to find them in censuses, directories, newspapers, court records, and/or military records.

ONE

⬧ ⬧ ⬧ ⬧ ⬧

Origins

Samuel Pickens first traveled to Alabama with his brother John in 1817 to begin purchasing land near St. Stephens for their brother Israel, the recently appointed land commissioner in the town. As land commissioner, Israel managed the sale of lands the U.S. government had acquired from natives of the region through warfare and other forms of coercion.[1] The Pickens brothers—Israel, Samuel, John, and Robert—all migrated from North Carolina, near Morganton in Burke County, to the Alabama Territory, where they expected to exploit fertile lands and the enslaved people who produced the cotton the Pickenses hoped would make them wealthy.[2]

When the Pickenses arrived in St. Stephens, government and banking in the Alabama Territory were dominated by men who had migrated into Madison County from the Broad River region of north Georgia. After the collapse of the cotton market in 1820, citizens suffering from the effects of the depression blamed the self-serving financial manipulation of Broad River

---

1. The territory consisted of approximately twenty-three million acres and had been taken from the Creeks (Red Sticks) after the Battle of Horseshoe Bend in the Treaty of Fort Jackson negotiated by Andrew Jackson. See Rothman, *Slave Country*, chap. 5.

2. Israel Pickens to Thomas Lenoir, May 5, 1817; Israel Pickens to Martha Pickens, February 16, 1817, both in Lenoir Family Papers, Southern Historical Collection; Rothman, *Slave Country*, 165–68.

political leaders.[3] Israel Pickens and allies around St. Stephens recognized an opportunity to reshape Alabama politics and reform a banking system they believed to be limiting the economic potential of the new state of Alabama.[4] Samuel Pickens, having secured state office as comptroller, used his connections around the state to build support for Israel's successful races for governor in 1821 and 1823.[5]

After Israel's second term ended, Samuel Pickens left government and moved to property he had been buying in Greene County, near Greensboro. The Pickens brothers had decided to move to Greene and nearby Marengo County, where the land was more productive and the disease environment less deadly than St. Stephens. With liberal loans from the state and private banks, Pickens joined his new neighbors in buying more land for cotton and more enslaved persons. By 1835 he was one of the wealthiest and best-connected men in Greene County.

Still unmarried, Pickens offered a promising match for the daughters of the emerging elite of Greensboro. Soon after moving to his land, about fifteen miles west of Greensboro, Richard Meade, a Virginia native who served with Samuel as a vestryman for the recently established Episcopal Church, introduced Pickens to his daughter, Mary. He and Mary began courting and married on September 11, 1830. At the time, Pickens was living in a home that was not much more than a frontier cabin. Wanting to provide a suitable home for his new wife, Pickens began building a large, impressive home on the Umbria Plantation, near Hollow Square.[6] But Mary did not live to see the completion of the house; she died in in December 1830 of unknown causes.

Depressed over the death of Mary, Pickens traveled frequently during the next few years seeking distraction from his grief. He frequently returned

3. Thornton, *Politics and Power*, 10–13.

4. Brantley, *Banking in Alabama*, 16–19; William Crawford to Pope, July 30, 1819, Bloom and Carter, eds., *The Territorial Papers of the United States: Alabama Territory*, 662–63.

5. E. L. Toulmin to Samuel Pickens Jr., November 2, 1820; unaddressed Israel Pickens letter, December 6, 1820; George Buchanan to Samuel Pickens Jr., July 30, 1821; J. Fisher to Samuel Pickens Jr., April 28, 1821; E. L. Toulmin to Samuel Pickens Jr., August 20, 1821, all in Pickens Family Papers; Thornton, *Politics and Power*, 14–16; Abernethy, *The Formative Period in Alabama*, 96–97.

6. William Edward Wadsworth Yerby, *History of Greensboro;* Alabama County Marriages, 1809–1950, Alabama Dept. of Archives and History; Matrana, *Lost Plantations*, 120–26.

to North Carolina to visit the family of Israel's wife Martha (also called Patsy), the Lenoirs of Fort Defiance.[7] During his stays at Fort Defiance, he met Louisa, the eldest daughter of Thomas Lenoir.[8] The relationship between Louisa and Pickens evolved from casual acquaintance to courtship and, by the fall of 1834, Pickens had decided to seek Thomas's and Selina's, his wife, permission to marry Louisa. Although the Lenoirs thought well of the Pickens brothers, they had never been enthusiastic about Alabama. Thomas's health being fragile, he feared exposing himself and his family to what he believed, despite Israel's assurances, to be the unhealthy environment of the Alabama frontier. But, as Louisa's mother wrote her brother William, Thomas and Selina, though hesitant, granted their approval, and the couple married on October 28, 1834, at Fort Defiance; they left Morganton, North Carolina, heading to Alabama two days later. Anticipating an objection from William about the "haste" of the marriage, Selina explained that she and Thomas considered asking the couple to delay but that they recognized Pickens as a man of "public and private" character, who "has been long known" to the family and Louisa's friends. Nonetheless, when Louisa left for Alabama, they worried. Thomas, she wrote, was "despondingly anxious about her safety" and "looks now as if he would never smile again."[9]

Tragically, Thomas's worst fear came to pass. Pickens and Louisa returned to Alabama and began their lives as master and mistress of Umbria Plantation. By the next fall, Louisa was pregnant with her first child. Julia Pickens, Israel's daughter, who was living with Samuel and Louisa at the time, wrote a month before Louisa delivered to assure her Uncle Thomas that Louisa was doing well. The birth of their son was difficult, however, and Louisa never recovered. She lived just long enough to name the boy Thomas, after her father. Devastated by the death of Louisa, Pickens fell into a deep depression, or "mental affliction," as he described it, that "impaired" his health. Concerned friends advised him to leave Umbria for a while so he would

---

7. Martha was the daughter of Revolutionary War general William Lenoir.

8. Julia Pickens to Eliza Lenoir, May 15, 1834; July 28, 1834, Lenoir Family Papers.

9. Selina Louise Lenoir to William A. Lenoir, October 30, 1834, Lenoir Family Papers. Her daughter was also named Selina Louise. In letters, family members referred to her by both names. To avoid confusion between mother and daughter, here Louise is the daughter and Selina the mother.

not be constantly reminded of Louisa. They suggested that he spend some time on the Bay of Pascagoula, between Mobile and New Orleans, where he might "benefit" from "sea bathing." His sister, Jane Duffee, who lived nearby, agreed to take care of Thomas, with the help of a slave who, still lactating after the recent birth of her own child, would be forced to act as Thomas's wet nurse. Samuel, accompanied by his brother John and William Duffee, left for Pascagoula just a few days after Louisa's death.[10]

While Pickens struggled with grief and depression for much of the period between 1830 and 1836, there were long periods when he left day-to-day supervision of his plantations to overseers, and he continued to buy land and slaves to produce more cotton. While traveling, he attended auctions of enslaved people in the southern cities he visited. For example, while in Richmond in 1833, Pickens visited Lewis Collier's slave auction business in the slave-trading district on Wall Street, near Shockoe Creek. While awaiting the auction, Pickens might have stayed in a boardinghouse on the property, near the "jail" where the enslaved were held until an enslaver purchased them. Pickens was typical of enslavers in that he preferred to purchase young people whose many years of productive labor alone would more than justify his initial investment. So, on this trip he purchased eight enslaved people who were all under the age of thirteen. Pickens took Martha, age ten; Mary, age ten; Arena, age nine; Polly, age thirteen; Pamela, age thirteen; Washington, age twelve; Robert, age thirteen; and John, age twelve, from their families, had them transported to Greene County, and put to work on his second plantation, the Canebrake, south of Umbria.[11] Pickens returned to Alabama in the fall of 1836 confident that he was laying a foundation for continued expansion of his plantations and the wealth enslaved people would produce for him. As he wrote to his brother Robert, he was as "prosperous as I had any reason to expect."[12] Pickens and most of his neighbors entered 1837 confident of another year of high demand and high prices for the enslaved and the cotton they grew. But after four years of expansion in the southwest

10. Samuel Pickens to Selina Lenoir, April 26, 1836, Lenoir Family Papers.

11. Bill of Sale, October 3, 1833, Pickens Family Papers. Many planters preferred to travel to Richmond to purchase slaves because they could save money and find higher quality labor (Gudmestad, *A Troublesome Commerce*, 14–15).

12. Samuel Pickens to Robert Pickens, November 20, 1836, Pickens Family Papers.

and increased production of cotton in India in response to high prices, cotton supply exceeded demand, driving down prices and triggering an economic depression that, with a brief recovery, would continue into the early 1840s.[13]

During this period, Pickens pursued a relationship with a young woman named Mary Gaillard Thomas, whom he met in Charleston at some point during 1838 or early 1839. Pickens and Thomas became engaged sometime in early 1840. He informed the Lenoirs of his engagement, seeking to assure them that he remained devoted to them and the memory of their daughter. "In forming new connexions," he wrote, "I shall never forget nor desert my old ones, and I trust I shall not be forgotten or deserted by them. By the dreams of an inscrutable providence the tie which bound us together has been severed, but you may rest assured that while the memory of that cherished object which formed the common link shall have a place in my affections, her surviving friends will ever find a home in my heart." He wanted them to know that he had carefully thought through his decision to remarry. He continued: "That the choice I have now made will be a happy one is yet to be tested. But I think I have the best assurances that such will be the case." He then explained why he thought he had chosen well. "In the first place, she sprang from a good family & race of people, has good sound sense, without frivolity or ostentation, has had the advantage of a first-rate education and if I am not greatly mistaken is possessed of an amiable temper."[14]

Pickens originally planned to marry in Charleston in the summer of 1840. Because of an outbreak of "country fever," as Pickens called it, Mary insisted that the risk of illness was too great for Pickens in the city, so she suggested that she and her mother sail to New York, where Pickens would meet them. Pickens agreed and in late May left Umbria, headed for New York, after stops in Salem, North Carolina, to visit his sister's daughter, and in Washing-

13. On the Panic of 1837, see Murphy, *Other People's Money*, 100–102; Roberts, *America's First Great Depression*, 40–43; Baptist, *The Half Has Never Been Told*, 272–78.

14. Samuel Pickens to Selina Lenoir, July 12, 1840; James Pickens to William A. Lenoir, September 7, 1840, Lenoir Family Papers. Her parents were Samuel Thomas, a doctor in Charleston, and Mary Gaillard. Thomas was the youngest son of Edward Thomas and Anne Gibbes. Gibbes was the daughter of William Gibbes, grandson of one of the original lords proprietors of South Carolina and a prominent Charleston merchant. Gibbes and Thomas married before the American Revolution and resided on Thomas's North Hampton plantation, near Charleston. For a brief biography of Anne Gibbes, see Wollaston, *Ann Gibbes*.

ton, DC, to observe the current congressional session. He met the Thomases in New York as planned, and they went to New Haven, Connecticut, where he and Mary married in St. Paul's Chapel. The Pickenses then traveled for a month, stopping in Hartford, Boston, and New York, before heading south in early November, first to Charleston and then Alabama. The couple, with Mary's mother, who would remain at Umbria until her death, returned to Alabama in late November.

For both women, life in rural Alabama would take some adjustment. Mary and her mother had lived all of their lives in Charleston. But when William Lenoir returned to Umbria in February or early March, he wrote his father that he was surprised at how well both women seemed to be adapting. "I am very much pleased with Mrs. Thomas and Cousin Mary (as I call her). I can hardly believe they are city folks—they are so industrious and domestic, and so kind and thoughtful and attentive to all around them and I even found an old pair of socks that I had worn in holes the other day neatly darned; how forcibly this brought to my mind the kind attentions of my dear mother."[15] A few months later, Mary gave birth to her first child, Samuel (1841). The next year the couple's second son, James, was born. By 1855 Samuel and Mary's family included four more children—Mary (b. 1845), William (Willie) (b. 1849), Louisa (Louty) (b. 1851), and Israel (Icha) (b. 1853).

Pickens, after years of inconsistent attention to his plantations, expected to settle into a life as a planter, husband, and father. In response to William Lenoir's suggestion that, after living in the "bright cities of the North," Pickens might be "weaned from agricultural pursuits," Pickens wrote, "I do assure you that I return with redoubled interest in those pursuits which, after all, are the foundation of all other occupations." Relying on the labor of enslaved people and overseers, Pickens had built a nearly self-sufficient operation consisting of multiple plantations and farms. By this time the enslaved population was increasing naturally. Young slaves he bought in the 1820s and 1830s married, formed families, and, as Pickens intended, produced more slaves. For example, in 1836, Pickens bought six slaves from William Burwell. Among them were Spencer, twenty-three, and Frankey, twenty-one. Spencer and Frankey married

15. Samuel Pickens to William Lenoir, January 4, 1841; William Lenoir to Thomas Lenoir, March 16, 1841, Lenoir Family Papers.

soon thereafter and by 1851 had five children—Francis (b. 1843), Susan (b. 1845), Tina (b. 1848), Narcilla (b. 1850), and Little Spencer (b. 1851).[16] This growing population of enslaved people not only produced cotton, but they also tended livestock and food crops. Enslaved mechanics kept the cotton gins and a grist mill working and tanned the leather used for saddles, harnesses, shoes, and boots. By 1850, Pickens owned three plantations—Canebrake, Goodrum, and Umbria—and enslaved nearly two hundred people.[17]

Pickens's business affairs and personal matters consumed his attention from 1830 to 1848, leaving little time for a public life. But in his correspondence with various members of the Lenoir family after 1840, he revealed a growing concern with attacks on the institution of slavery by abolitionists and free soilers in the northern states. He supported John Calhoun's abortive presidential bid in 1843 and thereafter embraced Calhoun's movement for southern unification in defense of slavery. After David Wilmot proposed his amendment banning slavery from any territories taken from Mexico during the Mexican War, Pickens emerged as a leading advocate for Calhounite resistance in Greene County. When Whigs and Democrats convened a meeting in Eutaw to "take action upon the subject of the proposed Southern Convention," Pickens served on the resolutions committee.[18]

Since 1848, political leaders from both parties had called on citizens to set aside party allegiances and unify in defense of southern rights from so-called "northern aggression." They, of course, found widespread agreement that the South must resist northern threats to slavery but had encountered considerable disagreement over tactics. This conflict deepened in reaction to the passage of the Compromise of 1850.[19] Party divisions in the fall of 1850 gave way to a split between those who defended the compromise as a settlement of the sectional conflict that protected southern rights and those who

16. Bill of Sale, William Burwell, January 1, 1836, Pickens Family Papers.
17. Damer, "The Vanished Plantation System," 90–94. Damer was the brother-in-law of James, Samuel Pickens Jr.'s second son. This article was typical of the post–Civil War celebration of the slave South. According to Damer, all the enslaved people who worked at Umbria were cooperative and happy. That was inaccurate, to say the least. Samuel Pickens to William Lenoir, January 4, 1841, Lenoir Family Papers.
18. *Alabama Beacon*, March 16, April 20, 1850.
19. Holt, *The Fate of Their Country*, 79–84.

considered the compromise a defeat for the South that would only encourage further "abolitionist" assaults on slavery.[20] Pickens emerged as a leader of the anti-compromise faction. In November, he and other Calhounites organized a Southern Rights Association in Greene County. The organizational meeting of the Greene County Southern Rights Association rejected radical demands for immediate secession. Resolutions adopted criticized the compromise for applying Wilmot to California and "dismembering Texas," doing "great injury and injustice" to the South, and exposing a "reckless disregard of southern rights and feelings." All the South got in return were the ambiguous New Mexico and Utah acts and the Fugitive Slave Act, which only promised to enforce the fugitive slave provision of the Constitution. To resist "designs of abolitionists against the south or who act or sympathise with them," the meeting called for the continued development of the southern economy through the building of railroads and expansion of manufacturing in order to free the region of economic dependence upon the free states. Resolutions also demanded that the region move toward cultural independence by only employing preachers and teachers "known to be southern wholly in all their feelings and opinions." To enforce "southern opinions," the meeting appointed a Committee of Vigilance and Correspondence "whose duty it shall be to procure and disseminate information, particularly in regard to the late and pending controversy between the Northern and Southern sections of the confederacy on the subject of African slavery as it exists in the Southern states, and also to guard the community against the efforts of abolitionists, and to cause to be arrested and to prosecute all those detected in the circulation of incendiary documents, or otherwise tampering with our slaves."[21]

Union parties organized in Greene County and across the state to promote the benefits of the compromise and to build popular opposition to the southern rights movement by framing all southern rights men as radicals.[22] The Unionist campaign was effective, the *Beacon* conceded, but warned that the voters had not embraced "ultra" Unionism. Rather, the paper argued, the voters had rejected disunionist "ultra doctrines." In the end, the paper concluded, "The signal defeat of the ultra–Southern Rights men, in the recent

20. *Alabama Beacon*, October 7, 12, 1850.
21. *Alabama Beacon*, November 23, 1850.
22. *Alabama Beacon*, February 22, 1851.

elections, will, we hope, have the effect of checking their ultraism; and in the end, strengthen the cause of the South."[23]

Pickens predicted that the success of "unionism" in Alabama and elsewhere was only a temporary truce in a sectional conflict that he doubted could be resolved. Addressing Lenoir's alarm about the "danger of dissolution," he wrote that he hoped that would be "avoided, at least till after our time." But, he continued, "I confess candidly that my hopes of a settlement of this question in a way to satisfy the South & do her justice have nearly fled. If the South had taken her stand firmly about two years ago & been united, there is no earthly doubt but that we could have had the line of 36/30 to the Pacific as a settlement." Seeing southern division, potential allies in the free states "had to go with their free-soil constituents." Pickens dismissed as naive Lenoir's argument that the debate over slavery and the near collapse of the Union might make citizens of the free states less willing to support future attacks on southern rights. Slavery had been thoroughly "discussed" for two decades, he wrote, and opposition to slavery had only grown in the free states. "It is not discussion on this subject that will cause the North to relax their oppressive measures against the South—the only thing that will move them to do us justice is the fear of dissolution." Pickens thought the threat alone would be enough to deter further "oppressive measures," for the Union, he believed, was more "favorable" for the free states than the South. "In my opinion," he contended, "all that will be necessary for us to do is to show an undivided front & to declare that in the event of any further encroachment on our rights that we will in a body withdraw from the Union. If we had done so before or if we even now should do so, I candidly think we need never be compelled to put our threat into execution. They will yield us anything we wish rather than the Union should be broken up. But to produce this effect on them, we must all stand up like men." Pickens then stated his support for "immediate dissolution or in other words secession" before qualifying his position as support for the "right" of secession. Pickens understood political realities at the time. Under the circumstances, he was "in favor of resorting to almost every other method of relief short of secession."[24]

23. *Alabama Beacon,* August 16, 1851.
24. Samuel Pickens to William Lenoir, June 8, 1851, Lenoir Family Papers.

Pickens died of unknown causes in 1854. To say the least, the death of Samuel created a potentially severe disruption in the lives of the Mary Gaillard Pickens, her children, and the people they enslaved. The Greene County probate court could have distributed Pickens's estate to the heirs, leaving Mary Gaillard with only a one-third share and turning over control of the children's shares to court-appointed guardians. Enslaved people would be divided among the family members or sold. To keep the estate whole until the children reached majority, Mary Gaillard filed a petition with the probate court requesting that she be named administrator for the estate, and the court approved the petition.[25]

Mary Gaillard now assumed responsibility for the management of three plantations. Like her husband, she relied on overseers and agents for advice and day-to-day operations, but she closely monitored production, income, and legal matters.[26] She corresponded with overseers and her factors in Mobile to give directions about expenses, purchases, and the disposition of enslaved people.[27] Viewing herself as an enlightened, Christian enslaver, Mary Gaillard sought to secure the loyalty of the enslaved by providing for their spiritual and material needs as she defined them. She was particularly concerned when she heard reports of mistreatment of enslaved people by overseers that might require her to intervene, something she found distressing.[28] But enslaved people exploited the tension that existed between enslaver and slave managers by appealing to her directly. For example, in the spring of 1859, slaves at the Canebrake plantation, who were "extremely anxious" about what would happen to them after the death of her husband, demanded she meet with them in person rather than complaining to an overseer. Despite

25. *Pickens Adm'r v. Pickens Distributees,* 35 Ala. 442 (1860).

26. Jones-Rogers, *They Were Her Property,* 63–64; Wood, *Masterful Women,* 35–36; Fox-Genovese, *Within the Plantation Household,* 203–5; Stevenson, *Life in Black and White,* 200–205.

27. Wood, *Masterful Women,* 4; Edwards, *Scarlett Doesn't Live Here Anymore,* 25–30; Genovese, *Roll, Jordan, Roll,* 7–25.

28. See Israel Pickens to Mary Gaillard, December 16, 1859; Samuel Pickens to "Mama," February 24, 1861, below. In response to a letter his mother had written expressing concern about how William Lawless treated the slaves, Sam wrote that he was confident Lawless would treat the slaves "kindly." Unlike her husband, Mary Gaillard wrote about her concerns for the physical well-being of enslaved people on the plantations.

her "dread of the undertaking," and after delaying for weeks, she concluded that it was her duty to visit "the servants" and address their concerns. She bought dresses to take to the women at Canebrake, hoping to reassure "the servants" of her benevolent intentions. As she wrote Sam, they would like the dresses even if they did not care for her.[29] She finally went near the end of May. After her visit, she wrote that the enslaved had already eaten but prepared supper for her Mary, Louty, her daughter, and a family friend named Joe Grigg. She wrote to her oldest son, Samuel, "We were kindly treated, and the servants each & all shook us warmly by the hands & welcomed us there. I asked Mr. High to give them a holiday on Saturday & he complied with the request. I am really glad that I went down, for I felt that it was a duty incumbent on me." Her visit reinforced her self-concept as an enlightened enslaver, though she appeared uncertain about the response of the "servants" to what she considered humane treatment. She wrote only that enslaved people at the Canebrake "seem to be quite happy."[30] Mary Gaillard qualified her conclusion about enslaved people's state of mind because she knew, from experience, that the appearance of acceptance, and even contentment, only momentarily obscured the fundamental conflict between enslaver and enslaved. Her "benevolence" was how she legitimized her power over enslaved people and would always be limited by her expectations for production and obedience. During the encounters she reported in her letters to her sons during the late 1850s, she acknowledged that enslaved people challenged her authority frequently.[31] After a visit to the Goodrum Plantation, she wrote Sam and James that "the servants seemed much gratified in seeing me. Most of them are satisfied, but as is usual a few discontented spirits are amongst them."[32]

Between the fall of 1859 and the outbreak of Civil War in the spring of 1861, Mary Gaillard, her children, and an enslaved man named William

29. Mother to Sam, March 17, 1859; Mother to Sam, March 30, 1859, Pickens Family Papers.

30. Mother to Sam, May 24, 1859, Pickens Family Papers. Isaih High was one of the Pickenses' overseers. U.S. Census, 1860.

31. Wood, *Masterful Women*, 41–43; Weiner, *Mistresses and Slaves*, 72–88.

32. Mother to Sons, June 28, 1859; Mother to Sam, February 12, 1858; Sam to Mother, February 19, 1858, Pickens Family Papers.

left Alabama for Virginia, where the Pickens children attended schools beginning in 1859.[33] Sam and James enrolled at the University of Virginia while Mary Gaillard remained in Richmond, where the younger children attended various schools.[34] Mary Gaillard soon regretted moving to Richmond. In her letters, she reminded both sons of how she suffered during their separation, especially when they did not write. Silences, she wrote, heightened her fear and anxiety that something was wrong with one or both. Mary Gaillard might have found some relief in the distractions and amenities Richmond could offer a wealthy woman, but she found the city unappealing. She described Richmond as pretentiously "extravagant."[35] Mary Gaillard was also unsettled by the reaction in Richmond to John Brown's attack on the federal arsenal at Harpers Ferry. When the Pickenses arrived in the fall of 1859, the city was in a near panic as rumors of slave insurrections spread through the region. Brown's raid and rumors in the local press of widespread support in the free states had fueled talk of "insurrection," Mary Gaillard wrote. Men were joining militia companies, preparing for war. She overheard men in her boardinghouse discussing the coming election in New York as a test of northern support for Brown and abolitionism. The "abolitionists" Mary Gaillard and the men referred to were New York Republicans, most of whom were neither abolitionists nor defenders of Brown. According to Mary Gaillard, one of the men believed that, if the Republicans did well, "the Union must be dissolved." Like her husband and these men she blamed the increased sectional tension after Brown's raid on the unreasoning attacks of "radicals" who would destroy the lives she and her children expected. She feared that, if "our Northern brethren" failed to "change their course" and reject the "abolitionism" of the Republicans, there would be civil war, "one of the greatest evils that could happen."[36]

When the Pickenses returned to Alabama in the spring of 1860, Mary Gaillard's fears of civil war grew as debate raged over how to respond to

33. William was one of the enslaved people who worked in the Pickenses' household on the Umbria Plantation (Umbria Account Book, Pickens Family Papers).

34. Mother to Sam, November 8, 1859; Mother to Sam, January 3, 1860, Pickens Family Papers.

35. Mother to Sam, December 5, 14; January 17; February 11, 1860, Pickens Family Papers.

36. Mother to Sam, November 8, December 5, 1859, Pickens Family Papers.

Brown's raid and the perceived Republican threat to southern slavery. In Greene County there was widespread agreement about the need to defeat Abraham Lincoln and the Republicans but deep division over the best way to do that. The county and state divided among Stephen Douglas, John Breckinridge, and John Bell. Bell, the Constitutional Unionist candidate, won a plurality of the votes in Greene County with Breckinridge, the Southern Rights candidate, a close second. Unlike 1852 when Sam Pickens Jr. bemoaned the failure of secessionists to overcome the appeals of unionism, in 1860 the election of Lincoln, and the fear that he and the Republicans would destroy slavery, transcended other divisions. After the election, for most voters in the county, the question was not whether to secede, but when—immediately or in cooperation with other southern states. In the election for delegates to Alabama's secession convention, Greene County chose immediatists, who joined the majority at the convention in approving an ordinance of secession. Pickens would have been gratified to see the people of Greene County, including his two oldest sons, Sam and James, join much of the South in defense of slavery. What neither he nor the secessionists of 1860 envisioned were the destruction and misery secession would bring to the nation, the "evil" of civil war Mary Gaillard predicted.[37]

37. On secession in Greene County, see Hubbs, *Guarding Greensboro*, 86–99. On the impact of the Freeport Doctrine and the conflict over the Lecompton constitution, see Thornton, *Politics and Power*, 365–82, and Holt, *The Fate of Their Country*, 119–24.

Secession and War

JANUARY–JUNE 1861

As the secession crisis unfolded in the fall of 1860, Mary Gaillard set aside her fears of war and prepared the family to travel to North Carolina and Virginia, where the children would attend school.[1] Mary Gaillard had decided to enroll her younger children at Albert Smedes's St. Mary's School,[2] in Raleigh, North Carolina. Sam and James returned to Charlottesville, where they would continue their education at a prep school for the University of Virginia named Locust Grove Academy, which Gessner Harrison, a friend of Henry Tutwiler, had opened in 1859.[3]

James and Sam attended their classes, while observing with keen interest the political struggle in Virginia over secession. Though neither was ever as

1. Hubbs, *Guarding Greensboro*, 86–99.

2. Albert Smedes established St. Mary's School for Girls, affiliated with the Episcopal diocese of North Carolina, in 1842. Alexander Wilson had established the Caldwell Institute in Greensboro, North Carolina, in 1835. He moved the school to Hillsborough, Alamance County, in 1845. Wealthy southerners from across the South sent their sons to Wilson's school and their daughters to St. Mary's. See Scott, "The Wilson School," 215–18, and Stoops, "Saint Mary's School."

3. Broadus, *A Memorial of Gessner Harrison*, 6–9. Harrison and Henry Tutwiler attended the University of Virginia at the same time and became lifelong friends. Tutwiler encouraged Harrison to retire from the University of Virginia, where he had been a professor of ancient languages for thirty-one years, and open Locust Grove Academy. Tutwiler was the founder of Green Springs Academy, where James and Sam went to school in 1859.

politically active in sectional politics as their father, both joined other students there and at the University of Virginia in demanding that Virginia join Alabama and the other Deep South states that had left the Union and would soon hold a convention to create the Confederate States of America.[4] Neither appeared concerned about how the incoming administration of president-elect Abraham Lincoln might respond to the secession crisis. They doubted Lincoln would use force against the Confederate states and sought to ease their mother's anxiety about the possibility of war. If war did come, they believed, it would be short and end with Confederate victory.

In the week after Lincoln's inauguration, James's and Sam's classes resumed at Locust Grove and life went on as usual. They joined many others in the seceded states and continued to dismiss fears of war. But they underestimated the new president's determination to restore the Union. After the Confederate attack on Fort Sumter, President Lincoln called for seventy-five thousand troops to suppress the rebellion. Virginia responded with an ordinance of secession that voters ratified in May.[5] Students at Locust Grove and the University of Virginia joined the thousands of Virginians who celebrated. Sam wrote of "stirring times" at the school. "Ever since the war news has been coming in[;] it has been utterly impossible to think of studying" he wrote. Students gathered at the apartments of professors and called for "patriotic" speeches. Sam praised the attack on Fort Sumter and Virginia's secession but sought to reassure his mother that any war between the Union and the Confederacy would be limited and short and have minimal impact on them.

Mary Gaillard did not share her sons' excitement about what she considered a precipitous descent into a war that could put her sons and the family's future at risk. After she received James's and Sam's letters celebrating the beginning of hostilities, Mary Gaillard's response on April 21 again advised them against joining the army. She reminded them of what their priorities should be and emphasized that service in the army was not one of them. She would consider taking the family out of the country rather than suffer through a war, she wrote. Sam promised her that he and James would remain in school.[6] Over the next few weeks Sam and James continued to reassure their mother

4. Cooper, *We Have the War upon Us*, 173–83.
5. Link, *Roots of Secession*, 239–41.
6. Mary Gaillard Pickens to Sons, April 25, 1861, Pickens Family Papers.

with confident predictions that Virginia's secession would convince President Lincoln of the futility of a "war of coercion," as Sam put it.[7]

The family returned home sometime during the early summer of 1861, before the first Battle of Manassas. By the time they arrived, the Greensboro Guards had mustered into the Confederate Army as Company D of the Fifth Alabama Infantry regiment commanded by Colonel Robert Rodes, an old acquaintance of Mary Pickens's.[8] As James wrote his mother from school, many of their friends and neighbors had joined the regiment. But Sam and James, as their mother wanted, remained at home assisting in the management of the family's plantations. Given the fighting then raging in Virginia, they would have to find a school in Alabama, if they returned to school at all.

︱︱

Charlottesville,
January 7, 1861

Dear Mama,

We arrived here safely today at 12 O'clock. We were compelled to remain in Richmond until this morning, as no train came this way on Sunday. The time passed pleasantly though, for on Sat. night we went to the theatre and were entertained with a play taken from "Guy Mannering," one of the "Waverly novels." It was well acted, & quite interesting. Sunday morning we went around to St. Paul's church and heard an excellent sermon from Mr. Minnegerode,[9] and at night another, also, from him. In the evening Jamie & I went on top of the Exchange hotel, whence we had a beautiful view of the city. Then walked down to the wharf and went aboard of a ship, through which the Captain kindly showed us, and explained to us the natures of the different instruments used in navigation.

Everything about the Farish house, and Charlottesville generally, seems

7. James Pickens to Mary Gaillard Pickens, April 26, 1861, Pickens Family Papers.

8. Hubbs, *Guarding Greensboro*, 122–25.

9. Charles Minnegerode was the rector of Saint Paul's Episcopal Church, sometimes referred to as "the Cathedral of the Confederacy." O'Brien, *Conjectures of Order*, 88–89; "Charles Minnigerode (1814–1894)."

exactly as we left it last spring. Almost the same set of boarders, Mrs. Coles included, is here yet. Even Omahundra and the sour looking house-keepers are still to be seen in their accustomed places. William, the waiting-man, is as polite & attentive as ever, & has made many inquiries after you all. And last, tho not least, our friend Jim of the 3rd floor gives incessant evidence of that uncommon fondness for singing & whistling, for which he was so famous, or rather infamous, when you were here. We went to see Tom Biscoe[10] soon after dinner and took him greatly by surprise when we entered his room. He was very glad to see us, & hear from you all and sends his love. He seems to be applying himself assiduously this year. Laura (?) enquired particularly after all. We have met with several more of our friends, but miss a good many that were here last session. Considerable excitement prevails amongst the students; some are going home every day, and it is thought that the number will soon be so decreased as to threaten a suspension of exercises of the University for the remainder of this session, at least. The students are forming companies and drilling, not with the intention of offering their services; but in order that should they be called into service they may be prepared to take some higher office than that of mere Private soldier.

We are glad to find that Dr. Harrison's school did not commence till to-day, since the Christmas vacation of two weeks. Tom got a letter from Cousin Emma saying that she had not recovered from her cold & would remain in Baltimore until she did. We hope soon to hear that you are all pleasantly situated at Dr. Smedes, & that Willy gets on well with Mr. Lovejoy.

The letter enclosed has been here some time, Mr. Webb not knowing where to forward it to. Jamie joins me in love to you and the children.

Your affectionate son, Samuel

————•————

10. Tom Biscoe was the son of Cordelia Hunt Biscoe. Cordelia was the daughter of Louisa Gaillard Hunt, Mary Pickens's sister, and Thomas Hunt. The Biscoe and Hunt families lived in Louisiana. See Wyatt, "Re: John Gaillard M. Judith Peyre, SC."

Belmont, Jan. 13th, 1861

My dear Mother,

I promised you, in a scrawl which I wrote you a few days ago, to write a long letter. I shall now endeavor to do so, and to give you a sort of sketch of our school, etc.

We went up, from Raleigh to Richmond, at which place we found that no train would leave there for Charlottesville, the next day (Sunday); so we put up at the Exchange & the next morning went to hear Dr. Minnegerode, who delivered quite a fine & interesting sermon. We heard another from him that night also. He spoke at length upon the crisis of affairs, tho' he did not—as most preachers do—make a real political sermon. He considered, he said, the present state of things, or rather the eventuality of it, as being a great epoch in the history of nations & of the world, and that great issues will arise from the restoration of the equilibrium of the two sections of this country. I do not recollect his sermon very well, but was very much interested with it indeed.

The morning after, Sam & I took the cars for Charlottesville at which place we saw Tom Biscoe. He was looking quite well and is studying very hard this year. [*Unclear name*] also was at the University. He has grown very much I think. They both wished to be remembered to you & the children. We took the cars the next morning & arrived at the depot near here—at 2 I think. We did feel quite lonesome as we drove in a crowded little hack, drawn by two miserable looking mules, to a place which we had never seen before & amongst faces new & unfamiliar to us. They gave us a very comfortable room, but poorly furnished, no fires in the morning & no water to wash our faces with, till the third day of our arrival. We have to rise at 7 o'clock to breakfast, and immediately after, in the same room, the Bible is placed before Dr. Harrison who reads a chapter and then prays. The same is done at night after supper about 8 o'clock. I forgot to mention that the occupants of the rooms into which we were at first placed having arrived, we had to give it up & are now in a negro cabin which Dr. H had vacated by some of his negroes & fitted up hastily for our accommodation. Added to this misfortune, two others are to be put in our room & we will then be four together. *I* do not like it at all & Sam is very vexed with it & says he is going to try very hard to get another room. I do consider it an imposition for a person to say at first he can accommodate pupils & after they come then stick them in a negro cabin with two other pupils. I trust we shall have room together & by ourselves. I like Dr. Harrison very much; he is so much like Mr. Tutwiler, both in looks, action & manner. We are acquainted with some eight or ten boys at present, and find it still lonesome & new. However, I think that we will begin to like it as we know the boys & get used to the place. Dr. H. has several assistant teachers here & amongst them, a Mr. Smith, who is an A.M. of the University of Va., & a brother of the Prof. of Geology etc. at the above place. He is a very pleasant man & is quite intelligent they say. He is teacher of Latin here. Dr. Harrison has no regular classes to teach, but goes from one class to another—both low & high—throughout the school, weekly, & assists by very plain & intelligible lectures both teacher & pupils. His lectures are quite interesting, & each pupil regrets that he (the Dr.) does not teach all his classes. They all like him & respect him very much indeed, & he treats them more like his children than his pupils. He speaks to them very plainly, of their duty, rebukes them sharply, tho' kindly, for their misdemeanors, & thus, does not gain the hatred but the love & respect of his pupils. T is true there are some who do not mind him, but there would be so everywhere & under any circumstances, & I reckon he does not pay much attention to them. The generality of them reverence him for he is popular all over the state of Virginia. He was very popular, I know, at the University where he taught for 30 years, and treated the students of his class so kindly & gentlemanly that they all shed tears when he bade adieu to them upon leaving the University. By the way, he was speaking to us this morning about taking Willie.[11] He says that he has classes into which he might put Willie, but there are only two or three of Willies' size here. As I said before, I think it is too advanced for Willie. And then, they say he does not pay much attention to the little boys & it is optional with them whether they attend a class or not. I hope we will hear in a few days that Willie is fixed at a good school. I think it is a very great pity that as you have got fixed so well as regards yourself & the others, Willie too couldn't find a place. I hope he will soon be fixed.

The country around here is very mountainous indeed & some of the scenes

11. James was referring to younger brother William. His mother had found a school for the youngest son, Israel (Icha), not "Willie." Mr. Harrison did admit Willie.

are very pretty. There is one range of mountains to the west of us which reminds me much of those around Charlottesville. We have had snow on them 'till lately, but I believe it has entirely disappeared now. It is quite cold however & I would not be surprised to find in the morning the ground white again.

Sam says he would have written to you but as I wrote he will defer doing so 'till another day. Tell Mary I will write a letter to her now, but if she writes me one I will be very glad indeed. Give our love to them all.

Your affectionate son, James.

P.S. Our box of books has not come yet, and we are in a sort of unsettled, unfixed state. We do not wish to buy others unless the box is lost. Write soon dear mama.

———•—•———

Belmont, Feb. 24th, 1861

My dear Mother,

I now proceed to reply to the kind and interesting letters received from you, and to beg your pardon for not having answered them more promptly. I will try and do better in future. We are very sorry to hear that you have had an attack of the Douloureux,[12] & hope that you are entirely free from it and may not have a return. You mentioned also that you had been troubled with liver complaint; this, no doubt, has been caused by not being able to take exercise, in consequence of the long spells of rainy weather; but now that the Spring is approaching and the weather becoming mild and pleasant, let me beg, dear Mama, that you will turn out with the children and completely walk off all such attendants of sedentary habits. This, together with mountain air and sulphur next summer, will, I trust, restore you to perfect health. I hope you have not been removed from the room which you occupied at first, as

12. According to the National Institute of Neurological Disorders and Stroke's "Trigeminal Neuralgia Fact Sheet," trigeminal neuralgia, or *tic douloureux*, is a medical condition characterized by stabbing pain to one side of the face. It arises from the trigeminal nerve that supplies sensation to the face. Attacks can last from weeks to months, but there are usually periods that are symptom free.

William[13] says it is much more comfortable than the other, and has smaller rooms adjoining for keeping the baggage in etc. Dr. Smedes has no right to deprive you of it unless the lady who engaged it previously, should return, & that is not the case, I suppose. Mama you ought not to feel yourself bound to be governed by the regulations of the school but should suit your own convenience in rising in the morning, taking meals etc., for William could very easily have your meals at more reasonable hours than those at which the school children have theirs. We are glad to hear that the children are happy and doing well in their studies, and hope that they will continue so.

Jamie got a letter from Mr. Joe Grigg a few days since, containing a good deal of news from our neighborhood.[14] He sent his kindest regards to you and the children, & said that he was delighted to get Jamie's letter as it was the first definite news he had heard from our party since we left home. He hopes that you will be perfectly satisfied with Raleigh, but has his doubts about it, as he had often told you. He says he goes to Umbria very often as the house is full of young ladies—Cousin Israel's three sisters, Hattie Uhlhorn, and Miss Martha James; and says he is very much taken with Miss H.U. He has been on a visit to Choctaw since Christmas & enjoyed it very much.[15] "Old Shanks" is the same old thing, wears precisely the same hat & clothes, & is as polite as ever. No mention was made of "Top Knot" & family, tho' it is to be hoped that they are still in the land of the living. The Sawyers were not mentioned either. Matt is at the trade and uncle Creed says he is rather green, but that he will make a blacksmith of him by and by.[16] I don't see how Mr. High misunderstood that Matt was to be put with Creed on the 1st of Jan., for

13. William was an enslaved man who worked in the family home at the Umbria Plantation and accompanied Mary Pickens to Raleigh (Umbria Inventory, 1853, Pickens Family Papers).

14. Joseph A. Grigg enlisted in the Confederate Army at Greensboro in 1861. He was captured at Antietam on October 1, 1862, and imprisoned at Ft. McHenry before being exchanged, paroled, and returned to duty in the Fifth Alabama (CMSR, Alabama, RG 109, roll 0141).

15. Cousin Israel was the son of Robert Pickens, brother of Samuel Pickens Jr. (U.S. Census, 1860). Hattie Uhlhorn was the daughter of Julia Hunt Uhlhorn, daughter of Mary Gaillard Pickens's aunt Louisa Gaillard (U.S. Census, 1850).

16. The family of Enoch Sawyer, who rented land from the Pickenses. Sawyer had served in the Mexican War. His family included twins Martha, or Markey as the Pickens children called her, and Mary, who would later marry Israel Pickens, or Icha, one of Sam's younger

I did not mention cousin Israel's name in the matter at all. Mr. Joe did not say how things were going on at the plantations: I will ask him to inform us, & to tell Mr. Lawless to write to you.[17] You need not be at all uneasy about his being too strict; I think he will get on smoothly and treat the servants kindly.

Dr. Grigg is well, and not doing much practice. Cous. Israel has a very trifling overseer, as usual, & the Dr. has to exert himself to keep the gates shut & stock out of the yard.[18]

We are very much obliged to you for the tooth powder, medicines etc. that you sent by Willy. Lou's antiseptic powder must be an excellent remedy. We gave some to a friend of ours here, who suffered very much with dyspepsia, & he says it gave him immediate relief. I should have been most happy to drink Mary's health on the 14th anniversary of her birthday, if I had had the where-with-al to do so, but as there was nothing here better than cold water, I was deprived of the pleasure.(I was very anxious to write to Mary also, today, but as I have not time, will do so as soon as possible.)

I don't know anything about the Dr. Moore of whom you spoke. We will not need our carpet, as the winter is almost over: I suppose it is safe, for Pegues was to have left it in charge of some responsible person.

Willy is getting on very well with Latin & seems to like it. He is also studying Arithmetic, History, & Geography.

In one of the "Baltimore Suns" that we sent you, we saw a notice of a melancholy occurrence in New Orleans, where a young man named T.H. Uhlhorn in attempting to cowhide another young man, was shot twice and killed.[19] We suppose it must be the Hunt's nephew, & if so you must have heard all about it: We sincerely hope, though, that such is not the case.

---

brothers. In 1861, Sawyer wrote General Leonidas Polk to request a noncombat position in the army because he was taking care of his elderly mother and had young children. Under the circumstances, he thought he should serve in a position that would not mean risking his life (Confederate Papers Relating to Citizens or Business Firms, National Archives, RG 109, roll 905; U.S. Census, 1860). Matt was likely a young slave who was learning blacksmithing from "uncle" Creed.

17. William G. Lawless was another overseer for the Pickenses (U.S. Census, 1860).

18. Beverly Grigg was a physician who lived in the Hollow Square district (U.S Census, 1860).

19. T. H. Uhlhorn was the son of Julia Hunt Uhlhorn (U.S. Census, 1860).

Jamie & Willie unite with me in love to our dear Mother, sisters, & brother. Trusting that you are all well & happy,

I am as ever,
Your affectionate son,
Samuel.

P.S. Give our love to cousins Eugenia & Emma.[20]
Howdye to Wm. & Katy.[21] S.P.

You asked what was Dr. H's opinion of the political crisis. I have never heard him say. I presume Lincoln will make known his policy in his inaugural address & if it be coercion, war will immediately ensue, but he will hardly attempt such madness. Even many of the abolition papers seem to be much disappointed in Lincoln, and to doubt his adequacy to the task before him.

Belmont, March 3rd 1861
My dear Mother

Your very kind and interesting letter came to hand more than a week ago, and I would certainly have answered it long before now but as Sam was writing to you and there was nothing new occurring, I concluded to defer doing so till another time. Nothing new round here to break the usual quiet and lonesomeness of the place, but these are left alone in their silent—reign. Indeed, if it were not for the variety & interest in our several studies & the regular weekly recitations, which afford something to do, the time would not pass so quickly; as it is the five days of the week slip gradually away, but when

20. First cousins of Mary Gaillard, daughters of Louisa Gaillard, Mary's aunt (Wyatt, "Re: John Gaillard M. Judith Peyre, SC").

21. William and Katy were enslaved people whom Mary Gaillard took with her to Raleigh to serve her and the other children. Katy was married to Simon, the son of "Old Simon" and his wife, Mary, and all had lived and labored on the Umbria Plantation for many years. Katy and Simon had at least one child, named Spencer (Umbria Account Books, 1853, Pickens Family Papers).

Saturday & Sunday come, when we have nothing to do, the time seems twice as long as the whole week has been.

As Lincoln's reign was close at hand and the paper was full of what was to be done at the inauguration, a great many of the students here having become very anxious to see the ceremonies performed, obtained leave of Dr. H yesterday & have left for Washington. We were very anxious to go, indeed, but knew that if anything serious were done it would not be very pleasant, and might be dangerous. It was to be a very grand affair and the ball to be given Lincoln is to cost several thousand dollars. Each ticket will cost $10. I think the black republicans are certainly making a great show and are evidently well pleased with the grand finale of their vote & the desideratum of the party—viz the election of their president. But I think that they will at last find out that it was one of the most unfortunate moves that was ever made, both for themselves & for the country. It is said that Chief Justice Taney will administer the oath of office to Lincoln, in the same manner as he did to seven preceding presidents. They say he is a very venerable & fine looking old man, and I reckon he must be very trust worthy and popular, as he has held his office so long.

I noticed in the last paper that the Peace Conference had adjourned—having accepted & agreed upon the Guthrie propositions;[22] but not understanding these, I do not know whether that agreement will be satisfactory or not, one thing I do know about it, & which I have heard several pronounce unjust, is one clause in the propositions declare that slavery shall be prohibited in the territories north of 36 degrees 30 minutes, & it shall only be recognized south of that limit; and that no territory north of that line shall be admitted into the Union as a slave state. I do not think it is just by any means. I think that slavery has a right to go wherever & as far soever as it can & that it ought not to be limited at all, for this would be denying to the south a right which she has ever possessed. We will hear more about the plan for agreement when those boys return who have gone to Washington.

I was very sorry to hear that you have been suffering with liver complaint & neuralgia and earnestly trust that that an abundance of exercise has relieved you entirely. Dear Mama, you should [*unclear*] the spring is opening

22. James Guthrie, senator from Kentucky, participated in the February 1861 Peace Conference. His "propositions" would have amended the Constitution to allow slavery to exist below the Missouri Compromise line (Cooper, *We Have the War upon Us*, 178–80).

and the cold and wet weather has ceased, take a great deal of exercise & walk off your former enemies. I am glad that the children are well and hope they will continue, with yourself, to be well and enjoy fine health. Then when the heat of summer comes on we will leave for the mountains and springs of Virginia. Often do we look back to the time spent, about four years ago, so pleasantly in the valley of Va., and think with pleasure upon anticipation this summer of the same. I hope that affairs may be brought to a peaceable conclusion & that another period of four years may pass away as pleasantly & peaceably as that under Buchanan has passed. I have, as I before said, nothing new or interesting, but rest assured, dear mother, that every letter we get from you all is *very* acceptable & interesting to us & is always read with avidity. I must close, hoping soon to hear from you. Tell Mary her last kind favor I received yesterday, am much obliged to for it, and will answer it very soon.

Sam & Willie join me in kindest love to you & each & all of the children. I will write to dear little Icha this evening if I have time.

Your affectionate son
James

P.S. Give our kindest love to the Hunts and tell them we are sorry they will not stay with you and go to the springs. Tell Wm & Katy how d ye.

————•—•—————

Belmont, March 23rd, 1861,
My dear Mother

Your last kind letter has been by me for a long time and I have not answered it, but must ask you to forgive me as I have been quite busy for several weeks. I find it very pressing to keep directly up with my classes, as there are so many exercises and grammar lessons to be learned that it occupies a good deal of our spare time. I would certainly have written immediately afterwards to you, to inform you of Willie's recovery, or state of health, but Sam & himself both wrote letters just at the time & so I concluded to wait a little. Willie is now as well as ever, as he has informed you, I suppose. He did not like to take his medicine at all but did so very manfully. Dr. H. would come in with the medicine & pretend to be in an awful hurry, saying that he must leave to attend to some business or other, just as soon as Willie would take the medicine. So Willie would soon come to a conclusion to take it at once. He never liked medicine, & is like myself in that respect, though I have taken so much in my life that one would suppose I had got used to it & did not mind it.

I have received several letters, from Mary, Lou & Icha, but must crave their pardon for my silence as I have been quite busy. I will most certainly write to them all very soon. I was very sorry to hear you had been indisposed and am glad that you are now well. Remember, mama, our constant advice to you—to take a great deal of exercise. If you would take long walks everyday I think they would benefit you very much & that your liver complaint would soon be cured. I expect there are some very good walks in Raleigh as the country around there seems to be quite level and open.

We have had a fall of snow since I wrote to you last, but it lasted only a night, as the next day a warm sun soon dispelled it. I have seen enough of snow since I have been in Virginia, & hope that the great quantities we have had for two winters may prove exceptional. Everyone here says that we have had a great deal more wet weather the last season than is generally to be met with here. We have had very few good days & even now it is cloudy and threatening either snow or rain, although on yesterday it was as clear and bright as a spring day.

They have got up a military company in this school and Sam, Willie and I are members of it. We like it very much as it is very good exercise and you are required to rise at 5 ½ o'clock in the morning. The days on which we drill are Monday, Wednesday & Friday on which last day the whole company is brought together & drilled in companies files & etc.; on other days they are divided out into squads under the charge of a lieutenant, who gives the commands etc. The boys (those who are members) are having a uniform made for the company & after they get guns they will show to very good advantage. Willie was formerly a member of a company in Richmond and understands a great many of the steps, orders, etc.

Dear mama do not consider this an answer, as it is very hastily & badly written, but as I have so much to do at present I know you will excuse it. I will write to you a better & longer one soon. I wrote to satisfy you concerning Willie, that you might not be uneasy about him, & to let you know how we all are.

34

The University students had a good deal of excitement last week, as a secession flag was hoisted by them upon the top of the rotunda, & the next morning when the other students perceived it they rent the air with deafening shouts. Prof. Bledsoe came out in the presence of the students, & said that he was on the same side of politics with the students, but said that he thought the exposition of a secession flag would not be approved of by the legislature & advised the students to take it down; they did so & secured it to another spot. Dr. H., who was standing in the crowd of students, waved his hat to the flag, and said that he did not know when Virginia would ever make herself honorable again. He is a very strong Southern man & vows if Virginia does'nt secede, he will quit his *native state* & go South.

Sam desires me to say to you that he received your kind letter yesterday and is under many obligations to you for it, and will answer it very soon. He and Willie join me in kindest love to you & all the children & to cousins Eugenia & Emma.

Your affectionate son,
James

I have to hurry to get this in the mail. I must acknowledge the receipt of two Church Intelligences from you; they are very interesting indeed and contain a great deal of scientific news. Remember us kindly to William & Katy. Sam says that he will answer the children's letters very soon.

Charlottesville
April 20th, 1861

My dear Mother,

Your last kind letter came to hand day before yesterday, and we are sorry to hear that you have been suffering with headaches and hope you have entirely recovered. Jamie, Willie, and I came to Charlottesville yesterday morning as there was very little going on at school and we had their clothes to get.

We are having stirring times now—so much excitement I have never before seen. Ever since the war news has been coming in it has been utterly impossible to think of studying. No one thinks or speaks anything but of the all-absorbing conflict which has begun between the North and the South. Our teachers are as much excited as the students. The evening before we left after the glorious news of Virginia's secession had been received with the greatest possible enthusiasm the whole school collected around the apartments of the teachers and called for speeches. Dr. Harrison gave us a most eloquent and patriotic address. Mr. Wood [*Section missing.*]

Give our love to Cous. Eugenia & Emma. Mama, I trust you will not feel at all alarmed either for yourselves or for us, for it is believed that Maryland & not the South will be the battleground. We are all well and hope that you and the children are also.

Please write to us often, as we will answer punctually. Jamie & Willy unite with me in much love to you all.

Your aff. Son,
Samuel

———•———

Raleigh N.C.
April 21st 1861

My beloved Sons,

As nearly one hour must pass away ere Chapel Service will commence, I thought I would devote that hour in speaking of the unhappy condition of our country and asking of you both what we had best do. There is great excitement here at the prospect of war and sad indeed are the hearts of many at the thought of having their homes made desolate. I am exceedingly nervous & troubled because of our separation, and pray earnestly that we may very soon be together. I trust in God that the war may be averted and peace restored to our hitherto highly favored land. You, my sons, are engaged in an honorable pursuit that of carrying on your education and I would advise you not to engage in War at your ages. I would like to leave our country at once, and go to a peaceful one where you would all be educated without the fear of War and servile insurrections, if we could do so, but Cousin Jane wrote to say that all our property would be confiscated if we left for another part of the world. I know not if this is the case, and would like you to inquire of someone who is perhaps better informed than she is. Oh! if we were together now, how much better satisfied I should feel. Do tell me what Dr. Harrison thinks of the times, and whether his school will be broken up. Willie wrote that you were all going to Charlottesville on the 19th, I presume to get Spring clothing. Do tell me how Biscoe is, and what he intends doing. I think he will pursue his studies and not go home until July. The girls say they have written to him; but he replies not. Eugenia & Emma are here and will accompany us to Va. If we go; but who can tell where we shall be on the 1st of June. That was the time for us to leave Raleigh, as Dr. Smead's school will close on the 31st of May. Alas! We know not where to go or what to do. I will write to Israel tomorrow for funds, so that we may be enabled to go at any time wherever you may desire or Dr. Harrison may advise. [*Unclear*] you speak to him on the subject and get his views; he is old and capable of giving sound advice.

We attended Chapel today, and Dr. Smedes omitted the prayer for the President of the United States & substituted one for the Governor of this Commonwealth.

All are well and I trust you are. May God! Guard & direct you all is the constant, fervent prayer your devotedly attached Mother,

Mary Gaillard Pickens.

P.S. Lou, Mary & Icha, strange to say are all in the room with me, and desire to be affectionately remembered to you all. My love to my three sons. M.S.P.

———•——

Belmont, May 4th 1861

My dear mother,

I have intended for a day or two to write to you but have not done so, however this evening before the mail goes I will try and write you a few lines.

I have been feeling very badly indeed for the last week and took some blue pills the other night but have had no relief from it. I am bilious I think but hope I shall soon be well again.

Oh, I am so anxious to be with you. I wish we were all together. Time passes off very heavily here and a week seems to me as a month. I hope that we may yet have an opportunity of visiting the Springs as you need the sulphur water & healthy mountain air of Virginia. I hope we will have no war as it would break up a trip to the Springs which is so requisite for you and the children. We heard Mr. Smith say the other day that Genl Scott says he is opposed to invading the South and Lee & Davis are opposed to taking Washington. So, he said, if they continue of the same opinions that there will not be any war. I hope that there will not be.

Oh mamma I want to be with you so much! I will be glad when the school breaks up as I am anxious very, very to be with you all.

There is nothing new at all here. Everything is going on quietly but not much is being done by either teachers or pupils. The Dr is busily engaged, almost all the time, in getting the classes together & finds it very hard to get them all, although he himself attends to it. A great many have left and I don't reckon there are many more than fifty here now. There are others who speak of going. I have heard nothing from either the Dr or Mrs. Joe since I wrote to the latter. But he hasn't had time to answer any letter yet.

Please tell Mary that I received two kind letters and am much obliged to her for them. I will answer them soon. And also Icha. I received a nice little letter from him and was more surprised than I ever was to see how well he had written. He is very smart. I will also answer his, soon. Tell dear little Louty I am looking out for a letter from her too.

Sam desires me to say to you that he received your kind letter day before yesterday & is much obliged to you for it. He says he will answer it very soon. Also to tell Mary that he will write her soon. Willie he writes punctually, so there is no need of saying he will write. He is quite well & enjoys himself very much. We are all anxious to be with you and the children.

Give our kind love to all. Sam & Willie join me in kindest love to you and the children. Give our love to cousins Eugenia & Emma.

Ever your affectionate son James.

Belmont, May 9th, '61

My dear Mother,

I am very much obliged to you for your long and kind letter in reply to the hastily written scrawl which I sent you from Charlottesville the other day. We have read it over and over with the deepest interest. I hope, dear Mamma that you will not permit the disturbed condition of the country to be a source of too great anxiety. Raleigh, on account of its retired situation, and its being headquarters for troops, will be a very secure place. There is no telling what course things will take. Some think it will be ruinous to England to have her usual supplies of cotton cut off for any length of time by Lincoln's blockade of our ports, and that therefore she will be constrained to recognize our government and insist upon having commerce with us and that Lincoln will recognize us also. I really hope it will be so.

Dr. Harrison frequently speaks of the war of coercion which the North is threatening to wage upon us and prays that success may attend our every effort to maintain our rights and to beat back the invaders. He says we can never be subjugated—no never. He exhorts all to practice economy and not to lavish their money foolishly, for that whatever they may have to spare can be well appropriated to the defense of our country.

I enquired about the route to the Springs and learn that we can go from Charlottesville via Staunton to the Greenbrier White Sulphur by road.[23] I sincerely hope that we shall not be prevented from visiting the Springs, for the sulphur water and mountain air would be of great service to us all and especially to yourself.

There is not much studying done here, and the classes are poorly attended. About thirty-five of our students have gone home and there are more who expect to go soon. I suppose St. Mary's is thinned out considerably, also. You must have all had hard work making mattresses etc. for the soldiers. There is a large number of troops quartered in Lynchburg. A good many from Alabama, among whom we have some acquaintances.

Please thank Mary for me, for the kind letters she has written to me, & tell her that I will certainly answer them very soon: also Louty's.

23. The Greenbrier Hotel was, and still is, a popular destination for those who could afford to visit and stay. At the time it was in White Sulphur Springs, Virginia, now West Virginia.

All join me in love to yourself, the children, and Cous. Eugenia & Emma.

Write soon to your affectionate son,

Samuel

———•—•———

Belmont, May 17th, 1861

My dear Mama,

I have been intending for several days to answer your kind letters but have not done so till now. I have not been feeling well for a long time & have'nt been doing much in my classes, but feel better today. I miss you very much and it has seemed to me like an age since we parted. I am growing very anxious to be again with you and the children and hope that the time, now short, will soon skip by, and that we may have an opportunity to go to the Springs. Oh Mama I would be very sorry if you could not go to the Springs as you would be so much benefited by the water, change of air, scenery [*word unclear*]. I think from what Dr. Harrison told Sam the other day, that Virginia would be as safe as anywhere else. He says that he thinks the mountains of Virginia would be a safe secure place. I hope that we may have peace once more and that ere long the establishment of the southern confederacy among the nations of the earth be a fixed fact. The vote on secession which is to decide Virginia, is to be cast on the 23rd inst. next Thursday after which time I think, and it seems to be a general opinion, that the North will tame down & Lincoln grow less in favor of war. I trust that this may be the case and that no such unholy, diabolical war will ever be attempted against the South. The last news is that Lincoln will convene the extra session of Congress (on the 4th July) in Springfield, Illinois, evidently being afraid of using Washington any longer. As regards this place, the Dr says it is perfectly safe and he intends remaining here during the summer. He has, boarding with him, two ladies from Louisiana with two brothers, or they may be cousins I do not know, at the Drs school. They are to stay here several years. The object in their coming was to be safe in case a war should be fought. Although I do not think there is any danger at this point of Virginia, yet I thought it was a singular move to come away from Louisiana up nearer the enemy. Besides if they had wished to embark for a foreign country they would have had better facilities, being near New Orleans, than they will have here.

We were very much obliged to you, my dear Mother, for your offer of money & would have written to you for it but we didn't know that you had any in the Bank. I wrote to Mary the other day and mentioned in my letter how much we wanted ($50). That will do us 'till next month I expect on the 20th of which this school breaks up; and as they will not have any examination, or rather as the examination will not be as large as it would otherwise have been if no students had left, I think it likely it may break up sooner. We have not more than forty-five and several are going to leave soon. There were about a hundred here at the opening of the session.

Saturday the 18th. I did not have time last night to finish this letter in time for this morning's mail. Our mail from this place has for the last three weeks been very irregular indeed for this reason. The old man at the depot, who has the mail sent over every day (or who was to have sent it) has got vexed because several boys have gone away without paying him & he has concluded not to bring our mail here any longer. The consequence is that some one of the boys has to go over to the depot every day & bring it over the best way he can & likely some is lost in this way. I think Dr Harrison ought to have it brought over as any mail is too important a matter to be entrusted to anyone without discrimination.

We are having delightful weather here, it being cool & pleasant and the sky clear as a bell. It is strange weather, however, for May, as we have to wear our thick winter clothes and find them. [*Page or pages missing.*]

———— • ————

Belmont, Va. June 2nd, 1861

My dear Mother,

I am much obliged to your for your kind letter which I've received and on yesterday, and will now proceed to endeavor to reply to it, though I have no news of any moment or interest to communicate to you. Dr. Smedes' school has at length closed and now would we be glad if we could all be together and that you & the children could go from Raleigh to some cooler & healthier spot.

Raleigh must be quite a warm place and therefore does not suit you. I wish that you could leave it and enjoy the fresh air of this state until our school breaks up which will be on the 25th of this month. We are eagerly and joyfully looking forward to that time, trusting that we may all be united then and that before that time things will have resumed their usual quiet and no war happens to prevent us from going to the waters of Virginia.

We were sorry to hear that Mary's eye is still inflamed & hope that it may soon get well. And we hope that the springs, if we go to them, will banish all symptoms of liver complaint and make her, yourself and all hearty, and restore all to good health.

I did not feel well when I wrote to you the other day, but since I have been feeling as well as usual. Sam, Willie & I do not take much exercise, i.e. Sam & I do not. Willie takes a great deal, but all we take is a walk occasionally. I think my not feeling well was leading so sedentary a life as I had all along from January when it was so muddy that we could not walk at all. If the Dr. had a gymnasium here it would be an excellent means of exercise and would be a great addition to his school, in point of health.

Our school is growing smaller and smaller. Four more are going off tomorrow morning which will reduce our number to not more than thirty-five boys. Dr. Harrison finds it quite difficult to get the classes together & really it is so very hard to study now that it is a task.

There are not more than six or eight who care to study at all, and when this is the case the classes get irregular & those who do study see no use in doing so. We attend our classes but do not do much.

We have just listened to the car whistle which on rainy days we can hear quite distinctly, and wish that we were all on board of it to be joined by you & the children. However, we hope that the remaining three weeks may soon pass & unite us again.

The other day we were all a little excited by a report which came down on the cars, that fighting had commenced at a junction near Alexandria, & that also Harper's Ferry was the scene of a bloody conflict in which several thousand men on the Lincoln side were said to have been killed & some fifty on ours. But, we soon afterwards heard that the report was false. No one can conceive why such reports get out or who it is that likes to start them. I do not think we ought to believe any more of them until we are certain of the truth of them.

It is very oppressive, and is cloudy, so I expect we will have some rain soon. I hope it will turn cool, as it has been quite warm for several days.

We received the check ($200) which you sent to us and we are much obliged to you for it. It was certainly our fault in getting out of money, as it was our business to write if we wanted it. We had no use for it though until after we had got our clothes when we found we had'nt quite enough.

We notice in the *Beacon* that Mr. Joe Grigg is a member of the "Greensboro Guards" which company is now at Pensacola on duty. I hope he will get back safe & meantime furnish us with accounts of his engagements, if he has any, and all about his battles etc. which I have no doubt would be very interesting. I wrote him an answer to a letter which I received from him in January, I believe, but have received no answer to it from him yet. I have not written to the Dr. as I am rather afraid of his criticizing wife and have delayed so long now that I don't know how to commence a letter to him.

You asked me the names of the ladies here from Louisiana; the name of a young widow here is Mrs. Trudore and there is another lady who came with her but I do not know her name. They are going to spend several years here, I believe.[24]

We are very sorry Cousin Emma's health is becoming so bad and trust that it will improve with Sulfer water, if we go to the Va. Springs.

I suppose you have seen an account of the postal regulations which requires an abolishment on & after 1st June of all the U.S. postage, making null the stamps etc. The rules for the transmission of letters is by prepayment in money, & the rates are, for every letter under 500 miles 5 cents; over 500, 10 cents. Our letters come under the firsts—5cts—as it is not over 500 miles from here to Raleigh. The Southern Confederacy Government intends this arrangement to continue until new stamps of the Southern Confederacy can be issued, which will be in the course of a month or so, I think.

We were quite astonished to see letters from Icha, who has made quite rapid progress in his studies, and has been paying strict attention to his lessons as he has learned to write & spell quicker than I ever saw one learn.

24. I have not been able to identify Mrs. Trudore.

I must at last close as I have nothing more to write about at present. I am looking for answers from Mary & Louty & will write to Icha soon, tho if he write again I will be very glad to hear from him. Hoping soon, my dear mother, to be with you all, I am as ever your affectionate son

James

Sam & Willie join me in kindest love to Mary, Louty, Icha & yourself, & to Cousin Eugenia & Cousin Emma. Tell William & Katy howdye—

THREE

Loyal Confederates, Reluctant Soldiers

APRIL–JUNE 1862

As the new year began, Sam, James, and their mother supervised the process of expanding the production of grain on the plantations in response to food shortages in Greene County and across the state. Both Sam and James continued to respect their mother's wishes, declining to volunteer for service in the Confederate Army. Then in early 1862, after the fall of Forts Henry and Donelson, the Union Army advanced south to capture the strategically vital railroad junction of the Mobile and Ohio and the Memphis and Charleston railroads at Corinth, Mississippi. If the Union Army successfully occupied Corinth, Confederate movement of troops and supplies across the South would be disrupted and Vicksburg and Mobile would be isolated. Major General Ulysses S. Grant advanced to nearby Pittsburgh Landing and awaited reinforcement from Major General Don Carlos Buell's Army of the Ohio, then in Nashville. General Albert Sidney Johnston, commander of the Confederate Army of Mississippi, then concentrated at Corinth, decided to attack Grant's army before Buell arrived. On April 6, screaming Confederates emerged from the woods near Shiloh Church, surprising Union troops, who fled the field. By the end of the day, General P. G. T. Beauregard, who had replaced the mortally wounded Johnston, informed Richmond that Confederate forces had "gained a complete victory." But, by the time Beauregard sent his message, Buell was arriving and, the next day, the Union

THE CONSEQUENCES OF CONFEDERATE CITIZENSHIP

Army launched a successful counterattack; the Confederate Army retreated to Corinth.[1]

With the Union Army bearing down on Corinth after its victory in the Battle of Shiloh, the Confederate secretary of war, Judah P. Benjamin, ordered General Braxton Bragg, commander of Confederate forces along the Gulf Coast, to move troops from Pensacola and Mobile to reinforce General P. G. T. Beauregard's Army of Mississippi, leaving only the troops then occupying Forts Morgan and Gaines at the mouth of Mobile Bay. Brigadier General Samuel Jones assumed command of the remaining Confederate forces in and around Mobile.[2]

When Jones arrived in Mobile, citizens of the city were in a near panic, having learned of the evacuation of Pensacola and fearing the same fate for their city. Jones wrote to Bragg that "the people are greatly alarmed at the report that this place is to be abandoned to the enemy." Governor John Gill Shorter had expressed his concern about the transfer of troops from Mobile to Tennessee and Kentucky in early January. Now, with troop strength reduced to new lows, Shorter feared that Union forces, recognizing an opportunity, would soon attack Mobile. He promised to send Jones a thousand thirty-day volunteers immediately and assured Jones more troops would be coming before the expiration of the thirty days.[3] Sam Pickens, contrary to his mother's wishes, decided to answer Shorter's call for volunteers. He left home in early April, certain that he would be returning soon, and traveled to a nearby port on the Black Warrior River to catch a riverboat for Mobile, where he was to report to a camp of instruction. His mother sent John, an enslaved man who had long been a "house servant" at Umbria, with her son to cook and attend to his needs.

By the time Sam reached Mobile, the Confederate Congress was debating a measure that would impose the first military draft in American history. Faced with Union challenges in the East and the West, and unable to raise enough manpower to address the demands of the army with volunteers, the

1. Eicher, *The Longest Night,* 250–52; Murray and Hsieh, *A Savage War,* 146–61.

2. Bragg to Benjamin, February 27, 1862; Bragg to Jones, February 27, 1862; Bragg to Jones, March 1, 1862, *The War of the Rebellion: A Compilation of the Official Records of the Union and Confederate Armies (OR),* vol. 10, ser. 1, pt. 2; Bergeron, *Confederate Mobile,* 22–24.

3. Jones to Bragg, March 6, 1862, *OR* ser. 1, vol. 10, pt. 2; *Alabama Beacon,* March 28, 1862; Linden and Linden, *Disunion, War, Defeat, and Recovery in Alabama,* 78.

Confederate government had proposed a conscription bill that would make all men aged eighteen to thirty-five subject to being called into the military for a term of three years. The bill as passed in mid-April 1862 allowed some exemptions, none of which applied to Sam or James.[4] Shortly after passage of the Conscription Act, Governor Shorter transferred the ninety-day men to the Confederate Army for the duration of the war, so Sam, because he was then part of the regular army, could not hire a substitute. Initially, it appeared, based on rumors circulating in camp, that Sam and the men in his company would be compelled to serve in units being formed in Mobile and Baldwin counties or be sent wherever the Confederate government chose. But the terms of the transfer did allow men to return home and enlist in a local company instead. Sam enlisted in Company D, Fifth Alabama Infantry, Army of Northern Virginia. He would be leaving for Virginia in the fall of 1862.[5]

Facing Sam's departure, Mary Gaillard was even more anxious about James's status. Neither she nor Sam thought James could cope with life in the army. They believed he could better serve the Confederacy by remaining at home and assisting his mother in managing the conversion of land to production of food for the armies and enslaved people, some of whom had recently resisted leaving their families to move from one plantation to another as James and Mary Gaillard had ordered. Under the circumstances, Sam agreed with his mother that James must find a way to remain at home and urged her to discourage any attempt by his brother to enlist. Sam saw two possibilities for James. He believed that James's fragile health might disqualify him from service. But, if the Confederate Army was willing to accept him, despite his "delicate constitution," then he should find a substitute, Sam advised.[6] At some point before he was to report, the Pickenses located and hired in Mobile a man named J. A. Rainsford, a "clerk" in the city and native of Glasgow, Scotland.[7]

4. Richmond *Daily Dispatch*, April 17, 1862.

5. *Alabama Beacon*, May 2, 1862.

6. James could not use the "Twenty Slave Law" because the Confederate Congress did not pass it until October 1862. On conscription and the debate surrounding it, see Moore, *Conscription and Conflict in the Confederacy*, chaps. 2–3; Doyle, "Replacement Rebels," 3–31; Sacher, "The Loyal Draft Dodger?" 154–60; Sacher, *Confederate Conscription*, 17–18; Mathisen, *The Loyal Republic*, 67–71.

7. Undated muster roll for the Thirty-Sixth Alabama Infantry, Muster Rolls of Alabama Civil War Units, SG025006–25100, Alabama Dept. of Archives and History.

||||||||||||||||||||||||||||||||||||||||||||||||||||||||||||||||||||||||||||||||||||||||||||||||||||||

Camp Shorter
April 11th, 1862.

My dear Mama,

I will pen you a few lines this morning to let you know that we are stored away safe and sound at Camp Shorter, near Hall's Mills. I intended writing from Mobile, but we were in such confusion—transferring our baggage, provisions etc. from the boat awaiting orders, and being mustered into service, during the evening of Wednesday when we arrived in the City—that I deferred writing, thinking we would probably remain there a day or two. On Thursday morning, however, we learned that we were to leave for this place at 10 O'clock A.M. So I had to hurry about looking for a pair of boots, which I finally succeeded in getting, and had not time to have my likeness taken nor to write. We had rather a pleasant trip down the river, but parting with my dear mother, brothers & sisters saddened my heart and depressed my spirits. I will write you a long letter soon and tell you more about our situation here, our stay in Mobile and our trip & etc. etc. Mr. Hutchinson is about to go up to the city & will take our letters, so I haven't time to write much. We are nicely quartered & faring sumptuously. Tell the children all to write to me & please do so yourself. Direct to me at Hall's Mills, Care of Capt. M.M. May.[8] Give my love to all & accept the same from

Your affectionate son,
Samuel

P.S. My best respects to Mrs. Grigg if she is still with you & to the Sawyers. The Dr. is well & will write I believe.[9] John sends howdy'e. S.P.

————•—•••———

8. May signed up as a ninety-day volunteer in Greensboro near the same time Sam did (CMSR, Alabama, RG 109, roll 141).

9. The doctor was Beverly Grigg of Greensboro, then the assistant surgeon for the Fourth Alabama Volunteers (CMSR, Alabama, RG 109, roll 141).

Camp Shorter
Near Hall's Mills,
April 13th, 1862

My dear Mother,

I had only time to write you a very short letter day before yesterday. As I am more at leisure today I will try and give you a longer one. It is almost impossible to write here, on account of the noise that is kept up around me. I commenced this letter today after returning from preaching—about 12 O'clock, and now I am writing by candle light. Well I must begin with our embarkation at East Port and give a sketch of our movements up to the present time, though nothing of interest has occurred as yet. As long as old East Port and our friends assembled on the bluff could be seen, every man on the boat stood out on the guards or on the upper deck to see the last of them; but when a bend in the river hid them from our view, we crowded into the Cabin around the Clerk's Office to try and procure comfortable quarters for sleeping. Capt. May got half of them State rooms only, as there were other soldiers aboard. So we got a room for each mess, of about eight; but we all managed to find a cot or bed on a table on the floor. By the next night, however, we had taken on so many more soldiers that the boat could not furnish bedding, but only a place on the floor for spreading our own blankets. We made out very well, though, in that line, and also in the fare. It was right dull one day as rain kept us in the cabin, but afterwards we enjoyed the fresh breeze and amused ourselves shooting at the water fowls. We arrived in Mobile about 12 M. Wednesday, but, as I told you, they kept us about the boat nearly all the evening—thus preventing us from attending to any business or from seeing the City. We slept on the boat the night we stayed in Mobile and got our meals at a restaurant where we had fresh fish and oysters. What a low flat country it is about Mobile. As you approach it, it looks like it was built in a marsh and almost on a level with the river. There are three rivers running side by side on the east of the city—the Mobile, the Tensaw, and the Spanish. I saw Mr. Green a few minutes.[10] His family is up the country. Joe and Henderson have also gone up for a short time, and Joe,

10. *Mobile Advertiser and Register,* August 20, September 25, 1861. Duff Green was the quartermaster general for Alabama and a partner in Israel Pickens's cotton-factorage firm.

they say, is quite sick. Hennie has been appointed adjutant of a regiment in Mobile. Mr. Green said he sent your papers up by Joe some time since, who was to carry them over to you, but had been prevented by the high water. Thursday morning we took the steamer Dixie and started for this place. We came down the bay about twelve or fifteen miles and then turned up Dog river which comes in on the West side. The bay is a right pretty sheet about eight or ten miles broad where we left it. There were several gun-boats to be seen steaming about, and two stationary batteries have been placed upon platforms built out in the water, commanding the channels to Mobile. We then came up Dog river—a small dark looking stream full of alligators—eight miles, and landed at the head of navigation. We marched from there to this Camp—two miles and a half—and began to clean up and fix our quarters. This is an extension Camp situated on a sandy pine ridge the only way by which the Yankees can come on land from the coast to Mobile—so I've been told. There is a drill ground cleared off a mile or more in length, and the houses are built in a row along one side of it. The houses are hastily constructed one story framed buildings, containing eight rooms. On one side of the room there are two troughs one above the other long enough for two men and broad enough for two lying abreast—thus accommodating a mess of eight. We fill the troughs up with pine straw and spread our blankets over. Then there are some shanties in which we cook and eat. John cooks very well and has the meals ready promptly at the hours appointed. I will now give you some of the Camp regulations. The drum taps at half past five A.M. for roll call. We are then dismissed, and at six we eat breakfast. At nine the drill begins and lasts until eleven. Between twelve and one dinner comes on, after which we take a nap or a game of Euchre, etc. Again at half past two we go out and drill two hours more; then rest till half after five when we have dress parade. The orders for the next day are then read out and the no. of men from each company detailed for guard duty, and for building the houses that were blown down some time ago. We eat supper before dark. The roll is called again at 8 P.M., and at 10 the drum taps for lights to be put out, when we go to bed, if we have not already done so. They will soon begin to drill us two or three hours a day more; that is if we stay here. It is not thought that we will remain much longer. Certainly there is no use for it. It seems that the citizens of Mobile became panic stricken and prevailed upon the Governor to call for the sixty companies for ninety days, but before many had time to get here he found out that there was no use for them and has put a stop to their coming. In Mobile he said that if we would give up our guns we might go home; that our arms were needed and not ourselves. It is a useless expense to the state to keep us, and I suppose he will disband the companies and press their arms into service. We will see before long.

Mon. 14th. I attended preaching here yesterday and heard another poor sermon. Mr. Hutchinson was to preach but did not arrive this evening.

We have very good water except that it is not very cold and I think this must be a healthy place, as it is a dry piny woods country.

Well this is really a long winded letter and I must bring it to a close. We have not been able to hear anything from our army at Corinth for four or five days. We whipped the Yankees badly and took a great many prisoners, cannon and small arms. Some of our men who were in Mobile a day or two ago saw Gen. Prentiss and seventeen hundred other prisoners.[11] We have heard that Fort Pulaski below Savannah has been taken, but have heard no particulars. I hope dear Mama, to hear from you very soon, informing me that you and the children are all well.

Give my love to Jamie, Mary, Willy, Louty and Icha, and tell them I will be very glad to get letters from them as often as they can write. I left Mary's letter with Gen. Green to mail. Dr. Grigg sends his kind regards to you and the children. He and Mr. Sawyer are both well.

Accept the sincere love of
Your affectionate son,
Samuel

P.S. Letters to us should be directed to Hall's Mills, Care of Capt. M.M. May. Mr. Sawyer says please tell his wife, as he forgot to tell her in his letter. S.P.

---

11. Union General B. M. Prentiss, captured at Shiloh, along with much of his command, was confined in Mobile for a short time before being paroled (Prentiss to Charles S. String-fellow, Assistant Adjutant General, CSA, April 13, 1852, *OR*, ser. 1, v. 10, pt. 1: 410, 842).

Umbria, April 25th 1862

My dear Son,

Your very affectionate and highly interesting letter was rec'd a few days since; but as Jamie & Mary are good correspondents, I deferred answering it until today. Altho I have nothing new to communicate, and my spirits are quite depressed, I know my letter will be acceptable if you only hear that all are well—such is the case, and we should be truly thankful for it. Since the conscription bill has passed, I have suffered great uneasiness of mind, and Jamie has regretted many times that he did not join your company. I too regret it exceedingly, for if he is obliged to leave us, I shall be truly unhappy if he cannot be with you. If he could now join your company, I would advise him to start on Monday, but I do not know if that would be allowed. I hope that the war will soon close, and all will be well; but God! only knows whether we are to be more deeply involved in trouble or speedily delivered out of the hands of our enemies. We are not well posted up in what is going on in the War department, only a few papers have been rec'd since the Dr went away and the last one stated that his paper would then be stopped. Jamie & I are going to subscribe to the *Reporter* as we cannot well do without it. The subscription has been raised to $10 per year.[12] On Tuesday last we attended St. Paul's Church, Greensboro by invitation to see Miss Ann Charles married to Mr Pearson, a nephew of Mrs Croom.[13] Never was such a kissing scene witnessed in public as we did, after the ceremony was over. Miss Ann looked pretty & interesting, and has gone to her new home near Tuscaloosa to enter upon her duties. Report says Mr Cobbs will be married to Miss Fannie Avery next month—how true, I cannot tell.

I fear we shall have some trouble about getting our servants' shoes. You must inquire if there be any chance of getting them in Mobile, as that would

12. Mary Gaillard was referring to the *Selma Reporter*.

13. Ann H. Charles was the daughter of Jonathan Charles, a neighbor of the Pickenses in the Hollow Square District of Greene County, who married John S. Pearson April 22, 1862 (U.S. Census, 1860 and 1850; U.S. County Marriage Records, Alabama, 1805–1967). Fannie Avery did marry Richard H. Cobbs on May 15, 1862 (*Alabama County Marriages*, online database). Cobbs was the rector of St. Paul's Church in Greensboro. He had held that position for two years when he married Avery. His father was Bishop Nicholas Hamner Cobbs, the first bishop of the Diocese of Alabama (Yerby, *History of Greensboro*, 194–95).

be better than to get them from the Stickneys, whose shoes are not well liked.

Unfortunately we are yet without a teacher. Several ladies could be got, but I think a young girl would not do much good among my children. I have written to engage Mr Williams' music teacher for Mary, but have not yet heard from him. I can send you some chickens, butter etc. if you are to remain. You must tell me in your next letter. All unite in much love to you. May God bless & protect you, my dear, dear son.

Your Mother

Lou will write & tell John about Suky.[14] Destroy all my letters, as soon as they are read. Kind remembrance to Friends.

Umbria, April 27th 1862

Dear Sam,

Again I take my pen in hand to write you a short letter, but as Mary & Mama have also written there will be no news for me to write. It is needless to say we all miss you very much indeed, and it seems to me several months instead of weeks since you left. There are few people in the neighborhood & it is only occasionally that any one is seen passing on the road.

We were at Wesley Chapel today and heard a fine sermon from Mr. Hutchinson.[15] The assembly was quite a small one and compared very strikingly with a few years ago—in times of peace—where the house was crowded.

The Conscription Bill has been passed and they say it will require everyone, without exception, to leave & fill up either companies, battalions or regiments which are incomplete.

I suppose I will have to go & if I am to, I will not go anywhere but with you. I wish you would speak with Capt. May & see if another member can

14. Suky was John's wife.
15. J. J. Hutchinson had been the Methodist minister in Greensboro. The Pickenses were Episcopalian but obviously attended other services at times (Yerby, *History of Greensboro*, 111).

join the company & if I can go there. Mama is at a loss what she will do if I go, but thinks of staying with Cousin Isabella in town. What would you advise her to do? I would not leave until I saw her & the children in security & safety. Mama is going to send to the Salt works to get some for the plantations & a little for this place. Mr. High sent up 14 sacks for the salt & mama is going to send for that quantity, if it is cheap, to try it. The 14 sacks will amount to $63.00, at $1.50 per bushel; but this is better than to buy from speculators. I am going to Eastport tomorrow & inquire the price etc. of the salt.

We heard today at church from Mr. Hutchinson that N. Orleans had been taken by the Yankee vandals, by an approach from the Bay side of the city. He says the telegraph operator bade the citizens of N.O. goodbye, saying he would not telegraph any more for them. Mr. H didn't know whether the city was shelled or not. Now you know all about the rumor & must write us. I don't believe it, & hope it isn't so. We have no news now as the Reporter has stopped—time out. Mama sent on to get it for six months, yesterday & we may get it in a few days. The price of it now is $10 a year. The *on dit* is that Nashville has been retaken, by our men. I hope that is so. Have you heard it confirmed?

If you have not already written about sending negroes to the upper part of the State, mama wants you to do so & tell her whether it would be best to send males or females, & of anything else in relation to it that you think would be best.

I enclose you a slip from mama about John's wife. Also I send you a Beacon & a thrilling & bold adventure of the Yankees on a Georgia railroad, which if you have not read already, you will find very interesting. That conductor Fuller deserves something handsome & a great deal of praise for his bold & enterprising procedure in the chase.

Katy became so bad & ungovernable that Mama sent her to the Lawlesses a few days ago. In exchange for her she took Ann & Robert to remain here awhile. Since Katy left, Simon has been remarkably changed in manner & rather displeased. Ann also is very sorry she has come etc. In fact they are all dissatisfied & give more trouble to us than you can imagine.[16]

16. Ann and Robert were married and had two children, Lindy and Mary Ann. In their inventories, the Pickenses identified enslaved families. See Umbria Account Books, 1853, Pickens Family Papers.

These lines are close & this is a longer letter than it looks to be; am as most of it is trash & I have no news to tell you I must close, anxiously awaiting the reception from you of an answer to my last.

Tell the Dr & Mr. Sawyer how d'ye & all my friends that inquire. All are well & unite with me in love to you. Be sure & write soon as I will expect a letter.

Your affectionate brother,
James

P.S. Tell John how d'ye

———•———

Camp Shorter
May 3rd, 1862

My dear Mother,

I must return thanks for the kind favor recd from you, and also to Jamie and Mary for one from each of them. It affords me great pleasure to hear that you are all enjoying good health but I'm sorry that you are so depressed in spirits. These are dark and troublous times but you know it is said that the darkest hour of the night immediately precedes the dawn. We must never despair, but trust in God for deliverance from our enemies. We may be made to suffer a great deal as a punishment for our sins as a nation, but I cannot believe that we—contending only for self-government—are to be subjugated and ruled by the despicable Yankees, a people so corrupt and depraved. I hope we will gain a victory at Yorktown and at Corinth that will check the Yankees for some time, if not put an end to the war. We had a rumor today of a terrible battle at the former place but do not know if it is reliable. Don't feel any uneasiness about the Conscription Act as regards Jamie. He could join any Company he might prefer until the act goes into effect, but he must not do so. He ought by all means to remain at home with you and the children, and being of a delicate constitution he ought to be able to get an exemption from military duty, but if he should not I think he ought to get a substitute. It is not certain what we will do. A report came from the city a few days since that we would be disbanded very soon, but it is not credited. An order is out today to the effect that all troops in the service of the Confederate States for ninety days will be allowed to enlist for the war in any regiment now being formed in Mobile or Baldwin counties, but in no others. This is to aid a few favorites about Mobile in filling out their regiments, and I am glad to see that not a man in our Company and none I believe in the regiments will join them. Mobile is behaving shamefully. It is not worth defending. Two regiments of Mobile men were disbanded today (Sunday 4th) in the city. That doesn't look much like defending it to the last, as Brig. Gen. Forney, in command of this district says he will do. The fact is the best part of the population is in the army, and the present one, composed in a great measure of Yankees and foreigners, have been engrossed in making money heretofore and are now employed in shipping their goods up the country for fear the city might be destroyed.[17]

Speaking of regiments, we had a regimental organization ourselves about ten days ago. The ten companies of ninety-day troops formed themselves into a regiment and elected Wm. M. Byrd of Selma, Colonel, Richard Randolph Lieut. Col., and a Lieut. Smith of Autauga Co., Major.[18] They are all nice men and will make good officers.

Now for a little business. I have spoken to all the large planters in our Company about getting negro shoes, and all say that they patronize Stickney and that they know of no other chance. And moreover that they do not intend to give their negroes but one pair a year, both on account of the expense and the scarcity of leather. I would make the negroes patch up their old shoes and try and make them last during the summer for I do not believe a supply could be had now. We must apply early enough to get the fall shoes in good time.

17. Brigadier General John H. Forney had recently assumed command of the Department of Florida and West Alabama. See Bergeron, *Confederate Mobile*, 24.

18. William Byrd was a former Alabama legislator and a lawyer in Selma, Alabama. During the secession crisis, he opposed secessionists in Alabama and in 1860 voted for William Bell, the Constitutional Union candidate. Like many others, once Alabama seceded, he defended the Confederacy. See Fitts, *Selma*, 45–46. Randolph was a planter from the Newtown District of Greene County (U.S. Census, 1860; Confederate Amnesty Papers, 1865–67, RG 94, National Archives). Lieutenant Smith was James M. Smith, who entered service at Prattville, Autauga County, Alabama, in March 1862 and was elected major in May (CMSR, Alabama, RG 109, roll 141).

And Miss Ann Charles is married. That kissing scene which took place after the ceremonies were over must have been quite interesting to the spectators, and I suppose more so to the participants. Accept many thanks for the chickens and butter you sent. The jar of butter was sent from the city here on a dray, together with other things for the Camp, but the chickens did not come. Next day the boat came down but no chickens, and I then sent Mr. Ross word to send them by the stage. Today I recd a message from him saying that he had entirely forgotten them every time an opportunity offered, and had finally concluded not to send them as it was doubtful whether I would get them safely. It is my opinion that chickens being a rarity in Mobile, Mr. R didn't try hard to get them away. I am under obligations to Mary for a beautiful pair of gloves and another letter.

I forgot to mention that Dr. Grigg has recd the appointment of Assistant Surgeon of our regiment. He would have been made Surgeon, but for the fact that our regimental officer had already been chosen from our Company. Also that Mr. Sawyer has been promoted to 3rd Sergeant. They both send kind regards to you and all the family. My best love to my dear Mother, brothers and sisters. I will answer Jamie's & Mary's letters very soon. Tell Willy and Icha to write to me—I haven't heard from them yet. Louty owes me a letter and must send it soon. Tell the servants all howd'ye. John sends howdye to all.

Hoping soon to hear from you,
I remain
Your affectionate son,
Samuel.

———— • ◆ • ————

Umbria, May 9th 1862

My dear Son,

Your letter of the 3rd reached me yesterday, and we were all highly delighted to hear from you. I had determined upon writing to you, ere your favor was rec'd, but did not feel very well and therefore deferred the pleasure. To-day I am very well, and will give you some of the passing events at home. All are well and as happy as we can be under existing circumstances—the horrors of war around us, and separated from you my dear Son, whom we all miss from our family circle more than words can express. I used to count the time of your absence and think we should have the happiness of being together at the expiration of the time for which you enlisted, but it seems you are in for the War, and cannot return to us until it is at an end. I trust that God! Will be graciously pleased to bring the War to a speedy close, and grant us a lasting peace. You tell me I must not be troubled about the conscription bill; but how can I be otherwise when Jamie will probably have to leave us: he will not consent to send a substitute, and on the 15th of this month the bill will go into effect. Some persons have told me that he will not be called into service now, but this I do not mind, for I know he will be subject to a call whenever an emergency arises. I am confident Jamie could not endure the hardships and fatigue of military life, and have urged him to provide a substitute. This is what William Withers intends doing.[19] Only 5 days are now left for Jamie to think upon it & determine what shall be done. Your advice on the subject may have some effect in convincing him to get a substitute; but where can one be found. I would turn out in search of one, if Jamie were willing for me to do so. I think our Governor will err in judgment if he calls out the few remaining men in this neighborhood. The negro who escaped hanging by absconding has lately been heard of, and search is now being made with hope of taking him soon. This must be kept a profound secret, Mrs. Sawyer says. She is now at home having spent two weeks with her friend and is quite well. I hope Mrs. Enoch will return home on Monday next.

Mary commenced music and singing lessons yesterday under Professor Damer, who says she has a fine taste for music and will make a beautiful singer in two months.[20] This is very encouraging and will doubtful stimulate her to be a proficient. The children need a teacher badly, and cannot get one until the war closes. They read and improve upon themselves in that way.

19. She was referring to the brother of Robert Withers, who was an aide to Major General Jones M. Withers, commander of the Second Division of the Army of Tennessee at the time of this letter (United States Confederate Officers Card Index, 1861–65). His family resided in the Hollow Square District of Greene County, near the Pickenses. William, his brother, hired a substitute so he could remain at home to assist his family in managing their plantations. See Will Records, Greene County Probate Court.

20. Thomas Damer was a music teacher for the Pickenses. He and his family had moved to Greene County from Baltimore sometime between 1860 and the date of this letter (U.S. Census, 1860).

Icha is still my scholar and improves very fast: he is a very smart & good boy. Jennie Vail is again staying with us: she is quite smart & interesting. Willie agrees with me in that opinion. They ride together on horseback every morning & afternoon with Mary. Portis' pony, James and Dr's are in constant use.

Mr. High was here yesterday and says he has a very promising crop of corn. His wheat is not good, being filled with rust. We got 6 bushels of stock peas for him last Evening from Mr. Kimbrough at $1 per bushel. Table peas he got from Dick Davis at $2 per bushel. Two hands are to be sent from the Canebreak to the northern part of this county, or the adjoining one, to work the crops of our poor soldiers. May Heaven smile upon our cause, give victory to our arms, and let the soldiers return to their homes. Then should our hearts be filled with the liveliest emotions of gratitude, and our lives devoted to his service.

Mr. Lawless was here a few days ago with his tax bill: he says his corn crop is very good but his "cotton looks sorry" in consequence of so much rain & cold weather. The servants are well at all our places, except poor Matt, who had two very severe convulsions on Sunday last, and Katy, who is now in bed. I fear her usefulness is almost at an end. If the war were over, I would send a servant to learn to sew. Times are getting so hard, I doubt if anyone would take an apprentice now. Mr. High says he would put Green to the blacksmiths' trade. What do you say? Shall we send him or keep him at home until the last of the year.

I was very much provoked with W.R. for keeping your chickens; it is one of the meanest acts I ever heard of but in perfect keeping with all I have heard of him. I will take care that no more chickens or anything else which he can make money on shall fall into his hands. I have the promise of more, and will send them on Monday next, directed to the care of Sam Webb, who I am told takes much pleasure in forwarding things to the camp. I have almost finished my letter, and have not said one word about the fall of New Orleans. I am truly sorry that such an important place should have fallen into the hands of our enemies without an effort being made to retain it. If Lovell is really guilty of having acted such a part, he deserves banishment, but I can't believe it is the case.[21] I wonder what the Hunts' will do. We learned from

21. Reference is to Major General Mansfield Lovell, the CSA commander in New Orleans when it fell. See Eicher, *The Longest Night*, 237–41.

the *Beacon* today that a terrible battle is expected to take place at Corinth. May we gain a glorious victory and put our enemies to flight.

We have subscribed to the *Selma Reporter*, which we hope to get in a few days, as it is unpleasant to be without news, particularly at this time when we feel such an intense interest in what is going on.

I have at last got my watch from Eutaw. Mr. Mayfield kindly brought it for me.

Your friends inquire kindly about you, and desire their kind regards to be sent to you. Mr. High has just sent a note in which he desires to be kindly remembered to you & Dr. Grigg. You must promise to destroy this and all my letters you have rec'd before I send you another scrawl. All the children write with me in warmest love to you. God! Bless you my dear, dear Son, and grant you may never be called to the field of battle, but return you to us in honor & safety.

Your Mother

Kind regards to all friends. Howd'ye to John from all of us.

———— ·—·— ————

Umbria, May 12th 1862

Dear Sam,

We are about to send to the river in order to see if there may not be a letter for some of us from you. I have written you two since I have heard from you; but of course I will not be so unreasonable as to expect you to write so often. Mama received your last letter the other day & we were very glad to hear you were well. She answered it last Saturday I think or may be before that.

I am writing this letter to tell you that Mama thinks she had better send you another servant. We heard this morning that your company were doing very hard work. Mama told me to tell you that as John has to cook, his time is mostly occupied & he would be of very little use in helping you. She told me to ask you had she not better send you a servant & to ask you which one would you prefer.

I think you had better take one, as you would be relieved of a great deal of trouble & it would be so easy to get one. Write soon & let us know & if you want one where to send him so as to reach the Company.

Our *Selma Reporter* first came this morning. It is a rare thing to see a paper here now. It had very little news in it. Norfolk, I expect you have heard, has been evacuated. It seems, as one by one our coast cities are left & our forces are drawn from them, that they are all untenable & will in course of time share the same fate. I earnestly hope & trust that Mobile will be an exception; & that all the labor our 90 day's companies & others are expending in filling up the channel, will not be in vain, but will be the means of preventing the infernal & accursed enemy from ascending with his gunboats our Warrior river.

The paper, under a cannon firing—announces the commencement of another great battle at Corinth. May God grant in his merciful wisdom to send victory to our arms, & to insure by a signal success over our enemies a speedy & lasting peace! It seems to me this war cannot last much longer. That an enemy so atrocious, so utterly regardless of right & so bent upon the destruction of an innocent people, will be permitted to carry out their fiendish purposes, seems to me impossible; but that they will be punished for their war of invasion & devastation, is certain.

On Friday Mr. Wheelan of Greensboro (the old man) died, having been taken sick on the Tuesday before. He died of pneumonia. This morning & just now, a funeral notice came from Mr. W. T. Stringfellow's who died recently.

I must close as it is time my letter had gone.

You must write soon when you get fixed etc.

You must let us know where to direct letters, so as to get to you.

Mama & the children join me in love to you

Believe me your affectionate brother,

James

This is a piece of an exercise book. It makes nice paper to write on.

———•—•———

Mobile, May 14th, 1862

My dear Mother,

Your long and highly-prized letter reached me yesterday and its perusal gave me great pleasure. I am glad to hear that you are all well at home, and hope you will continue in the enjoyment of perfect health. There have been quite a number of cases of the measles in our company and in several others of this regiment, but they have generally been mild and soon recover. I have only time to write a short letter this evening as it has to be put in the office by 3 o'clock in order to go by today's mail. You say that Jamie is unwilling to get a substitute, and of course it must worry you to think that he will be soon liable to be called out for military service. I therefore was anxious to write and urge upon Jamie the imperative necessity of his remaining at home. If he were to leave, you and the children would be there alone without a protector and no one to attend to business for you. It is not expected that every male member of a family should enlist in the army. Robert Withers' being away has made it necessary that William should stay, and Jamie's is a parallel case. And then as you say he could not well endure the hardships and fatigues incident to the military service. I spoke to Dr. Grigg about it and he says by all means Jamie ought to send a substitute. I am told that in Greene substitutes are very hard to find and are asking enormous hire. A good many men in the ninety days service here have been employed as substitutes and I suppose there are some yet who can be got. The Conscription Act has worried a great deal the men in the 90 days service who are subject to it. They are uncertain as to whether it can interfere with our present organization or not. It has been asserted by men in Mobile that as soon as the law goes into effect, we in the ninety days service *will be* immediately conscribed and put wherever the Confederate authorities may choose to send us. But I believe they say so in order to frighten men into the regiments now being filled out in Mobile & Baldwin counties. Gov. Shorter says that the ninety-day troops will serve their term out and be disbanded and sent home, where they will then volunteer or be enrolled. That is his opinion and may or may not be correct, for no one seems to know how it will be. That certainly would be the only just way of treating them as the men left home prepared to be absent only for three months, and are now in service here in a place under martial law where an order has been issued that no man can be transferred from their companies to those for the war unless it be in one of the regiments in Mobile & Baldwin counties. Now a good many of the men have relations in the army in Virginia, Tennessee etc. and would prefer going there. A number of our men, however, have gone into these regiments from choice, on account of having many acquaintances in them. I hope it will be as the Gov. says and that we will all go home for a short time in July and then make a new start for the war.

May 15th. I was detailed yesterday evening to go down to the wharf and load boats and consequently was unable to get my letter off. I have seen Joe Pickens several times and he always inquires particularly after you and the children. He was sick several weeks ago and is looking quite thin.[22] I am glad you have got your watch home at last. It ought to be in first rate order as it was in the hands of the jeweler for six months, I believe. I was exceedingly sorry to hear of the death of Dr. Harrison. He was one of the kindest and nicest old gentlemen I have ever seen. He will be much missed as a teacher as he was an excellent one, and the best linguist I suppose in America.

The chickens that you were kind enough to send me were kept here a week with little or nothing to eat and then sent to Hall's Mills and, as it happened, we had to come away the next day, so I made them a present to the sick people who were left in the hospital. After they fattened them up a little they, no doubt, made fine soup etc., and were better food for the sick than anything that could be had down there.

Mr. Webb is a better one to send things to than Mr. R., I suppose. I notice that all the boxes that are recd. are sent to his care. By the way he had a schooner or steamboat (I don't know which) to run the blockade last week,

22. Joseph A. Pickens, nephew of Governor Francis Pickens of South Carolina, lived in Eutaw. His father was Joseph Pickens, the brother of a former governor of South Carolina and president of the Bank of Alabama, Andrew Pickens. Popular myth has it that this Andrew Pickens was the brother of Samuel Pickens's father. This line of Pickenses, however, descended from Revolutionary War General Andrew Pickens, of South Carolina. See "Andrew Pickens, Jr. 16th Governor of the State of South Carolina."

In June 1861, Joseph requested an appointment as a lieutenant in the Confederate Army. According to his service record, however, he enlisted as a private in Company K, Third Alabama Infantry Regiment, the "Mobile Rifles," despite a glowing recommendation from his uncle. After service during the Peninsula Campaign, Joseph was discharged, for unknown reasons, and returned to Mobile, where he had enlisted (CMSR, Alabama, RG 109, roll 311).

and it was said at first to have bro't a good many arms, but it turned out that it had very few. There was one thing brought, though, that I wanted to get *very much* and send to you—and that was a bunch of Bananas; but it was not for sale, it having been sent to Mr. W. as a present. I had an opportunity at last to have my likeness taken two days since and sent it up by Mr. Herndon of Newbern, who was to leave it with Mr. Stollenwerck in Greensboro.[23] The artist was busy and did not make a very nice job of it. I ought to have my knife on the right side to have made it appear on the left in the picture, but I didn't think of it & the artist neglected to tell me. I would have made him take it over again but for being in a hurry, although that was the third trial. I am glad the children have commenced music again and hope they will improve rapidly. Mr. Damer really predicts fine success for Mary, and I have no doubt she will equal his expectations if she will exert herself and practice a good deal. Louty is too young to take singing lessons, but she can learn to play well on the piano. Icha you say is a good boy and is improving fast: he must write me a letter before long. I am glad to hear that the corn crop is so promising at the plantations. A large crop will be needed this year and it will be made, if we are only blessed with favorable seasons. I suppose Green might as well be at the trade now if Mr. High does not need him in laying by the crop.[24] You will have to find out if Mr. Mayfield is willing before sending Green there. Please give my respects to Mr. High and tell him I will be glad to hear from him.

John sends howd'ye to you and all, and says that whenever he has any nice fish to cook he thinks of you all at home and wishes you had them there. We haven't had as many here as we had at Hall's Mills, as we have to send to the market for them and they sell dearer too. I happened to be on the wharf yesterday evening when a fisherman returned with the fruits of his day's labor, and I got from him a string of the nicest trout you ever saw. Some of them were over a foot in length. I do wish you could have had them, you would have enjoyed them so much. Do they require specie for postage stamps up at home now? For if they do, I will get you some here as they take shinplaster [*a bank or private note of little or no value*] or any sort of money.

23. Frank Stollenwerck was a commission merchant in Mobile. He worked for J. A. Wemyss & Co. (*Snedecor's 1855–56 Directory of Greene County*).

24. Green was an enslaved man on the Pickenses' Canebrake Plantation (1857 Estate Inventory, Greene County Probate Court).

In addressing letters to me it is better not to send them to the care of Mr. Webb, but to Capt May as they will then be taken out of the office with the mail for the regiment. I must beg to be excused from destroying your letters as I prize them *very highly* and have carefully preserved every one I have ever received from you.

Tomorrow will be fast day and we will all attend church. I hope you will have an opportunity of doing likewise. I am obliged to Mary for a letter just recd., and will answer it soon. Also Willy's & Louty's. I am expecting a letter from Jamie. My warmest love to him, Mary, Willy, Louty, & Icha, and to you, my dear Mother. Hoping to hear from you again soon, I remain,

Your affectionate son,
Samuel.

———•·•———

Mobile, May 18th 1862

My dear mother,

According to the promise which I made you before leaving, I will let you know how I got down here etc. Upon taking the stage at the gate, I met in it a Mr. Hanna, with whom I was acquainted. He only went as far as Hollow Square where his place was taken by Mr. Howell. There were in the stage several interesting & agreeable gentlemen who whiled away the otherwise tiresome, dusty & hot ride to Scooba. We traveled very pleasantly while it was cool but it soon became warm & dusty. We took breakfast in Eutaw, got a relay of horses & proceeded on our way & after a long & tiresome day's ride at length reached Scooba. We had no sooner got out of the stage than the puffing cars came along, crowded to overflowing, from Corinth. We got our baggage & rushed to the train but were informed by the conductor that no others could possibly get aboard, & soon after the train moved off for Mobile. So we were left till the next morning before a possibility of leaving appeared. A more wretched night was never passed by anyone than Howell & I passed at the depot in Scooba—a night which I will never forget. We had to make out the best way we could for a bed & finally crawled into an empty car on a side track, when we worried the time out till morning. No trains came at all the next day (Friday) except some freight trains in the evening which were going only to Enterprise, a small village not far from Scooba. Again we were very much disappointed & had to lay over till 12 o'clock Friday night when the mail train from Corinth arrived. We got on board & after traveling nearly all of Saturday got here in the evening about 7 o'clock. We put up at the Battle House[25] & went immediately for supper us not having tasted food since the evening before & consequently very hungry. I have never had such a time as I had in Scooba. Without anything to eat or anywhere to sleep we spent a very trying time. We were very thankful indeed for your lunch & but for it I do not know what we would have done.

After supper we went to a restaurant as we got scarcely anything at the Battle House. While we were at the restaurant some one called me, but as I thought I knew no one there I did not answer but instantly looked around & saw Dr. Grigg. He seemed very glad indeed to see me & after we had finished a plate of oysters he went with me to the camp where I have been ever since. Sam was the first person I saw. He is in good health & looks better than I have ever seen him for a long time. Camp life agrees with him very well. He was sitting around a group of the soldiers listening to some very sweet music from two violins—one played by Mr. Sawyer. Sam says he was never more surprised in his life than he was on meeting with me. It was not long after that, that we went to bed.

They are under a large cotton shed on the river & have their camp utensils, cots, tables arranged in order, all together are very comfortably fixed. Sam says the accommodations at Halls Mills were much better. They had houses with rooms there. We slept on Sam's mattress & covered with a blanket. It is very pleasant here after sun set when the sea breeze from the Bay is continually blowing.

There are several large sheds here under each of which is a company. It is quite a lively scene near the meal times when all the cooks are busily engaged in preparing the food. They are living very well here indeed & the cooking is very nice.

Mr. Sawyer asked a thousand questions about his wife & family how they were, where were they & also inquired about you & all the children. He

25. The Battle House was and still is a hotel in Mobile.

looks very well indeed—tho' not fat as we heard he was—has turned out his beard which gives him an eccentric appearance, & stands the life, they say, very well indeed. All of my acquaintances in the Company were glad to see me & asked after their friends in Greene.

This morning (Sunday) we intended going to church but went, before, with Capt. May to take a bath after which it was too late.

Just now Sam is on guard duty, guarding some Yankee bridge burners who are confined not far from here. They detail a certain number from each company every day for guard & other purposes. This evening continued reports of cannon were heard in the city & in this camp—supposed to be the Yankees engaging Fort Morgan 40 miles distant. Pickets were called & have been stationed for several miles around the city. No attack is apprehended at this place, tho' they keep guard most of the time.

Well I must say I have written you a very wordy & long letter & you are tired; so I will close. Sam desired me to give his kindest love to you & the children, in which I cordially unite with him. Write soon my dear mother and let me know how you & the children are.

Sam would like a few articles of clothing which I forgot but I do not know what they are & will not send this evening.

Your affectionate son, James

———•———

Mobile, May 24th 1862

My dear mother,

Mr. Benners is about to leave camp for his home & I thought I would write you a few lines in order to let you know that we are well and mention when I will probably be back.[26] I concluded this evening to wait until Monday. There is a boat leaving this evening but as one will leave on Monday also I thought I would stay a day or two longer with Sam. There is no train leaving this evening & none will run til Monday. We have anxiously looked out for letters every day until we have come to the conclusion that there is

26. J. H. Benners enlisted as a ninety-day volunteer on March 29, 1862. After finding a substitute, he was discharged May 29 (CMSR, Alabama, RG 109, roll 311).

something wrong in the mails between Hollow Square & this place. Every other camp around this one gets a large package, it seems, constantly, but none comes for this company; in fact I believe the package of letters for this camp today amounted only to five or six letters.

A great many members of this company have hired substitutes for the expiration of their 90 days' service, and are leaving every day. Mr. Benners is one of these. It has a tendency to make those who remain quite anxious to leave; and this is very plain, as every one with whom I have talked seems to be very anxious to leave. I wish, oh greatly, that Sam would get one & return home. Mr. Green advised him to do so, but the only difficulty is that the military authorities will not allow but one or two a month to get substitutes.[27]

By the way, Mr. Green has advised me what to do. He said this evening that it would be best for me to go home & wait until I am called upon as a conscript; then he said I must take the substitute & go to a camp of instruction with him, have him examined by a surgeon, give in his name in my place & receive a written certificate to that effect from the officer commanding the camp. He says that nothing definite has been done as yet in the way of forming camps. That it is not likely that they will be formed soon, or that the conscripts will be called on to perform duty. He says that a number of instances have occurred here in which $500 or $600 have been given to substitutes & these have run away, consequently cheating the employer of both his money & the services which he had promised to render him.

We have seen Mrs. Green, Joe & Henderson & they enquired after you and the children. Henderson has joined a company belonging to a Col. Coleman's regiment and will be in service somewhere not far from here.

Sam & I walked over the greater part of Mobile yesterday & have seen about everything that is of any interest. Mobile is a very pretty city & there are some beautiful residences here, but it is not near so large as Baltimore or half as pretty. However, it is a Southern city & is pretty enough for Southerners, and when the war shall have ended, it is destined to become a great & magnificent one.

There are, as usual, vastly conflicting rumors concerning the war & a great

---

27. James was referring to Quartermaster General Duff Green.

68

variety of them. Some are "almost certain" that it can not last long, in fact all are, almost; while others go farther & say it cannot last over two or three months. It is evident, beyond a doubt, that the North to day, are more tired & sicker of the war than we of the South, and it is said that neither party will do much more fighting, but that the quarrel will be adjusted by long diplomatic harangues & a great talk. However it may end I hope that it will not take place unless upon honorable terms to the South & by a restoration the North of all Southern territory & property.

I was sorry to hear that [*unclear*] had left, as he promised to stay & look after the place, and be a sort of protector. It was a very shabby trick.

Sam & I walked all over town yesterday to see on what terms we could get sugar & molasses. Sam did not find any nice clear brown sugar at all, but all was a good article of the darker kind and at 35 cts per lb. The molasses was all at $1.35, not quite as dear as it was the other day when I wrote you the price ($1.50). We heard from a great many of the merchants yesterday, that they were expecting lots of both sugar & molasses from points on the railroad above here, and we concluded to wait longer, thinking that when it is received, the price will become more reasonable. We got the thread & needles etc. but saw nothing suitable for your [*unclear*]. We are going out again this evening and will make another attempt towards purchasing them. There are a few good stores here which have a good many articles in them, but most of them are very empty & charge enormously.

I will bring Howell home, and he can stay there until the camps of instruction are forming and the conscripts called out.[28] He can therefore work his mother's crop himself & release us from doing it. Sam talked to Howell & to his step-father, Mr. Willingham, about the bargain & they say they know something of the particulars, but that it was all Mayfield's doing. He told them that it must have been that his pay should depend on the length of time that he would be in service, that is, that he was to get so much per month. He ought not to expect all his pay in money, but receive part pay in cotton. If all

28. Joseph Howell, son of Eliza Willingham, stepson of Francis Willingham. The Pickenses were apparently providing assistance to Mrs. Willingham while Francis and Howell were away. There were other children in the family, but they were too young to provide much labor on the farm (U.S. Census, 1860, Alabama).

these particulars haven't been noticed in the contract, I will try and arrange them when I get home. We mentioned the case to Dr. Grigg, & he says that Mayfield is such an outrageous sharper that he has charged this big price & arranged it so that he will get the greater portion of it himself—tho' if I can prevent this taking place I certainly will do so, and adjust it satisfactorily.

Sam sends his love to you and says he has been expecting letters from home but hasn't got any for some days & thinks they must have miscarried. He joins me in kindest love to you & the children.

Your affectionate son
James.

————— · ◆ · —————

Mobile, June 6th, '62

My dear Mother,

I have been wanting to write to you for some time, but ever since Jamie left I've been on duty every other day, and so time has slipped by without my doing so. We are kept so busy here generally that the days seem to pass quite rapidly. The last time I wrote to Mary, I answered four of her letters in one. She is such a good correspondent that her letters accumulated faster than I could reply to them. I suppose Jamie had the pleasure of meeting with you all last Tuesday. I hope he had a pleasant trip up the river and, that he has gotten rid of his cold and sore throat. Received yesterday by the Demopolis a coop of nice chickens, a box of Cakes and a jar of Butter, for which we are very much obliged to you. I assure you they will all be *much enjoyed*. There was a slat loose at one end of the coop when I noticed it—sometime after it had been brought to the camp, and a good many of the chickens had gotten out and as there are other chickens loose about here we don't know how many to catch. Please mention in your next letter the number of chickens sent, if you know. John neglected to send the jars up by Jamie, but will send a stone jar & a colored preserve jar by the next boat. We had to leave the large stone jar at Hall's Mills.

Dr. Grigg got a furlough last Tuesday for 15 days to go to Col. James to see Herbert, who was very ill. I hope he found him getting better. The Dr. has been very busy with the many cases of measles and other illness that we have had in the Regiment.

Cousin Israel came down yesterday. He says his wife is not very well. His crop is very promising. I had the pleasure, the other day, of an introduction to an old friend of our family—Col. or Judge Collier Minge. He seemed very glad to see me and was surprised that I was so nearly grown. He inquired particularly about you and said he would be very happy to pay you a visit. His family is not in the city now, and every time he meets me he tells me how lonely he finds it at home in the evenings and presses me to go and see him and says if I should get sick to be sure to come to his house and he will take good care of me.

You have no doubt had full accounts of the battle of Chickahominy.[29] It was a terrible fight. There were not a great many engaged on our side but they were almost entirely Alabamians. They fought nobly and some regiments suffered severely. I have not seen a list of the casualties in the 5th Regt., but learned with deep regret that poor Gus Moore and young Chapman of the Greensboro' Co. were killed.[30] I hear also that several of Jamie's & my friends were wounded—viz. Dick Adams, Davis Williams & the Sheldons. Dr. Grigg showed me a long letter from Mr. Joe the other day. He was on a sick furlough at his father's. He said his health had been declining ever since he left winter quarters early in March. He is improving now though. The prices of provisions in Richmond he says are enormous. Beef 50 cts pr. Lb., Butter $1.40 to $1.75 pr. Lb.

Down here meal has been selling at $2.80 pr. Bushel, and bacon 60 cts. Per. Lb, Coffee $1.75 lb. Molasses $1.50 a gallon, and other things in proportion. Hard times for poor people.

There is a rumor here this evening that Charleston and Savannah have

29. He is referring to the Battle of Seven Pines, May 31–June 1, 1862.

30. By the time the regiment entered the battle, confusion reigned as Robert Rodes, the brigade commander, struggled to stabilize his advancing line. At one point Gus Moore had been a physician before entering the army. Alonzo Chapman, who had not been in Greensboro long, is the other man to whom Sam refers (Collins, *Major General Robert E. Rodes,* 126–32; Hubbs, *Guarding Greensboro,* 128–30).

both been taken by the enemy, but I hope it is like many other rumors—without any foundation.

John Dorroh is going up this evening, so I will close & send my letter by him. I hope to receive an answer very soon.[31] My best love to Jamie& all the children and please accept the same yourself.

Yrs. Very affectionately,
Samuel

———•—•———

Umbria, June 8, 1862

My dear Sam,

On last Thursday I wrote you a long letter and have been anxiously expecting an answer from you, but none has, as yet, come.

I may safely presume that, through the careless uses of the mails about Mobile & the reckless manner of delivering the letters to the camp, which they have there, it has not reached you. Mama received last evening a letter from you, from which we were all delighted to learn that you were well.

I am sorry that they still give the company so much unnecessary work, and that you have had so much of it to do. We heard that the Regiment would be disbanded by tomorrow (9th). I hope that this is true, and that you will be up on the Lilly—or whatever boat comes tomorrow.

John Dorroh has got a furlough, it seems, & has come home! Well, after this it seems to me that anyone might do the same who would ask for it. We heard that the plea advanced was "that one leg was shorter than the other." I'll declare, I thought he was as well & as sound as almost any one in the company, & I haven't seen any thing lately to change that impression—I believe it yet. Well they might all get furloughs now if they want them.

The news of the death of Gus. Moore & young Chapman was indeed sad, and unexpected. It is said that both had presentiments that they would never see their homes again—that they would be killed in battle. Dr. Guss. Moore was standard bearer, they say. We heard that, in addition to Davis Williams,

31. John Dorroh was a neighbor. He would later enlist in the Seventh Alabama Cavalry.

Dick Adams, etc, that John Moore was also wounded. I expect the wounded will come and remain at home.

I write only a few lines in order that you may know I wrote to you after getting home. If my letter has not reached you, it is bad business to send them by mail. It was a thick letter & heavy & no doubt was mistaken for money. But the one who mistook it was himself mistaken, as there were only a few samples & a strip of paper in it. You must write soon & tell me everything that has taken place since I left.

I send you three shirts, the Review, Napolean & a map. Also two Literary magazines for the Doctor. I enclosed you a piece called Beauregard in my letter. You will find it in the yellow back magazine which I send. There are some very interesting pieces in the magazine.

Your affectionate brother

James

P.S. Mama is writing you a letter & will give you all the news—but there is not much of that about here. She & the children all join me in kindest love to you. Remember us to the Dr & Mr. Sawyer. I send a box with John's things. Tell him how dye for us. JP

Mobile, June 14th, 1862

My dear Mother,

I intended to write yesterday by the Lily, but after going around and ordering the groceries put up and packing the little boxes and seeing them all put on board there was not time left to write before the boat started. I recd. by the Demopolis a box containing some clothes and books for myself and some things for John. I am very much obliged to Jamie for sending them. The book will interest me finely during the remainder of our stay here. I sent back two of the shirts as there is not room for them in my valise; also a blue flannel shirt. John returns pants as he has recd. some presents in that line and will not need any more. I will give you a list of things sent in order that you may know if anything be missing; viz 1 Bbl. Molasses, 1 Bbl. Sugar, 1 sack of

Salt [*sic*], 100 lb. sack of Rice, 1 Bonnet box (just out at East Port) and two other small boxes. I got only one bbl of sugar from Mr. Ross as I thought he would not like to sell too much on credit when he can get cash for it. Mr. Webb is expecting sugar and I thought I'd wait and get a barrel from him. I have no doubt he will sell on credit, also. Mr. R said he had no rice put up in ½ barrels but would send 100 lb sack. He has not made out his bill yet, but when he does I will send it up. If I have time to day I'll write on a slip of paper the prices of all the little articles and enclose it. I had money enough to pay for everything, so you need not send any down, for this Reg. will be paid off before disbanded and I'll have plenty to get home on. There was no choice in the bonnets scarcely. It was "neck or nothing." Mr. Sawyer was kind enough to go about with me looking for them. We found the ones sent at Mrs. Blair's and they seemed to us to be the most suitable ones in the city, but they may not be anything like what you and Mary wanted. There was but one other lead colored hair bonnet to be found and I'll describe it so that if you think you would like it better you can send back the one sent and I'll send you this one. It is a lighter gray and more of a lead color than the one sent—plain, without the hair border around the front. It was nearer the color but I thought not as pretty. Mary did not say whether hers must be straw or not but the Miliners said straw was worn. If the trimming does not suit, send it back & she said she would trim it over. She had no band boxes for sale and I borrowed that one on the promise that it would be returned. So you will please send it down on the Lily or Demopolis next week if you get this in time. I did not send the things by the Demopolis last Saturday because she did not expect to get up higher than Arcola. The Lily was to go Tuesday but did not leave till yesterday (Friday). I had bought the Salt before Jamie's last letter reached me. It was all taken by the State and could only be bought by getting an order from Gen. Green, and then only a half sack for each family. They sell it at $15.00 a sack, but if merchants had it they would ask $40.00. I bought the sack with Mr. Sample, a member of our Co. so you will please have it weighed and divided and set half of it aside for him. I told him if he could get along without it he need never call for his half. I paid for the whole of it. The very next day they found that there was so little salt left they stopped selling it, and now none can be had. Stockings are very scarce. I send you six pair at 75 cts. There were some very fine ones at one store at $1.50, but there were only three or four pair of no. 9 ½ and plenty of no 9. If those are not fine enough that I sent, return them and I'll get 6 or 12 prs of the fine ones—no. 9, if large enough. I also saw some nice Lyle thread stockings at $1 very thin, but as you did not say what kind, I took it for granted that cotton was meant, as that is most generally worn, I believe. I found the black flax thread and sewing silk, and had to pay an enormous price for them. Cotton tape sent. If you prefer linen I can send it. The hats for Willy and Icha are the best I could find. Willy's is a little smaller than the measure. Anything in the world that doesn't suit exactly, send straight back and it will be exchanged, particularly the bonnets.

Did you see the eclipse of the moon two or three nights ago. It was the first total eclipse I ever witnessed. Mr. Sawyer happened to see it and woke some of us up to look at it, and pretty soon it was known all through the Camp and a good many got up to see the sight. The moon became obscured about half past eleven o'clock.

Gen. Green has been quite sick nearly all the week but is convalescing now. Cous. Israel told me when he was down that Ellen Howe's husband had been killed in a skirmish about Corinth, I think. He was captain of a Co.[32]

Sunday. We have just returned from the Catholic Church where we heard a sermon and some fine music. I went more for curiosity than anything else, as I had never been in one during service.

I will get Mr. Sawyer to go around and look out for a piano. I think Mr. S believes all those objections that Mr. Damar raised to our piano are imaginary, though there may be something in it.

Please send my likeness back and I'll make the artist try his hand again. He was in a great hurry and made a rough job of it. I think the likeness did me full justice, but it was carelessly colored, and the knife was on the wrong side, and my head was too low etc. etc. Send it down & I'll have a better one taken. This has really been a business letter but I wanted to tell you all about

32. Ellen Howe Richardson was the daughter of Chiliab Howe and Julia Pickens, the daughter of Governor Israel Pickens (Texas Board of Health, Standard Certificate of Death, September 10, 1924).

The Howes had moved to Chickasaw County, Mississippi, after settling in Marengo, County, Alabama, sometime in the 1830s. Ellen's husband was John Richardson, a captain in the Forty-First Mississippi Infantry Regiment. Richardson was killed in a skirmish at Bridge Creek, east of Corinth, on May 28, 1862. CMSR, Mississippi, RG109, National Archives.

the things purchased. I neglected to acknowledge the receipt of the letters which came in the box. Please thank Jamie & Mary for several letters which will be answered soon. I am delighted that the time is drawing nigh when I shall return home and meet you, my dear Mother, and sisters and brothers. The weather is becoming excessively warm. Write soon. Love to all.

Your affectionate son,
Samuel

FOUR

Maintaining the
Ties That Bind

NOVEMBER 1862–MARCH 1863

In early November 1862, Sam, accompanied by John, left to join Company D, Fifth Alabama.[1] A few days after Sam joined his regiment, General Thomas "Stonewall" Jackson ordered Major General D. H. Hill's division to move south to New Market, Virginia. Hill's division, under temporary command of Brigadier General Robert Rodes, arrived near Guiney's Station on November 30. On December 2, after marching one hundred miles in five days, the division reached the Rappahannock River at Port Royal, near Fredericksburg, and set up camp.[2]

On December 12, Sam heard heavy bombardment from the Union side of the river at Fredericksburg covering the expected Federal crossing of the Rappahannock. Sam's division moved north toward the town and joined Jubal Early's division as part of the corps's reserve near Prospect Hill. In the initial Union attack on the Confederate position, a Union division under the command of General George Gordon Meade assaulted General A. P. Hill's division and broke through the center of the Confederate line. Early's division advanced to close the gap, while Hill's division moved to the right

1. Collins, *Major General Robert E. Rodes*, 42–45, 154–70; Hubbs, *Guarding Greensboro*, 138–41.

2. Collins, Major *General Robert E. Rodes*, 174–78; Hubbs, *Guarding Greensboro*, 136–47; Diary of Samuel Pickens, December 1–7, 1862.

to defend against a flanking movement.[3] The Confederates repulsed Meade's attack. General Ambrose Burnside then shifted the Union assault to Marye's Heights, defended by Longstreet's corps. After the assault on Marye's Heights failed, Union forces withdrew back across the Rappahannock during the cold, rainy night of December 14, so silently, Sam explained, that Confederate skirmishers did not realize they had left until morning.[4]

The exposure to cold and the physical demands of the army took their toll. By the end of December, Sam was sick with what he would later describe as a cold. Suffering from chest pain, nausea, and a lack of sleep, he went on the sick list. In his diary he described treatments that consisted of rubbing his chest with turpentine and powder of morphine, but his condition continued to worsen. The illness and crowded living conditions in camp made it nearly impossible to sleep. Captain John W. Williams, having noticed Sam's deteriorating condition, advised him to find a house nearby where he would be more comfortable while he recovered.[5] The next day, he sent John to find a place, but all the houses were full of refugees from Fredericksburg. Eventually, Sam found rooms at Hanover Court House and took them.[6]

When Sam resumed correspondence with the family in January, he wrote nothing about his illness to his mother, despite her insistence that he tell her everything. Instead, he told his sisters, Mary and Louty, the story and asked them to join him in assuring their mother that he just had a bad cold, though Sam believed he had pneumonia. He promised not to return to camp until the more substantial quarters the army had ordered built were completed. Sam expressed regret for his mother's "uneasiness" over his "break down" but notably did not commit to being more honest with her in the future.

At home, Sam's family continued to adapt to the world the war had wrought. The surprising news from home was that Mary and Tom Biscoe were engaged to be married. Typically, a sixteen-year-old woman of Mary's

3. Collins, *Major General Robert E. Rodes*, 179; Diary of Samuel Pickens, December 13, 1862; Rable, *Fredericksburg! Fredericksburg!*, 244–45.

4. Diary of Samuel Pickens, December 15, 1862.

5. Captain John W. Williams volunteered at Greensboro in April 1861 and was commissioned a second lieutenant (CMSR, Alabama, RG 109).

6. Diary of Samuel Pickens, December 31, 1862–February 1, 1863.

social standing would have completed her education before entering a period of courtship during which she would more or less interview potential mates. Mary would have spent time in Mobile, with Pickens relatives, or in Tuscaloosa, or nearby Greensboro where she would have attended balls, dinners, and other social events with eligible suitors. But the war made all of that exceedingly difficult, if not impossible. To the extent that there were opportunities for socialization, most of the eligible men were in the army. For young, single women the absence of men fostered a sense of urgency, a fear that they would not find a suitable husband.[7]

Suspicions about the death of a favored enslaved man, and complaints about Confederate impressment of enslaved people, revealed the Pickenses' uneasiness about the impact of the war on the people they enslaved. Mary Gaillard wrote of her "shock," and "the melancholy news" of the death of Simon, a trusted enslaved man upon whom Mary depended. Initially, James reported, he and others suspected that Simon had been poisoned by someone who considered Simon's relationship with the Pickenses a betrayal of the enslaved community. As he told the story, several people familiar with the case, including two local physicians, knew that there was a conflict between Simon and one of the other slaves. Another reason for James's suspicions was that Simon died during a local crisis over the return of Horace, a slave who ran away from a nearby plantation. Demands for slaves to work on fortifications in and around Greene County and Mobile were also, as James put it, "heavy." James understood the government's need for labor, but complained that the government provided inadequate care for ill and/or injured enslaved people.[8]

7. Jabour, *Scarlett's Sisters*, chap. 4; Faust, *Mothers of Invention*, 139–41.

8. *Acts of the called session, 1862 and the Second Regular Annual Session of the General Assembly of Alabama*, 38–41. See also Martinez, *Confederate Slave Impressment in the Upper South*, 9, 32, 101–2.

Petersburg, Va.
Nov. 11th 1862

My dear Mama,

I arrived safely at this place yesterday evening in company with Maj. Webster, Jack Wynne and a young man from Demopolis.[9] We came on through without stopping, except five or six hours in Montgomery, so we had a pretty fatiguing trip and didn't get much sleep until last night when we enjoyed a fine night's rest. Our route was through Columbia So. Ca and Raleigh NC, much the most pleasant one now as there is not such a crowd of travelers as on the other routes. I have taken cold in coming on; it commenced at Newbern where we had very poor accommodations. That night it blew up very cold and we were put in rooms without fire and not sufficiency of bed clothes. I am afraid Jamie and Willy suffered from that too. They had no overcoats to ride home in either. William exposed himself very much, also, by sleeping out in the carriage.

In Montgomery we had ourselves vaccinated, in order to be more secure from small pox. There is not much of it in the army and it will not be apt to spread, for I understand that the Regiments in which cases occurred have been detached and quarantined.

There has been a cold spell of weather up here. I saw snow on the ground about Weldon yesterday. It was said to have been quite a heavy snow storm and earlier in the season than they have ever known it. The weather has moderated considerably since, though. We expect to go on to Richmond tonight and may stop there a day to learn where the Regt is. We have heard that the army was falling back from Winchester but do not know if it be true. I wish I could tell you where to write to me so as to hear from you soon, but cannot do so until I get with the Regt. I sincerely hope though that you are all well. It was hard indeed to part with my dear Mother, Sisters and brothers, but it is what a great many are called upon to do in these unhappy times. Do not be at all uneasy about me, dear Mama, for I think I will get along very well,

9. In April 1861, D. T. Webster enlisted as a private in Company I, Fifth Alabama. In 1860 he lived with his father, John, near the Pickens family. By the time Pickens encountered him on the trip to Virginia, he was brigade commissary and had been promoted to major. Jack Wynne enlisted a few days before Webster (CMSR, Alabama, RG 109, and U.S. Census, 1860).

and after being in Camp & getting accustomed to it, will no doubt be better satisfied than I have been during the war.

Accept my best love, dear Mama, and give the same to Jamie, Mary, Lou and Icha. My kind regards to Mr. Enoch & the rest of the family, and to all other inquiring friends.

Yours affectionate son,
Samuel.

P.S. Robt. Withers was on the boat going up to Montg with us & told me he had heard from Mr. Staudenmayer.[10] His mother does not want him & does not think he would suit. They have heard that the was not of a pleasant disposition & very sensitive, I think he said. I told him (Mr. W.) that Mr. Mott recommended him highly, but he seemed to think a recommendation from our Episcopal minister by another was not of much importance. I hope you will hear more about him, Though, or of some other.

S.P.

———— •—•— ————

In Camp near
Gordonsville, Va.
Nov. 27th, 1862

My dear Sister Mary,

I would have written to you soon after I wrote to Jamie, but we have been on the move almost ever since & this is my first opportunity. On Thursday night last we recd. orders to cook up rations and be ready to march in the morning. So Friday morning a little after day light we left Camp and marched down the turnpike towards Staunton. It was a real forced march and as I had just gotten to the Regiment a few days before & had taken very little exercise, it went pretty hard with me. I do not think we stopped for eating and resting three quarters of an hour during the day, but kept on until near sunset, when

10. The Pickenses did hire the Staudenmayers later. L. R. Staudenmayer had been the rector of St. Luke's Episcopal Church in Jacksonville, Alabama, before the war (*Twenty-Fifth Annual Convention of the Protestant Episcopal Church in the Diocese of Alabama*, 6).

we halted in a piece of woods this side of Woodstock and camped for the night, having come at least *twenty miles*. I was so much fatigued that I could scarcely put one foot before the other. After cutting wood and building a large fire we cooked provisions for next day and then wrapped up in our blankets and lay down around the fire to get the rest which we so much needed. Soon after light in the morning we were again on the road and passed through the towns Edinburg, Mount Jackson and New Market, and at the last place left the Valley turnpike and turned to the east to cross the Blue Ridge. We camped that night, also, about twenty miles from where we started in the morning. I was more completely broken down then than ever before. My limbs were so sore and my joints so stiff that when I sat or lay down it was with the greatest difficulty that I could get up again. I couldn't lie in the same position any time scarcely without feeling cramped, so I hardly slept any. Just as we stopped in the mountains a pheasant was scared up and flew against one of the men in my mess and he caught it—so we had a nice game supper as far as it went, though it was rather scant for as hungry a crowd as ours was. Next morning (Sunday) we passed over the first range of mountains & from the top of it had a beautiful view of the valley we had just left. One or two villages & the country houses dotted about made quite a pretty landscape. We went fifteen miles & stopped some time before night. Monday's march was a *hard* one, but I was lucky enough to ride. Maj. Webster told me the evening before to come to the wagon yard early and he would show me one that I could get in. I did so & saved myself a hard day's march. The road was the most winding, circuitous, one that I ever saw. It was ten or twelve miles over the mountain that we crossed. That day we made nearly twenty-four miles. Next day I marched again and went about twenty miles. So in those five days we marched just about *one hundred* miles. The Troops were all nearly broken down and said it was by far the hardest marching they had ever done. It was, sad to see some poor fellows on those rocky and frozen roads perfectly barefooted. They were comparatively few, but still there ought not to be any in that condition. It is the fault of the Quartermasters in not keeping shoes on hand.

The night we got here (Tuesday) we had another game supper. A covey of partridges after flying about through the encampment lit near our fire, and were so badly frightened that they would not fly again and I caught two and some of the others got four more—making one apiece for the mess. John cooked them nicely & we enjoyed them very much. You have no idea how easily game is caught when it gets among so many soldiers. I have seen some rabbits and several squirrels caught.

Decr. 4th, 1862. Dear Mary, I did not finish my letter the other evening & as we have been on the move nearly ever since, I have not had an opportunity of closing it until now. Col. Hobson, Lt. Borden, Gilliam James & others came to camp that evening, and brought me two letters from you, one from Jamie & one from Lou.[11] I was very glad to get them, and hope soon to receive more of later date. But "Old Stonewall" keeps moving about so much I am afraid letters will be a long time in getting to us. Tell Mama she must never be uneasy at not hearing regularly from me, for we may be marching a week at a time, and during a march it is almost impossible to write for we are going from sun rise to sun set. I am much obliged to Louty for her kind offer to knit me "a good and substantial pair of suspenders." I would be very glad of them if I wore suspenders, but I'm not wearing them now. You can't imagine how useful the Sentinel's cap is that you made for me. I sleep in it every night & don't know how I could get along without it, for now we have no tent or shelter of any kind over us. We sleep very comfortably though, wrapped up in our blankets & with our feet to the fire. I have the best pair of blankets in the army. Every one that sees them admires them & wishes he had a pair like them. Well I will now tell you something of our movements since we left the camp near Gordonsville. We rested there on the 26th & 27th after the five days march and on the 28th started again—passed through Orange C.H., and it appeared to me we traveled a very roundabout way, going on small, out-of-the-way roads & sometimes through plantations etc. We marched four days at the rate of sixteen or seventeen miles a day, going within four miles of Fredericksburg and camped near Guinea's Station on the Richmond &

11. Edwin Lafayette Hobson. Until promoted to major, Hobson had been the commander of Company D. By the end of the war, he would become the commander of the Fifth Infantry Regiment. In 1860, Hobson was listed as residing in Greensboro, Greene County, but his plantation was located in the German Creek beat near the Pickenses' Umbria Plantation. See CMSR, Alabama, RG 109, 142, and U.S. Census, 1860. The lieutenant he refers to is Joseph Borden. Borden's property in German Creek bordered Hollow Square. Gilliam James was a private who enlisted in Company D in 1861 (CMSR, Alabama, RG 109; U.S. Census, 1860). For the location of individual properties, see Snedecor, *Hand drawn maps of the Precincts of Greene County, 1858*.

Fredericksburg R.R. Here we rested a day (2nd Decr.) and yesterday marched twelve or fourteen miles to our present camp. We are very near the Rappahannock River and five miles from Port Royal. Genl, Stuart & his cavalry are scattered along the river as pickets. Well Mr. Joe is at home now & I suppose you have seen him. Give my love to him and tell him I am very sorry he did not get there before I left, as I would have been so glad to have met him. Tell him he must take a good furlough & enjoy himself as much as possible.

You must write me word if Mama has heard from Mr. Nicholson of Mobile. I think Mr. Staudenmayer ask too much. In these hard times if he could get board for himself & family $400 or $500 he ought to be satisfied, and I believe he would take that. However, Mama may prefer Mr. Nicholson when she hears from him. Tell Mama when she writes to mention of Mr. Simms purchased the colt & what he gave. Also how's the shoe-making coming on now. I know Peter is in his glory.[12] How about the rent of our land? Has Mr. Stickney taken it? Tell Jamie to tell Mr. Lawless to get Dr. Moore's boy to fix the screw at the Goodrum Place as soon as possible, so that it can be covered, for if that is not done it will rot directly. I am looking anxiously for a letter from Mama saying how all are & giving all the news from home. All letters to me had better be directed to Richmond & they will be sent to the Brigade wherever it may be. Cunny James has been discharged from the service on account of bad health and I suppose he will return [*word missing*] before long. [*A portion of the page is torn away, so only portions of sentences can be seen until the bottom of the page. Pickens told Mary how much pleasure he derived from receiving mail from home. He apologized for using a lead pencil. He also wrote something about franking his letters himself.*]

Give my very best love to Mama, Jamie, Willy, Lou & Icha & accept the same from

Your affectionate brother
Samuel

P.S. John sends howdye to you all & his love to his wife. Mention how his family are when you write. Tell Wm, Duddy, Simon & all the servants howdye for me. S.P.

---

12. Peter was an enslaved shoemaker.

N.B. Col. Hobson left my boots in Richmond & I am glad he did so as I am not needing them now. I am much obliged to Jamie for sending my Almanac.

S.P.

———•———

Umbria, Nov. 30th 1862

My dear Sam,

Your kind and welcome letter came to hand yesterday and we were all very much delighted to hear that you are well. I am very glad that you met with no accident in traveling and finally reached camp safely. You cannot imagine how very lonely & depressed I felt the morning you left, at Newbern. After waiting on the platform at the depot until the last roll of smoke from the departing train had disappeared & naught but the sound of the rattling wheels were left, Willie & I went back to the hotel where, after waiting—in hopes that it might get warmer—until 7 o'clock, & finding, on the contrary, that it grew colder, we told William to hitch up & were soon off at a fine rate. We took a different route coming back from the one we went, which avoided the sand; and traveled much faster. In two hours and a half, after we left Newbern, we were at the door here. It was a very quick trip; but as it was so cold and the roads so good the horses didn't mind it at all. Tom Biscoe & Mr. Joe reached Mr. Sadler's on Frid. Morning, 14th. I was very much surprised when I heard that Tom was with Mr. Joe.[13] The Dr. stopped at the gate that morning & told me that they had come & rode on. Mr. Enoch & I, after breakfast went up & sat for a few hours with them. They were both sadly disappointed at not seeing you. I invited Tom down & he has been with us ever since. He has changed but very little since we saw him in Richmond; except that he has turned out side whiskers (he is the same person), like Col. Hunt. He looks like the Col.[14]

---

13. Tom Biscoe was at Hollow Square recuperating from wounds he suffered at Germantown, Maryland, during the Battle of Sharpsburg (CMSR, Louisiana, 1861–65, RG 109). William G. Sadler's farm was in the Hollow Square Precinct near the Pickenses' Umbria Plantation. In 1860, Sadler identified himself as a "planter" with six enslaved people (U.S. Census, Slave Schedule, 1860).

14. Biscoe's maternal grandfather.

He is now Captain of the Co. of which he was 1ˢᵗ Lieut when we saw him. He has a great deal to say & is very pleasant & agreeable. Mr. Joe is the same Mr. Joe that he ever was, in looks, good spirits, etc. etc. He was very glad to see us indeed & was very sorry when he heard you had left. He has been to see us two or three times, but we do not see much of him. The Dr has not been here since you left, except for a minute or two once or twice.

We have had the most singular weather for November, you ever heard of. It hasn't rained since the morning you left. We waited all the time, hoping that it would, in order to sow wheat, but it hasn't rained yet. On the 19ᵗʰ we had a little, but not enough to lay the dust. We had waited so long to no purpose and the season was so far advanced that Mama & I thought it would be better to risk it. In fact, Henry Williamson told me that if wheat was not sowed then, it would be too late. So on the 25ᵗʰ they commenced the job, and finished it yesterday morning the 29ᵗʰ. The ground, to my surprise, after so long a dry spell (for you know what little rain we have had the past two or three months) was moist & in pretty good order. It did not clod in plowing at all. It has been warm ever since we sowed, so I think it will soon come up. We put a tablespoonful of blue stone to a bushel of wheat which Mama said was the old plan, I think. Mr. High's opinion of the quantity couldn't have been right, as it seems to be too much blue stone for a bushel.

Mr. Sawyer carried the samples to town and actually got—what do you think?—fourteen cents for the cotton. Simms, he said, seemed very obliging and quite willing to favor Mama as much as he could.[15] Mr. S. considered himself, of course, as having done a great thing. Well, he did deserve credit for getting fourteen cents for cotton for which he said he would not begin to give thirteen cents. He finally got two certificates of bonds (a division of the whole amt. into two parts) one of which Mama has sent on to Richmond by Frank Stollenwerck to have sold at par. Mr. Stollenwerck has established a

15. James H. Simms was a merchant in Greensboro (Snedecor, *1963 reprint of Snedecor's 1855–56 directory of Greene County, Alabama*). He was a produce-loan agent. The Confederacy's produce-loan program encouraged planters to exchange cotton for Confederate bonds. The Confederate government then used the cotton as collateral for loans (Todd, "The Produce Loans," 46–54).

business in taking these certificates & selling them.[16] That is, a great many are disposing of them through him. In regard to shoes, those for the Goodrum Place are done, and they will commence with the Canebrake shoes on Tuesday. Mr. High sent the other day a large quantity of leather (42 lbs. sole & ten hides upper). I do not know whether this is all that Harry Johnson will send or not. It will be plenty for the shoes for the Canebrake, but not enough for half-soling the shoes at both places besides.

This is a half business letter & the more of it I write the more disgusted am I with it. I will only say that Charley Stickney refused to take the place at $800.00 and has rented a place of Mr. Nelson. Where his place is, I don't know, unless it is the old Randolph tract. He says "As I have obtained of Mr. Nelson ample land for planting purposes, and on reasonable & accommodating terms, I must respectfully decline your offer." Mama does not know whether to rent it out another year or to plant it by the Goodrum Place force. What do you think had best be done? Mr. Studenmayer wrote saying he would come for $600. And Mama replied engaging him at that price, but has not heard from him since. He has a notice in the Church Intelligencer, directing all his letters to be sent to him at Charlotte, N.C.; so Mama concluded he intends remaining in that place. In the event he does not come don't you think the best plan for Mama to adopt is to go to Greensboro?

But enough! I have no doubt worried you by this time, so I must close. You must write soon and as often as you can. Tom desires me go give his love, and Mr. Joe his kind regards to you. Mama & all the children join me in warmest love to you.

Ever your affectionate brother,
James Pickens

P.S. Tell John how de ye for us all.

16. James was referring to bonds the Confederate government issued in return for subscriptions of cotton (Todd, "The Produce Loans," 46–54).

Mon. Dec. 1st,

P.S. Icha took too much exercise yesterday & had fever last night, in conse-quence. It has not left him this morning, but will in the course of the day, I hope.

Mama, Tom, Mary & I went to church in town yesterday and, fortunately, Bishop Wilmer preached. It was a very good sermon.[17] I believe Tom is very much pleased with him.

Tom's furlough will be out on the 4th inst. And the other day he insisted on leaving today, & finally made up his mind to go & could not be moved; but by dint of hard persuasion he consented to stay another week.

He says he will no doubt see you often, as he is in the same Division.

Mama answered your letters the other day, so you will probably get it before this goes.

While I write it has commenced to rain. I hope it will be a good one, as the wheat would soon be up.

Will you not go into winter quarters? All seem to think that the cam-paign is over for the winter, in Virginia. In that case they ought to go into quarters.

Well, I must close, hoping soon to get an answer from you.

Yr brother,
James

Aunt Sucky sent her love to John and says she and all are well.

———•—•———

Umbria
Dec. 10th 1862

My dear Son,

It is a long time since I had the pleasure of writing to you, but as Jamie and Mary are fond of their freres, and the former wrote to you at Winchester,

---

17. Bishop Richard Hooker Wilmer, Episcopal bishop of Alabama and an ardent defender of the Confederacy, spent much of the war in Greensboro. See Whitaker, *Richard Hooker Wilmer*, 167.

you have not been without home news. I intended writing a long letter to you today, but Mr. Joe came in and spent the day here: he is in high spirits and seems to enjoy life as much as anyone I ever saw. He requested me to send his love to you. I think he intends remaining in this neighborhood until Christmas is over. The last time he was here, he told me that Mr. Webster had recd a letter from Va in which the writer mentioned that your Regiment had been ordered to Gordonsville, 90 miles distant from Middletown, and that you "had broken down" on the march. This of course has made me very uneasy and unhappy, as I knew you had been suffering with severe cold. Mr. Joe made a joke of it and said he would have a laugh upon you. But a Mother's fears are easily excited, and you know I do not form an exception to the rule. Tell me my dear Son how you are, and why the army has fallen back. Some suppose you are going into Winter quarters there, but I fear it is because a battle is anticipated. Do my dear Sam tell me everything and be not afraid to do so lest it make me unhappy. I would rather know from you what is going on, and if you are sick. Oh! How much trouble and anguish has the war cost us, and how much will our enemies have to answer for at the last day. My only trust is in God! that His will mercifully deliver us out of the hands of our enemies and let you return to us soon in honor and safety. I cannot fe el happy until you are with us.

I recd a letter from Julia Howe a few days since, saying our enemies were only 65 miles from her house and that she wishes to send their servants (30 in number) to us to save them from being taken. She thinks it advisable that the white family should remain and prevent, if possible their home from being destroyed.[18] I have invited them all to come and stay with us, and consented to take their servants, who are to be hired out if places can be obtained. I have offered the Eubank place to them, if they wish to raise a crop, and told them of Mrs. Dufphey's place to be rented 22nd Dec.[19] As there is no probability of hiring their servants, I think they will take our place, which Mr. S declines giving $800 for. He says "Mr. Nelson has rented land to him on reasonable & accommodating terms." The Randolph place, where he is putting up new cabins now and getting things ready to move by Christmas. I am not sorry he is going from us; but I think he will be. Biscoe is still with us and has added much to the happiness of the family: he is lively and plays with the children.

18. Julia Howe lived near Meridian, Mississippi, an important railroad junction.
19. She is referring to Jane Pickens Dufphey, her sister-in-law, who lived nearby.

We are much attached to him, and would fain keep him here a long time; but he speaks of leaving on Monday next. He requested me to send his love to you.

A letter recd today from Mr. Staudenmayer informed us that he & his wife will be with us a few days before or after Christmas. I rejoice to think the children have some prospect before them of being educated and recovering some of the lost time caused by the war. I despaired of his coming and determined to ask the aid of Bishop Wilmer in getting another. Dr Lawry is on a visit to his mother and he with some others of the family spent last evening with us. He expressed his opinion of you in the handsomest terms, saying as you were not here, he could do so with propriety. You know how much it is worth. Mr Enoch is now the happy father of 6 daughters—one having been added to the family within the last week. He has been occupied of late in making salt, and finds it so easily done, that he advises me not to buy any. But Mr Lawless & High both prefer buying to making and say they must have 11 sacks: 9 for their use, and two to return to a neighbor from whom Mr. L borrowed last spring. Mr H was surprised when he heard it, saying he had sent so many sacks to the Goodrum place, he did not know how it had been used. Salt is $50 a sack in good weather and $60 in case of rain. We sold our cotton at the G. [Goodrum] place 74 bales for 14 cents per lb and got 2 certificates for bonds—one of which Mr. Enoch sent to Richmond with his to have it sold at par: here the discount is heavy—10 percent. The rest of the cotton I would have baled & sold but Mr L has no rope.

What do you say about the Canebrake cotton? Shall we sell it or keep it. Mr. Stickney says he intends keeping his, and expects a large price for it when the war is over. Dr. Grigg says there is great risk of fire and advises all to sell who owe money. We shall have enough from the sale of the G cotton to pay all we owe. You must instruct us what to do.

The children are all well and very happy: some of them anticipating much pleasure from a visit from you at Christmas. Jamie is engaged in having fences built & shoes made. All unite in warmest love to you. I will write again in a few days, and hope to hear from you when the messenger returns from the office. May God! bless & protect you, my dear, good Son. Yr Mother William[20] sends howdye to you. Remember us to John.

20. This is the enslaved William.

—— • ——

Hanover C.H., Va.
Jan. 6th, 1863.

My dear Sister,

I will now reply to the letter that I had the pleasure of receiving from you about ten days since. As you notice from the caption of my letter I am now at Hanover Court House, and I suppose you want to know why. Well the reason is this: I got a leave of absence from camp and came down here where I can get a plenty to eat and have a nice quiet time for a week or so. I (did you ever see half so many Is in your life?) had taken a pretty bad cold and couldn't sleep any scarcely at night. Our tent was on the side of a hill, and we had very little straw to lie on, & all crowded together, we had a most uncomfortable time. After passing four or five restless, sleepless nights, and my cold not improving any, Capt. Williams told me I had better try and get in at some house in the neighborhood: so I started John out to find one. He walked around two days without finding a place where they would receive me; every house was crowded with refugees from Fredericksburg. So I got a leave of absence and came off in the wagon of the sutler of our Regt. & kept coming until we got here, as I had been told that it was a good place. Have been here now three days and am very much pleased with it. This Hotel, a large frame building, the court-house and jail constitute the village. Being out of reach of the army it is a quiet & pleasant retreat. I have a comfortable room & bed which is a great treat and first rate fare for these times which is a still greater treat. After living on beef and biscuit alone & then getting here to this good country fare, I tell you I can scarcely restrain my appetite. If I'm here long I think it will fatten me up. Now Mama is so apt to be uneasy when there is anything the matter that I want to impress it upon her that I am *not sick*, but came away from camp only because I had a cold & there was a bad spell of weather coming on, & wanted to get in a house where I would be comfortable and free from exposure. That is all and she must not have a moment's uneasiness. I will try and write every few days and you must all write oftener. I believe that you, Mama, Jamie & Louty, who are all good correspondents, do write but from the irregularity of the mails I don't get the letters. The mail is closing so I'll send this to let you write within a week or two direct to me at Hanover Court House, Va.

My warmest love to Mama, Jamie, & all the children & accept the same from

Your aff. Brother,
Samuel

———•———

Hanover C.H., Va.
Jany. 16th, 1863

My dear Mama,

You're most welcome letter of the 10th ult reach me a few days since, having taken a month to get here. I recd at the same time one from Jamie dated the Dec. 26th, and was very glad to get such late information that all were well, for I was becoming quite uneasy. The mails must be badly managed for letters are much longer in coming here than they should be, and I know that my letters do not reach home in due time either. Sometimes, two letters mailed a week apart will get here together. You ought always to direct to me at Richmond and the letters will be immediately forwarded to the Regiment wherever it may be stationed at the time. The reason your last was so long in getting here is that it was sent to Gordonsville and probably lay there a week or two before being forwarded.

My dear Mama I am sorry you were uneasy about me at hearing that I "broke down" on the march from the Valley. A person in the best health would not be able to keep up on a hard march unless he were accustomed to it. Mr. Webster might have mentioned the good many others—old members of the Co. that "broke down," as he calls it. All complained very much of the march and said it was by far the hardest they had ever taken. Mary recd from me, a few days after you wrote, an account of it.

I regret very much to hear that cousin Julia Howe and family have to break up their plantation on account of the approach of the Yankees. It is much better to do so, and move their servants off in time, though, for thousands have been lost in this state by waiting too long. I hope they will accept your offer of the Eubank place. It would be much better than hiring the negroes out, and they would get little or nothing for them.

I would insist upon our overseers making salt at home. Lawless, particularly, as he has not made any at all yet, and could get a great deal out of the old Smoke-house at the Goodrum Place. Salt has been as high as $2.50 per lb. in Richmond, but has fallen to 40 cts. However, the State and county furnish a certain no. of lbs. to each citizen at 5 and 8 cts per lb. The cotton sold well. You will now be able to pay all debts—even those due your good North Carolina creditors, though I believe they are as perfectly satisfied with your note as they would be with the money itself. I did not know what course to advise with regard to the Canebrake cotton. I heard that the government had stopped buying, but do not know if it be true. The ginned cotton at the Goodrum Place ought by all means to be packed out if it can be done; and I was under the impression that Mr. L had some rope, but stopped packing because the screw was in such a bad condition. Mr. Enoch Sawyer thought that cotton rope could be made out of very coarse thread that would answer.

If Tom Biscoe is still with you, give him my love and tell him I hope he will remain until his wound is entirely well, for there is no use in his hurrying back before he is fully able to resume the duties of his command, and especially during the Winter when the armies are quiet. Give my love to Mr. Joe Grigg, also. In my letter to Louty I begged that you would send me $50 by him, but if he had gone before that reached you, it will not make much difference, for we will be paid off very soon. It is too great a risk to send money by mail. Although in Camp we have no way of spending money except with the sutler for cakes, apples, sugar and coffee, and such things, still it goes pretty rapidly. Our traveling expenses from home were much heavier than I expected. We failed to get transportation furnished us a part of the way, and then John's expenses were a good deal. Speaking of traveling reminds me of meeting, in coming on here, Matthew Duffy, the old proprietor of Blount Springs. He seemed glad to see me, and made many inquiries about the family; and told me to tell you that he would take great pleasure in giving you any information concerning our tract of land in Blount, and would attend to paying the taxes on it, if you would write to him requesting it. His post office is Blount Springs, where he lives altogether now.

I suppose you have long since seen accounts of Bragg's victory in Tenn.[21] and the capture of a garrison at Galveston, Texas, and the steamer "Harriet Lane," with the destruction of a gunboat. Also, the reported loss of the Yankee ironclad, the "Monitor," off the coast of North Carolina.[22] I am in hopes we shall soon hear of other losses in Lincoln's fleet, as the wind has been blowing a gale for two or three days past. Yesterday and last night the weather was as mild as Spring, but this evening it has blown up very cold. Please thank Jamie and Louty for the kind favors recd at the same time that yours was. I enclose two pieces for Jamie's scrapbook that were to have gone in my letter to Lou. Please present my kind regards to the Sawyers and to Dr. Grigg. I am well again and will return to camp by the first opportunity that offers; so letters to me should be directed to the Regt as usual. There is a gentleman going to Richmond this morning and I will send this letter to be mailed there. Please give my warmest love to Jamie, Mary, Willy, Louty and Icha, and accept, dear Mama, the same from

Your devoted son,
Samuel

———•—•———

Umbria, Ala.
Jan 13th 1863.

My beloved Son,

Our hearts were gladdened today by the receipt of a letter from you to Jamie. You can scarcely imagine what joy pervades our family circle when a letter from you reaches us, and how each face is lightened up as it passes from one to another. I was sorry to hear that you had rec'd only a few letters

21. Pickens is referring to reports then in circulation that General Braxton Bragg's Army of Tennessee had defeated a Federal Army of the Cumberland under the command of General William Rosecrans at the Battle of Stones River, near Murfreesboro, Tennessee. The Army of Tennessee had actually suffered a defeat and were retreating into East Tennessee as Pickens composed his letter (Daniel, *Conquered*, chap. 6).

22. Eicher, *The Longest Night*, 200–201. The *Monitor* sank on December 31, 1862, in a storm off of Cape Hatteras, North Carolina. A Confederate force recaptured Galveston on January 1, 1863, sinking the USS *Harriet Lane* in the process. See McPherson, *War on the Waters*, 129–30.

for many I assure you have been sent from us to you, thinking they would in some degree make amends for the loss of our society. Next to the pleasure of seeing a friend comes that of hearing. So many of our letters have either miscarried or been suppressed. I am glad you got your blanket. I suppose Biscoe & Mr. Joe have arrived at camp by this time. I hope the former will be with you or so near that you can have constant communication. He is an uncommonly good young man and has endeared himself to all of us. I wrote to you that I intended sending on a box of good things to you by Mr. Joe; we mentioned it to him but he only laughed without saying it would give him pleasure to take it. The next time we saw him he seemed much put out at having to carry a pair of boots for Mr. Brown, so we concluded not to trouble him with our box. He was quite a disappointment to us; however another opportunity may offer to send you something.

Lou has just come in with the chill, which has doubtless been brought on by imprudence. She ate a raw turnip and went into the yard without covering. I must attend her.

January 14 Lou had fever until this morning. She is better now and, I hope, will escape chill tomorrow. Rev. L.R. Staudenmayer and his "fair companion" have been with us two weeks. He is a good-looking gentlemanly man about 45 years old, and speaks the English language well enough to be understood by us all. He is patient in teaching, and extremely desirous that the children should learn under him. They are all much pleased with him, and have commenced their studies very well. Dear little Israel, for we have dropped his nickname, is pronounced a bright boy by his teacher, who seems to have taken a fancy for him, and he is studying Grammar, Geography, definitions and Arithmetic. Jamie, I am glad to say, is pursuing his studies, and he and Mary say French together. She is also studying Latin, together with all the English branches. I hope Willie will study hard & endeavor to make up lost time. He has impressed in manners, and seems ambitious now to improve his mind. Louty is so smart I have no fears about her. We have doubtless a first-rate teacher, who, being a minister of the Gospel, will discharge his duties conscientiously & faithfully all together in a different manner from our friends Weatherly & Lilly. We couldn't go to church last Sunday, so he proposed having service at home. We met in the drawing room and after prayers had an exhortation on obedience. Some of the servants attended service. Mom Lindsay has just paid a visit to Lou and she requested me to send her love to you, and to say she wishes you all the good luck, which this world affords, and hopes you will soon be at home. All at home unite with her and these good wishes. I am so anxious to see you that if I heard the war was over, I would be tempted to leave home, children & all and go to meet you. Oh! When shall we be delivered out of the hands of our enemies? I trust the time is near at hand when our independence will be acknowledged by all nations of the Earth.

Mr. High has gone to the saltworks to get salt for us, and will return home tomorrow night. I gave him $750, borrowing 90 dollars from the Canebrake servants to make up that sum. After buying salt, paying his expenses down & up the river on a steamer and paying freight, I don't think there will be much money left out of the $750. All at the plantations are well except Matt, who has been worse lately. Dr. Moore refuses to attend him, unless we will have him taken to the Goodrum place: this cannot be done as he is feeble & confined to his bed. Aunt Franky has great faith in an old colored Dr. (not Abraham) and wishes to employ him. I think we must gratify her as probably it will be the last & only thing she can do for poor Matt. Sam Dufphey agreed to get us 11 bushels of salt—a poor return for three months services of Alford & the use of 3 kettles. Mr. Lawless has got only a part of the salt, and whenever he has sent for the balance, Sam has been absent from home. Let us in the future have no business transactions with relations. I have good reason for wishing to avoid it. I could not get change until now to send Suky her money but will do it today or tomorrow. Simon says he has not made her shoes because John gave him no leather. Harry Johnson has paid us all he owes and about one half or more of the servants are without new shoes. We are trying to buy or rather exchange for the leather with him. I have not yet rec'd any money for the cotton sold at the G Pl. [Goodrum Place] One check I have given to Mr. A. Stollenwerck to sell, but he has not handed the money to me. I am anxious to have the money ready for the Lyle land whenever we shall be called on to pay it. Mr. Logan told me it would be due this month.

I presume Jamie and Mary keep you well posted up in all home news; but I am sure they have not told you a secret, which I am about to communicate. Well! It is this—Biscoe and Mary are engaged to be married. I gave my consent for I think him a good, an honorable young man and worthy of Mary.

She is young, but I suppose she will complete her education. Mrs. Sawyer says "you must always send my love to Sam." So says Mr. E also. All the children said much love to you. Accept the same from your devotedly attached

Mother

I will write to you very soon. I have written this in the midst of noise, confusion & repeated interruptions. Tell John howdye. Take good care of yourself my dear Sam & buy warm clothing and every thing you need.

———— · ● · ————

Umbria, Ala.
Jan. 26th 1863

My dear Sam,

We are anxiously looking for a letter from you, and sincerely hope to hear that you are restored to health. I have been quite uneasy about you and wished times without number, that I could have had the pleasure of nursing you. But so it is that we are separated, and are denied the satisfaction of ministering to each other's wants. A merciful God will, I trust, soon put an end to such an unhappy state of affairs. I look to the bright side of the picture, and think how very happy we shall soon be, locked in each other's arms. Son, if my prayers are heard you will soon return to us, and make us all happy again. Jamie has written to you and told you of the death of poor Simon, but as there is so much irregularity in the mails, you may not receive his letters. I was never more shocked in my life, than I was when William came to the house in the night to announce the melancholy news. I had seen him late on Friday night holding Mr. Lawless's buggy at our door, and was terribly shocked to hear of his death a few hours after. What a loss to us, at this, or any other time. He was uncommonly smart and good, and a great favorite with the family. The shoe business, I fear, is almost at an end, tho' Robert & Edward both improved under Simon's instruction. How forcibly impressed upon our minds in the solemn fact that "in the midst of life we are in death."[23]

23. From the Book of Common Prayer.

I regret very much that so few of our letters have reached you. Jamie, Mary, Lou & I are constantly writing to you, and it is a shame that the post office department is so badly conducted, when so much uneasiness and unhappiness are caused by it. I know not where [?]. At all events you have lost many letters. It would be almost incredible to tell you how many letters we have sent to you. The children are all well and doing well at school. Willie will not study hard and consequently will not improve as he might do under such an able teacher as we have. I think we have been peculiarly fortunate in getting him. He is a pleasant gentlemanly man and good tempered withal. Israel & Lou have commenced Latin today.

We have not yet rented the Eubank place, and several persons have advised me to let it lie out & improve. Dr. Grigg intends going to housekeeping and thought he had secured Ben Evans' place two miles from us. Yesterday he told me that "possibly" he might want the Eubank house, as there was some uncertainty about his getting the other place. If we could rent the land advantageously, I would prefer doing so. But really I am glad we got rid of C.S. Emma Logan wishes to rent the Lyle place, if she can get an overseer. If she does not take it, Capt. J. May wishes it. $100 is said to be the value of it. Mr. Wheeler declined taking it. Mary recd a letter from Biscoe a day or two since. He wrote from Richmond on the day of his arrival there—14th Jan., and spoke of going to port Royal. He said he hoped to see you frequently. It has been reported here lately that D. H. Hill's division has been ordered to N. Carolina, but I hope it is not true. Do write immediately and tell us how you are, and where you will probably be this Winter. It seems to me that you have been from us at least one year, so heavily does time pass away now. Tell John Suky was here yesterday in good health. I gave her $10 and told her to come for the other ten whenever she wants it. She was very glad to receive it, and sends her love to John. Her baby has a bad cold, which almost every one else has at present. Sucky is hired at the same place this year. I was quite sick last night, but feel as well as usual to-day. Jamie was an attentive nurse and wanted to stay all night in my room. Dr. Johnston's pills for liver complaint have cured me. I am writing at the desk in the parlor. Your friends make kind inquiries about you, and all send much love, including Fannie M. If she loves you as the old grand Mother does, you will have a large share of her affection. Mr Enoch gets along pretty much at the old rate. He comes to see us & is very friendly. The overseers are preparing for another corn crop. What do you think of our planting the land opposite to the house in corn? It will save some hauling. The children send warmest love to you & the Servants howdye. Remember us kindly to John. May Heaven smile upon and bless you, my dear, good Son.

Yr devotedly attached
Mother

———•———

Umbria, Jan 24th 1863

My dear Sam,

It has now been a week since I last wrote to you & promising you a regular correspondence, will give you a few lines; meanwhile, am anxiously expectant for an answer from you to my last.

Since I last wrote, in the brief space of a week, one or two incidents have transpired which will be both painful & interesting to you. In a word, we are all much shocked & very much grieved this morning quite early, to learn from William, who came up from the quarters with news, that little Simon was dead. I cannot describe the feeling that I had on first hearing the news. Seeing him no longer than last night as well as he ever was & in good humor & waking up to learn of his death, produced a most painful effect upon us all, & to day has been one of the most melancholy that we have spent for a long time. It seems that Simon retired last night jus as usual, after eating a hearty supper, lying down in front of the fire. Katy awoke about 2 or 3 o'clock this morning & called him several times, & on receiving no answer, said to Catherine who was up, in fun, "Why your daddy must be dead, he's so fast asleep," dreaming not for one moment that that had really taken place. She got up then, & trying to renew[?] him, soon found out that he was dead, & from that time 'till morning almost [?] with grief & sorrow. Daddy Simon also attempted to wake him but instantly perceived that life had fled. One of Simon's arms in relaxing and falling from his body fell in the fire-place causing his hand to be burned & shriveled. No cause has yet been found, of his death, though I will proceed to relate what has afterwards transpired, which seems almost a conclusive fact. Dr. Grigg came in this morning, having been sent for by Mama, to have a post-mortem examination. He had no sooner examined Simon than he told me privately that he was convinced from evident proof that he was poisoned! My, how terrible! It is truly sad to see anyone to whom you are attached (and we were all attached to Simon, you know, as good, obedient, honest & faithful a servant as ever lived.) I say it is sad to see one in the prime of life put [?] down by a natural death; but, oh, how much more is this sorrow deepened when foul means were [?] the work! Mr. Enoch is of the same opinion that Dr. G is, & says it is clear to his mind that he was poisoned & he even has an idea & so has the Dr. of whom the perpetrator is. The Dr. has not had an examination yet, except for himself.[24] He tried to get Dr. Parrish, Osborne, or Webb, but could get neither. He then sent this morning for Dr. Moore & is to have the examination to-morrow. I hope they will arrive at the cause & investigate the matter from beginning to end. We had no servant amongst them all who was more willing & ready to do anything & everything for us at anytime, & who took delight in doing little things for us. He was also very useful at any trade or business to which he applied himself & was very ingenious & smart. His loss to us will be great & irretrievable. He was one of, if not my favorite, of all the servants.

He had just cut out a pair of shoes for himself & intended making a pair for Spencer to day, when he was called away.

I sincerely trust that he was not poisoned; but if he was I hope the person may be found out & never allowed to come on the place again or else be sold. I don't think one who would do it is worth having.

Another incident has occurred which produced no little excitement in the neighborhood. The boy Horace, who ran off to Miss last year, was seen the other day on Mrs. Torbert's place & being pursued by some one, Mayfield[25] I think, ran for some little distance & surrendered himself. Mayfield then took

24. Sam was concerned about Simon's death. Dr. Grigg's and Dr. John R. Moore's autopsy concluded that Simon had died from congestion of the heart or lungs (Diary of Samuel Pickens, February 14, 16, 1863).

25. A. J. Mayfield, a neighboring planter in the Hollow Square District. Mrs. Elizabeth Torbert was the widow of Cyrus A. Torbert. The family lived in the Hollow Square District and enslaved sixty-nine people in 1860 (U.S. Census, 1860).

him & carried him to jail in Eutaw where he put him for safe-keeping. The neighborhood called a meeting last Thursday at Hol Sq [Hollow Square] for the purpose of finding out the sentence which the people wished carried out in regard to Horace. It was unanimously resolved that the same sentence which was agreed upon at the meeting which we attended last year, should now be carried into effect. The sentence of that meeting was that the boy should be executed when caught. It seems that Mayfield is Administrator of Mr. Torbert's estate & refuses to give the negro up to the people as he said that in that case he could be prosecuted by law & made to pay the value of the negro. However, at the meeting a "bond of indemnification" was signed by the whole crowd, which released Mayfield from all responsibility in the matter & put it upon those signing the bond. He refuses, however, to give the negro over to the people & is beginning to be regarded as trying to defend him. No one knows the result of the matter but all this [?] long law suit will have to be gone through with before it is ended & all, of course, say & know that the act of turning the negro who was found so deeply implicated, loose upon the community would produce a bad effect upon the other negroes who would be emboldened to try their plans again & some think this will be the result.

Well, I must say, I have written you a long sad letter, filled only with some sorrowful & exciting news. But it was all I had to tell you, and I am forced to bring it to a close hoping that more pleasant matter for a letter may form my next to you.

Mama & all the children are well & all have been joyful & glad of a letter which Louty received the other day from you saying you were nearly well & telling us a great deal which we were truly glad to hear of you. I hope we will receive letters more regularly from you & also get them to you better. We have written to Dr. Cunningham in Richmond please to forward all letters to you which we direct to his care. Whenever you move from place to place just drop him a line informing him of your post-office.

I must close this as I have no doubt been fatiguing in my descriptions.

All the children & Mama join me in kindest love to you. Hoping soon to hear from you, & to receive regular letters, I remain ever your affectionate brother,

James.

Sunday, 25th

P.S. I will write you the result of the examination.

Tell John, please, that we rode to Evans' the other day & enquired after Suky, who was very well indeed. She will be there another year, I think. It was so late when we went that we didn't expect to go there & did not carry her the money which we were to give her, but will send it to her soon.[26]

J.P.

———•—•——

Camp in Caroline Co., Va.
Febry. 19th, 1863

My dear Mother,

I will now write and thank you for several ever dear and welcome letters received since I wrote to you last. I would have answered them sooner but there are so many interruptions in camp that it is almost impossible to write at all regularly. Very often just as we get seated and fixed for writing, the drum beats and calls us off on some duty. We have a drill in the morning directly after breakfast, roll call at 1 P.M., another drill at half past 2 and Dress parade about half past 4. So you see how the day is divided up: and once a week I am on duty all day; for instance, Monday I was on guard, Tuesday it snowed hard all day, and was too cold to write, and yesterday I was detailed to work on the roads or on fortifications. The weather was so bad, however, and snow on the ground four inches deep, that, after trudging about several miles to report at Brigade and Division Headquarters, we were excused. And even when at leisure there is very often a crowd in the tent playing cards or laughing and talking, and under these circumstances I find it difficult to write, tho' am trying it now, with a party busily engaged in a game of Poker. I hope, therefore, that you will take this as an excuse for all errors and shortcomings.

From your letter of Jan. 16th, written the day after you heard that I had

26. It appears that Suky had been rented to the Evanses. This may be the Abner P. Evans family, who lived in the Hollow Square District, near the Pickenses. Evans enslaved twelve people (U.S. Census, 1860).

gone to Hanover C.H. on sick furlough, I was extremely sorry to see that you were so uneasy about me, but appreciate it highly, and am happy in the belief that such anxiety could be felt only by a dear Mother who loves me much. My sickness was not so serious as you feared but I had taken a bad cold and had severe pains in my breast. Dr. Tom Hill of Newbern (acting Surgeon) said he had not the proper medicines for me, but gave me several doses of Quinine and at bed time a dose of morphine, but we were then so uncomfortably fixed that I could not rest at night, and after spending nearly a week without improving any and passing almost sleepless nights, he (Dr. H.) advised me to try to get into some private house in the neighborhood. John walked all about trying to find a place for me but could not, every house being filled with the poor Fredericksburg refugees. Dr. Hill then gave me a leave of absence and I rode down to Hanover in Ellison's wagon. John went to Richmond and brought me a box of Jew David's (Hebrew) Plaster which I applied to my breast, and being in a comfortable house, soon got relief. After my return to the Regt we exchanged our fly for a good full tent, moved from the cold, bleak place on a hill, down into the bottom where it is much warmer and sheltered from the wind. We have plenty of straw in the tent now and a nice little Yankee stove which we bought for $10. It is made for Camp use and is very light, being made of sheet iron, and is shaped like an inverted funnel. We find it very convenient as it requires very little wood to make the tent warm. So snugly are we fixed up now that we would like to remain here, but I'm afraid we shall have to move before long. It is believed that a large portion of the army on the Rappahannock has been taken away, probably to act as a land force against Charleston. Several Divisions of Longstreet's Corps have already moved down towards Richmond. The Richmond papers think that very soon a desperate battle will be fought in Tenn. & should the Yankees be victorious that they will sweep down the Miss. valley and attack Vicksburg in the rear, where another terrible fight will ensue. Charleston & Savannah are expecting an attack, also, and I suppose you saw Genl Beauregard's address, calling upon all who are able to come forward for their defense, and advising the noncombatants to leave the cities. So it seems that the Yankees are going to make another grand effort, and if we defeat them, which I trust in God will be the case, it may end the war. The news from the N. West has been favorable of late, though we do not know that it can be relied on.

In your letter you urged me to get a furlough & go home. I assure you that nothing on earth would have given me so much pleasure and if my health had required it & it had been possible, I certainly would have exchanged this air for that of glorious old Umbria. I am in excellent health now tho,' and need nothing in the way of clothing or blankets. My outfit is as good or better than any I've seen. I know that I have three of the best blankets in the South. The one that you lined & sent on to me is wide enough doubled for two of us to sleep on and is almost as good as a mattress. You must have intended it for that purpose when preparing it. I was mistaken in supposing that you sent me the candy that Joe Grigg gave me. He says the [unclear] candy for which you will please return my thanks to him, when you see him. And Dr. has gone to house-keeping, as he could not stand Mr. Sadler's charges. I saw a letter from him to Mr. Joe in which he said that you let him have corn cheaper than he could have gotten it elsewhere, offered to loan him spoons until he could get some, & had done a thousand other kindnesses for which he said "May the Lord bless her & restore Sam hale & hearty." He really seems very friendly.

Mr. Joe begs to be kindly remembered to you and all the family. He says he will write to Jamie in a few days. I have not met with Tom Biscoe yet: he is some distance from us, tho' Mr. Jow & I intend going to see him. The secret you told me respecting him & Mary sounds more like a jest than reality, as Mary Is a school girl and very young. I hope Icha is entirely well again. How happy it would have made me to have been with you on Mary's birthday.

Santee, Caroline Co., Va.

March 9th, 1863

My dear Sister Mary,

As an opportunity offers of sending a letter directly to Greensboro I will avail myself of it and write one to you by Mr. McCall who goes home on furlough.[27] Oh! how I do wish it was so that I could go home, too. What joy it would give me to be with the dear loved ones there once more. (The ink,

27. W. Alexander McCall, from Greensboro (Hubbs, ed., *Voices from Company D*, 412).

which was borrowed, has been called for, so I shall have to use a bad pencil.) But furloughs are now granted only to those who have not been home since enlisting in 1861. I hope, though, that the war will soon come to a close, and that we may all return to our homes to stay. It is feared, however, now that since the Northern Congress has passed a conscription bill to increase their armies & voted an unlimited supply of money for "Old Abe" that the war will be protracted. I hope to no great extent, though. Last Friday I read a letter from Jamie & one from you, & am much obliged to you both for them. Your pony must be very gentle, as you venture to ride her. Did they continue to break the two colts at the Canebreak? I suppose you would all be very glad if Cousin Jennie should come to go to school at Umbria, for you would have a nice time together. Give my love to her & also to cousins Isabella & Julia when you see them. I have had the good luck to get hold of a book or two to read lately. It is rarely the case that we can have anything at all to read & consequently they will be a great treat to me. I've just finished Scott's "Lord of the Isles," which is a beautiful & very interesting poem; and intend reading "Lady of the Lake" & several others. I have also one of Cooper's novels—"The Pioneers." If it had been possible to have gotten books I could have read a great deal in Winter Quarters. I suppose at home Spring begins to shew itself in the budding & blooming vegetation; and the farmers are preparing to plant their crops. While at Hanover C.H. I saw some corn that a soldier brought from one of the counties on the coast & it was so pretty that I asked for an ear & brought it to camp. I will enclose some of the grains in this letter, and you & Louty, Willy & Icha must plant them in your gardens and see who will raise the prettiest ear. It is said to be fine corn for stock, and on the ear looks prettier than any you ever saw. And Mr. Staudenmayer & John are planting a new Strawberry bed, are they? One was badly needed & I hope they will succeed well with it. Jamie ought to have the fruit trees trimmed & pruned, if he has not already done so. I will write to Lou in a few days. Please give my warmest love to dear Mama & all the children, & accept for yourself the same. Answer this soon.

Ever your affectionate brother,
Samuel

P.S. John sends howd'ye to all & enquires after his family. Tell all the servants howd'ye for me. S.P.

This day one year ago this army left Winter Quarters.

———•—•———

Umbria, March 9th 1863

My dear Sam,

More than a week has now glided by and still no letter from you has reached us. We have begun to feel uneasy lest you may have had a relapse & a return of your cold.

(By-the-way, the mail came just now and with it a letter for mama from you, dated 19th ult.) We were rejoiced greatly to hear from you, that you are once more in good health.

Mama thanks you for your most welcome letter and says she will answer it very soon.

I feel ashamed at having delayed writing so long, but have really been through the rubs since I last wrote, an account of which I will hastily relate to you. Last week I was ordered as all other conscripts were, to report at Eutaw to the examining Surgeon. Sat. Mon. & Tues were the three days on which the Surgeon would be at Eutaw. Well, to commence, Sat. was one of the rainiest days I ever saw & of course didn't go. By the way, however, the Surg was not in Eutaw on that day but was in Greensboro where he examined the papers of all the town exempts but I knew nothing of it. On Mon. I went to Greensboro to know what to do, as Geo. Briggs said there would be no use to go to Eutaw.[28] Found out from him that I would *have* to go & that I had only one day left to go in (Tues.) & the river was then, we heard, seven miles wide at Jenning's ferry. However, I determined to risk the trip & accordingly taking William along, a sort of companion de voyage (by the by I was glad of it) we proceeded to the ferry which comes now up to the stage stand. We found old uncle Nick, the former ferryman, in good time to row us over. But just as we were getting in the skiff, three others drove up & persisted in going along, as they were anx-

28. George Briggs was the constable in Greensboro in 1860 (U.S. Census, 1860).

ious to cross. Now what do you think of six people in an ordinary sixed skiff, a trunk & to cross one of the strongest tides I have ever seen! It was a great risk, & all had to keep as quiet as possible. Once or twice the skiff, becoming unsteady by the motions of one or two impatient ones, came near tipping. Then we had to feel our way through brush, briers, etc on the side of the river (we didn't face the current—it being too strong) and a very slow time of it we had! We went two miles down the road from the ferry to the river & three miles up the river; but winding about as we did went almost seven miles which took us nearly 3 hrs. We then landed at Finche's ferry 3 miles from Eutaw to which place we walked. I finished my business, got a discharge from the surgeon & William & I proceeded back to the ferry, where we took the skiff & returned to stage stand in one hour, a third of the time we were in going up.

The river is very high indeed is five miles wide (instead of seven as we heard) and was rising when we last heard from it. The ride back on the swift current was delightful and the scene, a long, broad sheet of water reaching on both sides as far as you could see, with pines & other trees almost submerged, was very novel & pretty. I fortunately found a buggy on getting to this side of the river, in which I rode home. William walked as I couldn't get him to ride in another buggy which was there but for the ride in which he would have had to pay $1. William was very considerate, but as he had walked six miles that morning must have found it very fatiguing to walk five additional miles. Was very glad after the trip was over and would not take it again for anything, hardly.

But enough of this egotism. I have actually filled four pages with more trash than I expected to find need for in a *short* description.

You must excuse the haste in which I have written the foregoing. Mama & I intended going to town to send some things on for you & Tom, but it has turned so cold, and as Mama does not feel very well we have given it [*unclear*] till tomorrow. I was hurrying to finish my letter in order to send it on by Mr. Pasteur who intends leaving day after tomorrow, but as it will not go today I will add a little more to it.[29]

29. Pasteur enlisted in the Fifth in 1861. He was wounded and captured, with Sam, during the Battle of Chancellorsville. In October 1863, having been judged unfit for service, he was detailed to the Quartermaster Department Office in Greensboro as a tax-in-kind collector (CMSR, Alabama, RG 109).

I am very glad that you have a good tent and that you have a warmer & more comfortable place for it than you had before, and also that you have a stove. This must be a great comfort indeed and a great addition to a tent. I hope you may not find much more use for it, but that the war may soon end & see you returned once more home. Mr. Staudenmayer is very hopeful & thinks that the 1st of April will certainly bring us good news from the Emporer Napolean, whom he thinks will recognize the South beyond a doubt & probably intervene, either amicably, if possible, or forcibly, if other [unclear] fail.[30] It is certainly a very pleasant thing to indulge *hope* of recognition and intervention, and this buoys up the hearts of a great many who without it would be cast down. But it has, in so many instances proved but a fallacy, we have been deceived so often that I sometimes think foreign nations have no idea or intention of doing one thing in our favor, but that to us alone, is left the work & glory of achieving our independence. I sincerely trust whichever manner we come out in the end that that end is not far but that it may soon appear. You cannot tell how glad we would be to welcome you back, how we count the months & days you have been away & how anxiously we look forward to the future to hasten your return to us.

Vegetation with us is very forward this Spring & already the trees are beginning to put forth their new leaves. Peach & plum trees have been in full flower & some have had leaves for two weeks. Until lately we have had very wild spring weather; but a day or two ago it turned very warm became almost like summer & finally rained very hard. Last night we had a very severe thunder storm & a pelting rain for about half an hour after which it turned very cold & now is again regular. March weather—cloudy, cold & raw. Hope the weather you are having is more pleasant, as it is not only very unpleasant to be out in it but detrimental to health. After this month, tho, we may look for warmer & more agreeable weather.

We heard this morning of the death of Mrs. Willingham, who recently lost a second son—her first ones dying when Sam Dorroh did.[31] What great

30. Emperer Napoleon III in the fall of 1862 proposed that France, Britain, and Russia propose a six-month armistice during which the blockade would be lifted. Russia refused; the British cabinet discussed the idea but rejected it (McPherson and Hogue, *Ordeal by Fire*, 325).

31. W. H. Willingham died of typhoid at Sangster Station, Virginia, near Manassas, on October 3, 1861. Dorroh died a week earlier on September 25, also at Sangster Station. Both

distress must be in Mr. W's house now! First a son then another and now his wife, having gone. She is to be buried in Greensboro where her two sons were buried.

Alfred was returned from Oven Bluff week before last, very sick. Dr. Moore attended him & pronounced his case typhoid pneumonia & entertained but little hope of his recovery. Subsequently, his case has taken a change. The Dr found that he had measles & is now much better. Alfred was found to be sick at the bluff, was put on a boat & left at a landing on the river too sick to move. Geo. Erwin's wagon happened to be at the landing when he directed Alfred to be put in the wagon & taken to our Canebrake place. Mr. High then sent him to Goodrum place. It is a very mean thing to have hands ordered out & then when they are sick to have them attended to no better than if they were inhuman. It is doubtless owing to the carelessness of government agents, many of whom have no other concern than their own interests.[32]

Matt is no better than when you last heard from him. He has pneumonia Mr. H. says.

We have commenced planting a little corn (or rather, are preparing to do so) in the field to the right of where the wheat is. Beyond the wheat & next to the woods we are going plant some Chinese sugar cane. Charley Stickney kindly gave us some of the seed. In the field by the gin house we are going to have a clover patch, as it is only in this way that a good pasturage can be procured for the calves, etc. Uncle George has the sole supervision of the garden & is getting on with his seed-planting pretty well, but is now

---

men had enlisted in the Fifth Infantry in April 1861. The second Willingham brother, Claudius, died January 27, 1863, in Richmond (CMSR, Alabama, RG 109). Claudius was living in Mississippi, near Corinth, where he enlisted in the Sixteenth Mississippi Volunteers in May 1861 (CMSR, Mississippi, RG 109). The Willinghams were the sons of Phillip and Francis Willingham, who lived in the Hollow Square Precinct in 1860. Phillip Willingham worked as an overseer (U.S. Census, 1860).

32. Alfred was one of the enslaved people the Confederate government impressed to work on the construction of fortifications at Oven Bluff, on the eastern shore of the Tombigbee River, in Clarke County to defend a gunboat production operation and the salt works of the county (*Clarke County Genealogy and History Network*). Enslavers frequently complained about government agents' treatment of enslaved people. On planter objections to Confederate impressment policy, see Martinez, *Confederate Slave Impressment in the Upper South*.

prevented from continuing it on account of the wet & cold weather we have lately had. Hope the vegetables get of eatable size & when fruit is in season, if not before, that you may be with us to enjoy them. How much more would we enjoy them if you were with us to share them.

Capt. May has rented 150 acres of the Eubank's tract for the year & has commenced operations for a crop there. Mama endeavored to rent the whole of the tract, but not finding a tenant for it, let Capt. M. take the above part of it. It is well that we rented even a part of the place as the houses will be occupied; whereas if it had laid out they might have gone to ruin. No one has taken the Leyle's place, so I expect it is to remain tenantless for the year. I heard that Mayfield is glad of this as he can now fatten a quantity of cattle & other stock on it. It ought to be fenced off I think & so might the Eubank's place at some time when hands from one of the places can be spared.

I haven't seen the Dr. for some time, but when I last saw him he was well; he had recovered from an attack which was brought on by too much exercise. He & Mr. Burge had several cat hunts in Eubank's swamp, in which they caught two pretty large ones. After the last hunt, the Dr. was taken with chills & fever and was sick for several days but is now well again. Mr. Enoch spent the evening with us Saturday last (day before yesterday.) He inquired particularly after you & desired us to give his love to you; the Dr. also did the same.

Well, I believe I have exhausted my fund of news, which was limited, at best. It has now been nearly two weeks since I have received a letter from you; however I am constantly expecting one & will continue to write regularly to you until I get one. I know it is impossible for you to answer all my letters.

Mama sends you $100.00, which I enclose.

Mrs. S. is a very pleasant little woman & interesting—also quite smart & intelligent. You would be very much pleased with her.

Have you heard that Cous. Isabella is to be (or has) married to a Mr. Williams of Mobile, has broken up at Cousin Julia's & is going to live fifty miles from that city on the railroad? Were you not surprised to hear it? You will be more so to know that he is a livery stable keeper.

It seems singular how, all of a sudden she should have determined to give herself to such a lot.

Well, I must draw this miserable excuse for a letter to a close hoping soon to have a long letter from you. I have not had the letter from Mr. Joe which he promised to write, altho' many days & a few months have elapsed since he left. Give him & all our friends my love.

Mama & the children send warmest love to you. Accept the same my dear brother, from Your ever affectionate,

James.

P.S. All send howdye to John. Tell him when we saw Sucky last (a few days ago) she was well & sent her love to him.

J.P.

———— ·•· ————

Umbria, Ala.

March 17th 1863

My beloved Son,

Accept my heartfelt thanks for your affectionate letter, dated 19th Feb, which I would have answered sooner if a severe attack of rheumatism had not almost deprived me of the use of my arms. I am not altogether relieved, and may have it as severely as ever, if a rainy spell, of weather should come on. But this we are not to expect at this season, so I will, as usual, look on the bright side of the picture, and hope that I shall never be troubled by that painful disease again. Jamie had it in his wrist lately and suffered very much for several days; but I soon cured him by rubbing with [*unclear*] and putting a piece of flannel on the part affected. I am a better doctor or nurse for others, than for myself. I mentioned the remedy, so that you may use it on yourself or others who should be so unfortunate as to have rheumatism. I hope you will take good care of yourself, and avoid all the evils incident to exposure.

Since the early part of January we have had rainy, gloomy weather and the Warrior River is now almost as high as it has been. We are now enjoying pleasant Spring like weather which I hope will last as we are busily engaged in planting our garden and corn in the field opposite the house. One of our neighbors, Mr. Smaw, speaks of planting a large cotton crop as he did last year.[33] I think no one should plant any thing except grain and wish the tax on cotton may be so heavy as to prevent the losing money people from trying to amass wealth in such times as these. The war has developed the character of very many persons, and extortionate prices are charged even by those who might have been considered liberal & patriotic in times of peace. We sold some of our corn at $1.25 and some at $1.50. The balance we concluded to keep, so as to be able to get shoes and leather, which can be got only for corn or something to eat. But the government agents impressed 600 bushels a few days since at $2 per bushel. I have heard that they are taking wagon loads of meal from some plantations; as yet they have taken corn from us. Perhaps they found less than our overseers represented to us.

I was delighted to hear of you through Dr. Grigg on Sunday last; he had rec a letter from Mr. Joe stating that you now weigh 25 pounds more than you ever did before. I remarked to Jamie "how handsome he must look." I do not admire fat people but as you were quite slender when you left us, 25 lbs. must have improved instead of disfiguring you. We went to the Prairie Church to hear Bishop Wilmer preach and see the rite of confirmation administered to Mr [*unclear*] Nelson and Mr. Edward Bryant and 3 Colored persons.

In my last letter, I mentioned the illness of Alfred; he is now better, and I hope out of danger, tho very weak and spitting blood every day. Dr [*unclear*] has stopped visiting him, so he must consider Alfred as convalescing. He was very low. His wife Mary Ann is now sick with pneumonia. Poor Walter died on the 12th of this month; he was attacked with pneumonia which ended his life. Dr. Osborn attended him. He was willing to die and was calm and collected in giving advice [?] to his friends, and instructions to have his funeral sermon preached by [*unclear.*] Aunt Franky & Spenser were much distressed at his death.[34]

33. William Smaw owned a large plantation next to the Pickenses' Umbria Plantation. He was another North Carolina migrant. See Snedecor, "Map of Greene County, Alabama, Precinct 6 Hollow Square," in *Hand drawn maps of the Precincts of Greene County*, and U.S. Census, 1860.

34. Alfred, Mary Ann, Walter, Aunt Franky, and Spenser were all enslaved people (Samuel Pickens Jr. estate inventory, 1857).

The children are all well and getting on fairly well with their studies. They find their teacher very cross, unmercifully so, and make loud and heavy complaints to me. I have however determined not to interfere though I am strongly tempted to do so in Israel's case today. The school was dismissed at ¼ past 4 o'clock with the exception of poor little Icha who has to remain one hour more. I think the confinement is too long for most of the scholars. A ride on horseback every afternoon keeps Mary alive. Lou grumbles over her French exercises and thinks she is oppressed. I am satisfied that we have a good teacher, who would give entire satisfaction if he was blessed with a tolerable share of patience.

William Withers has joined a Cavalry Company in Mobile and will start tomorrow morning for that place. Robert Withers will soon leave home for Tennessee. I have not been to see them yet. In fact I go nowhere except to the Sawyers. Enoch walked home with me tonight and said "you must always give my love to Sam." Your time I know is fully occupied, but you must write as often as you can. We are so anxious about you. May God preserve you unhurt and restore you to us soon is the fervent, oft repeated prayer of your Mother. Lawrence Wood died on Sunday with pneumonia. All send much love to you. Remember us kindly to John. Suky & all are well. The servants and Sukey make many kind inquiries about you. [*End of letter.*]

———•◆•———

My dear Sam,

Again have I deferred writing to you for now more than two weeks, and it would seem that I have been waiting to receive a reply to my other letters in order to write; but this is not the fact. I have been intending to write for several weeks, but have been prevented, first by going to the Canebrake last week to see how things were getting on there, as I had not been since you & I were there last fall. Then, having two such good correspondents as Mama & Mary, I knew you would be posted up on news & so I deferred 'till this week. And now, as it is, I can provide you but a stale letter, having nothing of any interest to form anything of a letter. Tom Moore is going to return to the army next Wednesday, so I will send this by him as it will probably go more direct than by mail. I thought Tom had got a discharge, but he told me yesterday he had not.

I rec'd yesterday a very welcome letter from you, dated 4th inst., from which we were all glad to learn that you were well. You speak of camp life being monstrous. It may be to you, but as to the descriptions of it which you give us, [*phrase unclear*] and I am always sorry when I reach the end of your very interesting and highly prized letters, and only wish I could repay you in the interest which this [*unclear*] affords me.

We heard that Lawrence Wood was dead, but this proved untrue. He is very weak tho' and is lingering away. I can hardly realize the healthy person he was when in the Company at Mobile last year, to be so sick, and with consumption, Dr. Moore thinks.

I must relate an occurrence which took place on my way from Canebrake the other day. "Dr" of course got frightened, near the Randolph house at a calf in the fence corner & making a pivot of her hind legs whirled instantly around, and before I could regain my "equilibrium" was drawn by the attraction of gravitation to the earth; in other words, got thrown. I was, however, perfectly off my guard and having an umbrella in my hand could not manage the reins in time. Well, I had then to walk the rest of the way home, but I took it through the field, cutting off half the distance. Speaking of Dr. she is a very poor dependence for a horse, and I think is getting worse in regard to shying at vehicles etc. passing than ever: then again, she is too slow in gait for convenience. However, she is better than none, and will answer every purpose, while the war lasts.

That dinner which you had must have been a splendid one indeed. As regards the cabbage, peas and Irish potatoes you are ahead of us in vegetables, the only dish & the first from the garden which has been on table yet, being onions. We have a good many things up tho,' which will be very nice in about a month, at the end of which time I hope peace shall have been proclaimed & that you may be with us again, to share them.

You have a very good mess, and I suppose must have a great deal of humor & pleasure amongst you. Mr. Joe carries fun wherever he goes and adds greatly to the life of the mess, I know.

We have been having nice Spring weather, lately; and the trees are beginning to put forth their leaves. Some are quite full of leaves.

Altogether, it may be called an early spring as I think it was much later last year when they commenced to put forth. Last night we had almost a hurricane of wind from the N.E. I have never heard such violent wind before. A mulberry at the S.W. corner of No. 3, was blown down & an orange tree on the Newsons.

All are well at the Canebrake when I was down last week and everything seemed to be getting on well. Mr. H. will finish planting in a week or less time, I think. The whole place is planted in corn. That planted on the eastern part of the place has come up very nicely indeed. Lawless is not getting on so well. The land lying back of the mill is under water yet and has been for five weeks I think. Now he has a great many sick from bad colds; so he will be later in making a start.

They have called very heavily upon us for hands to work on the river defences & on fortifications at Mobile. They called not long ago for two for the latter work & the other day for one for the former. I think we have five hands now away. However, if they improve the defences, it is very important & should not be complained of.

You have no doubt read the glorious news from Vicksburg which confirms still more the belief of all in its ability to withstand the forces of the enemy. They were driven off, one vessel was sunk and another so badly hurt it is believed it also will sink. Day before yesterday being fast day (Friday) Mama, Mr. Staudenmayer & I went to church & heard one of the best sermons from Mr. Cobbs which I have ever heard him preach. Mr S. assisted Mr. C. in the services.

Mama had violent pains last night, the result either of bad cold or of liver complaint, she thinks; but is better today. You must persuade Mama to take exercise, as it would be of great benefit to her. Well I must close as I have given you the little information I had.

All send love to you. With kindest love to you I remain your affectionate brother,

James.

P.S. I send two calendars. I will look out for another letter soon. Tell John howdye for us all. Mama encloses you $100 thinking you may have need of it.

Did you hear that Mat died? He died on Thursday night—12th ult., with pneumonia.

Mat was a very good boy indeed & would have made a useful servant.

I received all the copies of the News which you sent me and am much obliged to you for them. They are very interesting indeed.

Mon. 30th Mama is much better today & is up. It was a very bad cold which she had taken.

Write very soon, and whenever you can steal an opportunity.

Remember me to all friends and tell Mr. Joe if I don't receive the letter which he was to have written, very soon, that I will write to him.

Y'r Brother, J.P.

P.S. Tell John I haven't had an opportunity of enquiring after Ben & his mother but will do so & send answer in my next.

FIVE

Reckoning with the Cost of War

APRIL–JULY 1863

On April 29, while preparing to go on picket duty, Sam and the Fifth Alabama learned that "the Yankees" were crossing the Rappahannock again.[1] Rodes's brigade, now under the command of Colonel Edward A. O'Neal, received orders to march toward Fredericksburg and form a line of battle in some pine woods near Hamilton's Crossing, facing the Rappahannock below Fredericksburg, and prepare to turn back a Union force under the command of General John Sedgwick, which had begun crossing the river, in the initial phase of the Battle of Chancellorsville.[2] The brigade remained in that position for the rest of the day. Sam confided to his diary that he could not sleep much of the night of the 29th "[*from*] the excitement of the day & speculating on what the morrow would probably bring forth." During the brief sleep he did get, he wrote, he dreamed of returning home to the life he had before the war. Fearing he might not survive the coming battle, he wished that his dream "could be soon realized."

1. Sears, *Chancellorsville*, 121–23.
2. Report of Colonel Edward A. O'Neal, *OR*, ser. 1, vol. 37, pt. 2: 950–51; Diary of Samuel Pickens, April 27–29, 1863; Eicher, *The Longest Night*, 475–78; Sears, *Chancellorsville*, 249. Rodes had assumed temporary command of D. H. Hill's division after Hill left to take command of the Department of North Carolina. Edward "Allegheny" Johnson was to take permanent command of the division when he recovered from a year-old ankle wound. See Collins, *Major General Robert E. Rodes*, 183–87.

Early on April 30, before dawn, O'Neal's brigade moved about half a mile to a line of "rifle pits" that were "muddy & water in the bottom." It was raining, and Union guns on Stafford Heights across the river began firing on the entrenched Confederates as Sedgewick's corps continued its advance. "There was cannon firing," Sam wrote, "kept up slowly all day—shells passing to right & left of our position whizzing by & bursting but none over us." A while later General Rodes ordered the brigade to move to a position in the rear of the rifle pits, into some woods. They remained in this position that night, maintaining, as Sam put it, "a vigilant watch in the breastwks that we had occupied in the morning."[3]

The next day the brigade moved again, this time marching up the river, along muddy roads, to the Plank Road between Fredericksburg and Orange Court House. Union forces had completed their crossings above Fredericksburg and were advancing from the west, in the rear of the Confederate Army. General Lee ordered three divisions of Jackson's corps to reinforce Lt. Gen. Richard Anderson's and Maj. Gen. Lafayette McLaw's divisions, which were moving to block Hooker's advance from the west. When the men reached the Orange Plank Road, they stopped, stacked their knapsacks, turned west, and prepared for battle. The brigade then crossed an open field to woods so thick that it was "not possible to preserve anything of a line." That afternoon, in front of the Fifth, Anderson's and McLaw's attack took Union forces by surprise and bitter fighting ensued. Sam did little more than march several times through the woods, for Rodes's division was held in reserve. At about 9:00 in the evening, the men went into bivouac in a field near an orchard. Sam described his physical condition by that time as "completely broke down."[4]

Late in the night on May 1, Lee and Jackson met and decided upon the bold plan for Jackson's corps to sweep around the Union Army's right flank and launch a surprise attack on the Yankee rear. Rodes's division would take the lead. Early on May 2, O'Neal's brigade marched west on the Plank Road,

3. Report of Colonel Edward A. O'Neal, OR, ser. 1, vol. 37, pt. 2: 950–51; Diary of Samuel Pickens, April 27–30, 1863; Eicher, *The Longest Night*, 475–78; Sears, *Chancellorsville*, 249. Collins, *Major General Robert E. Rodes*, 183–87. On Civil War soldiers' dreams and their meaning, see White, *Midnight in America*, chap. 2.

4. Report of Colonel Josephus M. Hall, Fifth Alabama, OR, ser. 1, vol. 25, pt. 2: 957–58; O'Neal Report, OR, ser. 1, vol. 25, pt. 2: 951; Collins, *Major General Robert E. Rodes*, 198–200.

turned left, passed Catherine's Furnace, and then headed north ten to twelve miles to near the intersection of the Orange Plank Road and the Orange Turnpike. By afternoon, Jackson's corps had passed the right flank of the Union line and was in its rear. The Confederates formed a line of battle, perpendicular to the Orange Turnpike, with Rodes's division in front. O'Neal's brigade took up a position at the center of the line, in some woods, to the left of the Orange Turnpike. The attack began around 6:00. During the fighting, Sam was captured by counterattacking Union soldiers and transported to Old Capitol Prison in Washington, DC, where he remained until he was exchanged later in May and returned to his unit near Richmond. He saw how well supplied and equipped the Union Army was as well as the plentiful food and other goods in Washington and was troubled by the contrast with the shortages Confederate citizens and soldiers suffered.[5]

Sam's family knew that fighting had resumed in Virginia and suffered through another silence awaiting news of his and Tom Biscoe's fate. In the letters that follow, his sister Mary and his mother wrote of their anxiety as they hopefully awaited word of Sam's and Tom's survival, but also described the routines of daily life that provided some relief from the burden of worry they all bore. Some historians have argued that such letters undermined soldiers' morale by reminding them of the struggles of loved ones at home and of their own lives before the war. Yet, the Pickenses' expressions of distress and anxiety while wondering if Sam and Tom survived, combined with sometimes lighthearted descriptions of social life, appear intended to remind Sam of how much he was missed and what he would return to when the war was over.[6]

Sam's mother heard news of his survival from a neighbor, and the victory at Chancellorsville confirmed her belief that God had heard her prayers. That he survived while so many others, including his friend John Cowin, died, relieved her anxiety, for the moment. But she understood that Sam's survival at Chancellorsville might be only a temporary reprieve; she could join Cowin's parents in grieving the loss of a son at any time.[7] Only the end of the war could guarantee her son's safe return, and she prayed for that every day.

5. Diary of Samuel Pickens, May 11, 1863.

6. On the impact of letters on soldier morale, see Hager, *I Remain Yours*, 149–50.

7. Faust, "Christian Soldiers," 86: Rable, *God's Almost Chosen Peoples*, 140–41, 258–59; McPherson, *For Cause and Comrades*, 62–65.

When Sam returned to Richmond, he wrote a letter to his mother about the battle and his time as a prisoner. He devoted the better part of three days composing a sanitized version of his experience in the Battle of Chancellorsville, including a slight wound from a near miss. In the letter, he constructed a narrative in which events unfolded in a relatively organized way. But in his diary he described scenes of random shooting and killing and characterized the battle as chaotic. The diary description suggests a test of his faith in God's control of events that was missing in his letter. He appeared troubled by a randomness to all the killing that seemed to contradict his confidence that God had a plan. Yet confronted by the existential threat war posed, and with time for reflection, Sam's doubts had given way to his faith in God's deliverance.[8]

In the aftermath of the Battle of Chancellorsville, General Lee decided to invade Pennsylvania. If all went as planned, he hoped a Confederate victory on free soil would force President Lincoln to negotiate a peace settlement. The Lincoln administration was then under intense political pressure from Peace Democrats, or "copperheads," to bargain with the Confederacy for an end to the fighting. Lee knew as well that the Confederacy's ability to sustain the war much longer was severely limited. The condition of the army and the country, Lee determined, would only continue to deteriorate if he remained on the defensive in Virginia.[9]

The Fifth Alabama reached Carlisle, Pennsylvania, on June 27 and remained there until the 30th. The next day, July 1, the men broke camp at 6:30 a.m. and marched to Gettysburg, where Union and Confederate forces were already engaged. When the Fifth arrived west of the town, Sam wrote that it was ordered to double-time "through wheat fields & ploughed ground & over fences" to join a flanking movement against the Union line. Union troops on the Mummasburg Road forced the disorganized Alabamians of Colonel Edward O'Neal's brigade to retreat, leaving the left flank of General Alfred

8. The literature on Civil War soldiers and the importance of religion is vast. See, for examples, Faust, "Christian Soldiers," 86; Linderman, *Embattled Courage,* 105; Phillips, *Diehard Rebels,* 9–10; Watson, "Religion and Combat Motivation in the Confederate Armies," 31–36.

9. Stoker, *The Grand Design,* 279–81; Eicher, *The Longest Night,* 490–91; Guelzo, *Gettysburg,* 26; Guelzo, *Fateful Lightning,* 338–39; Glatthaar, *General Lee's Army,* 268–69; Levine, *The Fall of the House of Dixie,* 146; McPherson, *Battle Cry of Freedom,* 646–48.

Iverson's North Carolina brigade exposed. The North Carolinians suffered heavy losses.[10]

On the second day, General Richard Ewell's corps was to attack Culp's Hill and Cemetery Hill as part of a rolling assault along the Union line. Ewell decided that his three divisions should attack simultaneously. General Edward "Allegheny" Johnson's division would secure Culp's Hill; General Jubal Early's division would assault the east side of Cemetery Hill; and Rodes's division would attack the west side of Cemetery Hill. Late in the day, the division began moving through the town to a line of battle just east of the Emmittsburg Road. Under heavy fire from Union artillery on Cemetery Hill, the division lay in a wheat field, waiting for orders to advance. Henry Hay's Louisiana Tigers, Tom Biscoe's unit, and Isaac Avery's North Carolinians, believing that Rodes's division was in position and attacking West Cemetery Hill, led the assault on East Cemetery Hill and briefly opened a gap in the Union line. But, as Lee reported, Rodes's division was not in position "to co-operate with General Early." By the time Rodes had his troops in line of battle, Union reinforcements arrived on East Cemetery Hill and forced Hays and Avery to retreat. As Sam wrote in his diary, he expected to attack Cemetery Hill that night, but after lying in a wheat field for a few hours, the Fifth retreated to a sunken lane near the town.[11]

Early on the morning of July 5, Ewell's corps was the last of the Army of Northern Virginia to withdraw from Gettysburg. As the army made its way toward the Potomac River crossings, Confederates fought off Union troops harassing the army's rear. Unable to cross the swollen Potomac, the Army of Northern Virginia dug in near Hagerstown, Maryland, expecting a Union attack. Knowing that his mother and his family were seeing the casualty re-

10. Rodes, *OR*, ser. 1, vol. 27, pt. 2: 555–56; Report of Colonel Josephus Hall, Commander, Fifth Alabama Infantry, *OR*, ser. 1, vol. 27, pt. 2: 595–96; Collins, *Major General Robert E. Rodes*, 267–70; Guelzo, *Gettysburg*, 170–72, Murray and Hsieh, *A Savage War*, 308–10.

11. Report of Robert E. Lee, *OR*, ser. 2, vol. 27, pt. 2: 319; Report of Major General Jubal Early, *OR*, ser. 2, vol. 27, pt. 2: 470; Rodes Report, *OR*, ser. 1, vol. 27, pt. 2: 555–56. The performance of Ewell's corps continues to be a subject of debate among historians of the Civil War, though generally overshadowed by Confederate operations against Cemetery Ridge. See Collins, *Major General Robert E. Rodes*, 288–90; Pfanz, *Gettysburg*, 276–79; Guelzo, *Gettysburg*, 351–60, 384.

ports and stories of the battle, Sam, while in the line at Hagerstown, praying that he and his comrades would soon get back into Virginia, wrote a brief letter home to let everyone know that again "a Kind Providence" had spared his life through the "bloody battle."[12]

Santee, Caroline Co.,
April 18th, 63

My dear Sister,

It has been some time since you have had a letter from me, but I'll try and make amends by writing to you today and promising to do better in future. Tom Moore arrived here a few days since and brought me a letter from Jamie with one hundred dollars in it and a box containing two bundles & a small package for Tom Biscoe, and a very nice pair of gloves, two packs of envelopes, a lead pencil and some sealing wax for me; also a nice letter from Icha.[13] I am very much obliged to Mama for this money and articles sent, and to Jamie and Icha for their kind letters. Tell Mama that she has sent me so much money lately that I shall have to beg of her not to send any more till I write for it, as I have more than $300 on hand now. She need not be at all afraid that I'll not write as soon as it is needed. We had a rain a day or two ago and I have been waiting for dry weather and roads to go and see Tom and carry his bundles. We have had an order to leave Winter Quarters and move to where wood is more plentiful and to accustom ourselves to do without cabins or tents; but the Col. of this Regt has asked permission to remain here longer, on the grounds of its being a healthy locality & and I hope we will be allowed to do so, for the bad weather is not over with by any means. We have cold rainy spells that would be very disagreeable if we were without shelter or protection.

12. Collins, *Major General Robert E. Rodes*, 295–406; Brown, *Retreat from Gettysburg*, 277–78; Diary of Samuel Pickens, July 6–14, 1863.

13. Thomas G. Moore attended Green Springs Academy with James and Sam. He enlisted in 1861 at Greensboro. When Sam wrote this letter, Moore was the company courier (CMSR, Alabama, NARA, RG 109; ledger of standings, studies, and absences of students at the Green Springs School, University of Alabama Digital Collections).

Let me tell you now of what a nice time Mr. Joe Grigg is having at present. The Commissaries are catching fish out of the River near here for the soldiers, so as to give us a little change in diet, and Mr. Joe is one of the two sent from our Co. to assist in drawing the seine, guarding the fish etc. They have splendid sport hauling the fish out by the hundreds, at each drag of the seine, and it is needless to state that they live on fresh fish, and of the choicest kinds that are caught—such as Shad, Perch and Rock. They catch Herrings principally, though, and they are very nice, but troublesome to eat on account of the great number of bones. The whole Brigade has had one day's rations—1 ¼ lbs. to each man—and the commissary expects to be able to furnish two days' ration of fish a week. Mr. Joe has sent privately to our mess several strings of Perch, Cats, Herring, and a shad or two. I do wish you all could have some of them at home to enjoy. By the way, does Uncle Lev ever send Mama any fish now? It is time they ought to be catching plenty of them now in Alabama.

Tuesday 21st. After writing the foregoing on Saturday evening I had a chill and fever and deferred finishing my letter till now, so that I might tell you how I succeeded in breaking the chills. On Sunday morning I took a blue pill[14] which I needed; and yesterday morning a dose of salts in red-paper tea and then during the day twelve grains of quinine made into pills: so last night I was fortunate enough to miss my chill entirely. That is the first time that I've been unwell since January, and I hope it will be the last chill or sickness of any kind that I will have while in the Army. Health is a great blessing, and as long as a person possesses it he can make out very well almost anywhere. On Sunday Tom Biscoe met some of the men from this Co. at church and when he heard that I had been sick, he came over to see me and sat an hour or so. I was very glad to see him and took advantage of the good opportunity to deliver the bundles that came in the box for him. I must thank you for an interesting letter which I received yesterday and Mama also, for one recd the day before. I am very sorry to hear that Mama has again been troubled

14. At the time, blue pills were used as a remedy for a range of conditions. They had little if any effect on the conditions for which they were prescribed, according to medical historians. The pills consisted mostly of mercury, so long-term users, such as Abraham Lincoln, developed symptoms of mercury poisoning. See Hirschhorn, Feldman, and Greaves, "Abraham Lincoln's Blue Pills," 315.

with Rheumatism. She is quite a martyr to it. Tell her I am much obliged to her for the offer to have some shirts made for me, but have a good stock of clothes & and don't think I shall need them. You really had poor luck in your late fishing excursion. I hope you will do better next time and bring home a good string of fish. I've no doubt Jamie makes a first rate farmer & will raise good crops. Tell him he ought to return Ben Melton's visit. Ben will think him very unsociable if he does not. You can't help liking "Kenilworth"—it is such a fine novel. "The Talisman" and "Ivanhoe" are also excellent. In fact all of the "Waverly Novels" must be good; but I have not read many. Not long since I got hold of a copy of "Lady of the Lake" and found it a beautiful poem. You had it at Dr. Smedes,' did you not? I have read also "The Lady of Lyons"—a play by Bulwer, which I suppose Mama has seen on the stage and "Vicar of Wakefield" for the 2nd time, and am now reading Irving's "Crayon Miscellany." It is a treat to get a book in Camp. And Lindy is to be made a seamstress! It is a little amusing to think of such a thing—tho' she may do better at that than she did as house servant or chamber maid, for the sedentary life will suit her exactly—if she can keep awake. You must not let Ann or [*unclear*] hear that. I hope you will succeed well with your flower-garden. I'll certainly send you some flower-seed if any can be had. Remember me kindly to the Sawyers, Dr. Grigg, Capt. May & Mr. High; and give my warmest love to Mama & all the children, & accept the same from

    Your affectionate brother,
    Samuel.

———•———

May 3rd 1863

My dear, good Brother,

    I know you think I have treated you badly in not writing to you before this, but dear brother Sam I have been very busy with my studies. I had been scolded by all of my correspondents for not writing oftener, but I really will endeavor in future to write to you two or three times a week. If I were not going to school I would write almost too often. Mama and Jamie have gone to Greensboro to church. I could not go as I woke with a headache and I knew the ride would be too long for me. I have been enjoying myself very much lately, going fishing and visiting. Last Saturday Markey, Sallie, Willie, Lou, Icha and I went fishing with Dr. Grigg to Hines Creek. We got a great many bytes, but they happened to be mosquito bites. We caught only a few fish. I caught the largest one, it was about as large as my hand. I think we went too late. Friday evening Markey, Sallie, Willie and I went for Ms. Betty Wynne and Ms. Lavinia Farrell. We then ran down to Erie and paid a visit Miss Ida Dorroh. We enjoyed ourselves very much. Markey, Sallie and I rode out yesterday evening and had a very pleasant ride.

We are going fishing as soon as the river falls. How I wish you were here to go with us. Betty Wynne and Lavinia Farrell are going and I think Dr. Grigg and Mr. E. are going too. I expect to have a delightful time. I expect the Dorrohs will join our party. I think I will go tomorrow evening to see Mrs. Grigg. Mama, Lou and Mrs. Sawyer went to see her on Friday evening. Dr. Grigg was in one of his funny humors and was very agreeable. Betty Wynne seemed to be very sociably inclined, she and Lavinia promises to come here soon. I have not seen cousin Jennie since Christmas, she has been very unsociable. Cousin Isabella is married and has gone to Mobile to live; she carried all of her children except cousin Jennie. Cousin Julia has a beautiful little girl. I have not seen it but have heard that it is beautiful. I must get a better pen and see if I cannot do a little better. Cousin Tom said in his letter that you had a chill. I hope my dear brother that you are now well. I wish you were here. I could make some nice things to tempt your appetite. Do if you are sick come home and I will take good care of you . Oh! How I wish this awful war was over. I would then be so very happy. I don't feel very well today. I feel very nervous so much so that I can hardly hold my hand, so you must excuse my very bad writing. Ms. Borden was married the other day to a Mr. Clark from Eutaw, a brother of Mr. Pickens Clark and during the day on which the wedding took place, [*section unclear*] Mrs. Clark died of heart disease. I feel very sorry for the old man, he is said to be looking very badly and is not expected to live long. You remember that they lost three out of their family last year and one had to have his arm amputated, Pickens Clark.[15] I believe I told

15. Joseph Pickens Clark enlisted in the Eleventh Regiment, Company D, in Eutaw, Alabama, in May 1861 and was appointed sergeant major. The Eleventh Infantry joined the Fourth Brigade, Longstreet's division, soon thereafter. The arm amputation was the result of

you [*unclear*]. Jimmie and I went & returned home at daybreak. We enjoyed ourselves very much although we had no dancing. Capt. Melton to whom the party was given started on the stage on the morning on which the party was given or rather the morning on which the company left their house. I feel so very sleepy that I must lie down and take a nap. Convention will meet next Thursday in Greensboro so we will have Thursday & Friday. All join me in warmest love to you. The servants send Howdye to John. Tell John Howdye, and tell him that his wife is quite well and so are his children. Give our love to Mr. Joe and remember us kindly to Mr. James. Do write very soon. Excuse this horribly written letter.

Your devoted sister

May 12th, 1863

My ever dear Sam,

After suffering intense anxiety about you lately, my mind was relieved when Sunday last whilst on my way to church by hearing that you had passed through the late battle in safety. I cannot tell you my beloved son how deep was my gratitude to my Heavenly Father for his merciful kindness in preserving your life amidst the dangers to which you recently passed. I trust His protecting care and watchful Providence will take over again in the day of battle, should it so happen that you are again to meet the enemy. I pray you may never be engaged again in another battle. Mr. Hardaway visited us on Sunday and yelled out "your son is safe." He then handed me the telegram in which I was sorry to see John Cowin's death announced.[16] I am truly sorry for his poor parents. The old man cried half an hour when Mr. Wynn announced the painful tidings to him. The battle is said to have been one of the bloodiest

---

wounds Clark suffered in action in the Battle of Gaines Mill, June 27, 1862. His brother Henry was killed in action at Gaines Mill (CMSR, Alabama, RG 109).

16. Cowin had enlisted at Greensboro in April 1861, joining his father and brother. He had been a student at the Green Springs Academy at the same time James and Sam attended the school. Cowin graduated from a Philadelphia medical school but chose to enter the army as a private rather than a surgeon. Sam appears to have been fighting alongside Cowin when

of the war. The number of wounded in your company was very large. I was extremely anxious to hear from you, to be assured that you were not hurt. I shall not rest satisfied about your safety until I hear from you. I am more than anxious to receive a full and well authenticated account of the battle as soon as you can. I was truly glad to find that Mr. Joe was safe. Give my love to him and tell him all are well at his mother's house.

Martha James has not come yet, but is expected. . . . We, that is Jamie & I, have attended Church three out of four days. The church was so crowded on Sunday that Jamie had to stand, until he was near fainting. . . . Mary and himself have gone home sick this afternoon; she has been in bed almost all of this day with high fever caused by a violent cold which she caught by imprudently taking off her flannel during a cold spell. The weather in April was very variable and some times as cold as in Winter. Bad colds of course were the consequence. I am now suffering with the worst one I ever had. I had rheumatism so badly yesterday that I was obliged to go to bed. I would have written to you frequently had I not this terrible disease to contend with. When the war closes, and God! grant it will soon end, I will try the hot springs of Virginia. [A report reached them] that our great General Stonewall Jackson is no more. Can it be true? I still hope it is not so. We heard a day or two since that his left arm had been amputated; that we considered a great loss; but thought he would be capable of much service to his country notwithstanding the heavy loss he had sustained. Oh! I do hope the report of his death is not correct. Let us hear of all the particulars of the great, the bloody battle. We are in painful anxiety about Biscoe's fate. Do relieve our minds as soon as possible. We saw in the papers that his Regt had been entirely engaged in the terrible conflict. I trust in God! that Biscoe is safe. He . . . endeared himself to all in the family. He is a . . . fine young man. Jamie has withdrawn from Mr. Staudenmayer's instruction and leads an active life on the farm. Our corn looks well and our wheat will be ready for harvesting about the last of this month. . . . I am sorry Jamie does not pursue his studies under Mr S as it is a golden opportunity offered to him; but really the man

---

he was hit in the femoral artery and bled to death during action on May 3 (Diary of Samuel Pickens, May 2, 1863; Hubbs, *Guarding Greensboro*, 155–56; Hubbs, ed., *Voices from Company D*, xv; CMSR, Alabama, RG 9).

is so bad tempered I cannot wonder that Jamie wishes to have nothing to do with him. . . . He is a good teacher in many aspects but his temper is a barrier to his communicating his knowledge to his pupils.

The servants inquire kindly after you and desire to be kindly remembered. Tell John howdy for us and that Suky & his children are all well.

The children, except Mary & Jamie, who are rather complaining, are well and as happy as their teacher will let them be. They send warmest love to you. Give my love to Biscoe if he is near you and kind regards to Mr. Joe.

May God! bless & protect you, my dear good Son, and return you to me soon.

Your devoted mother.

May 15th '63

My dear Mama,

I am happy to tell you that I am again out of the hands of the Yankees and back in our Southern Confederacy. We arrived in Petersburg day before yesterday and came on here yesterday evening. I wrote to you from Washington on the 7th inst., so I hope you have already learned that no injury befell me in the battles. I telegraphed to you this morning of our arrival in Richmond.

We gained another victory but it was dear bought, since it cost us many lives and particularly that of the great and [*word unclear*] Genl Jackson. His loss is irreparable and has cast a gloom over the army. We had a pretty hard time of it. Marched nearly all day Friday and Saturday 1st and 2nd inst with scarcely anything to eat, and went into the fight Sat. evening hungry and tired, but we drove the Yankees before us like chaff before the wind and the greatest difficulty was, in our exhausted condition to keep near enough to the Yankees to shoot them. When we came to a line of their breastworks they would stand & fight a while, but as our men rushed upon them yelling—off they would go again. Their artillery fought much better, but nothing stopped the impetuous charge of our troops & they captured three batteries (or parts of three) during the evening. Thus the enemy were driven a mile and a half or more, and Genl Jackson said if he had an hour more of sun he would have had them surrounded so they would have been compelled to surrender or cut their way out. Unfortunately the great hero was mortally wounded about 8 O'clock P.M. by our own men. We heard the sharp volleys of musketry, and cannonading, but little thought what a serious loss we were sustaining.

That night the troops made their suppers on Yankee commissary stores which were very abundant as they carried eight days' rations. We enjoyed it exceedingly having had about nothing at all to eat for two days, and then it was better than we were accustomed to—for we got crackers, [*word unclear*] sugar & coffee, and some got fresh beef and mutton.

Next morning our commissary wagon came up and while the rations were being distributed the enemy commenced shelling us. We then moved into a piece of woods and soon made an advance through many thick woods. There were two lines of battle in front of ours and we expected to be used as reserves to support the others; but they bore to the right and went to the left, so that when we came upon the enemy we were face to face with them. As we approached the position of the enemy they shelled the woods furiously and men were killed or wounded all along our lines. We advanced steadily to within, I suppose, one hundred and fifty yards of the redoubt and then such a storm of shell, grape shot and minie balls met us that we were ordered to lie down, and stayed in that position some time. We were near to the edge of the woods (on a hillside) and the Yankees entrenchments were on the top of the hill in open ground. We could see the gunners loading their pieces and the red flames leap from the cannon's mouth [and very close] and had we not been lying down and protected somewhat by the hillside very few if any would have escaped for most of the missiles passed over our heads. As it was just [?] as many were killed and wounded. Poor John Cowin was wounded [*rest of sentence unclear*]. Col. O'Neal of the 26th Ala. Regt. who was in command of our brigade [*unclear word*] a slight wound [*word unclear*] the command then devolved upon Col. Hall of our regt, and his place was taken by Capt. Renfrow, the senior captain in the Regt.[17] I do not know if a charge was ordered or not, but Capt. R who was as brave a man as ever lived ran in front of our Regt waving his sword

17. William Thomas Renfro entered the Confederate Army in May of 1861 at Talladega. At the time of the events Sam described he was the commander of the Talladega Artillery company. He was wounded on May 3, 1863, and died on May 8 (CMSR, Alabama, RG 109).

and calling to the men to follow him and immediately fell with four wounds and has since died. Several men ran to him to carry him off when three out of four were instantly shot down. We kept on to the breastworks and from there poured a fire into the Yankees as they retreated. There were not many of us who got to the breastworks and all who did were killed, wounded, or captured. Now we were fired upon from the left, as we at first supposed by our own men, but soon perceived a line of blue Yankees emerge from the woods that had flanked us, & a fire from three directions was opened upon us. Some of the men sheltered themselves as well as they could by lying in the cannon pits and were captured there, while others ran across the open field to a piece of woods—the only direction left in which no enemy was to be seen. A good many of these were shot down, but four of us from our Co., one of whom was Geo. Nutting bearing the colors, reached the woods unhurt. How we passed safely through such a shower of balls from three directions, the Lord only knows; and to Him is due our eternal thanks, and gratitude. While crossing the field a shell which had spent its force rolled along by me and had it exploded it would have torn me and several others to pieces. After getting in the woods a ball grazed my thigh—cutting thro' my pants and drawers and just breaking the skin and left a bruised spot. We had not gone far in this direction when we came upon another line of Yankees who were retreating from the fire of one of our batteries and when they saw us some started to run and fired upon us, but we cried to them that we would surrender and were taken on to their rear. It was some time, though, before we got out of the range of our batteries, and some of our prisoners suffered from it as well as the Yankees. As we were carried on toward the river and saw the enemy's formidable fortifications, his masses of troops splendidly armed and equipped and the quantities of superior artillery, I must confess that I was a little afraid he might prove too strong for Genl Lee; but since we were blessed with victory I will never be uneasy again. They took us across the Rappahannock at the United States Ford on a pontoon bridge to a camp for prisoners, and next morning (Mond 4th) about day light we were hurried away in great confusion by our batteries throwing shells at the camp. We marched six or eight miles to where Genl Hooker's Head Quarters had been all winter—near Falmouth—were there paroled and that night sent by railroad to Aquia Creek where we took a boat and arrived in Washington City next day. There was a large crowd of men, women, & children and negroes assembled to see the "Rebel prisoners," and the streets thro which we passed were lined with eager spectators. We were quartered in the Cliffburne barracks in the outskirts of the city and fared very well for prisoners. We had no communication with any of the citizens and only with the soldiers who guarded us. They were mostly foreigners and heartily sick of the war. In the North provisions, clothing and everything is so plentiful and so cheap that really the people don't seem to us to be suffering much by the war; but I suppose they must be. It was tantalizing to us to see fruits & luxuries of all kinds and not be able to enjoy them as our money would not pass. I ate a few oranges, apples, dried figs etc.—and always thought of you & wished you had some—particularly when passing thro' the streets—I saw bunches of ripe bananas. Monday 11th we were put aboard of a boat & sent via Fortress Monroe to City Point on James River & thence came to Petersburg on the thirteenth (13th inst.) All the time that we were in Yankeedom I consoled myself with the fond hope of being able to get a furlough and go home; but in this I am disappointed for it is said that we will be exchanged & returned to our Regiments in a few days. It is a great disappointment for I would give any thing in the world to go home now & be with you my dear Mother, and my sisters and brothers. I trust you have not suffered anxiety on my account & hope my telegraph will reach you in due time telling you where & how I am. I have not yet learned the exact loss of our Co. On Saturday five were wounded, and on Sunday one killed, and fifteen or more wounded, and sixteen that I know of take prisoners (among whom were several of the wounded.) Col. Hobson also was wounded on Saturday. Our officers captured were not sent back with us. Please give my kind regards to Mr. Enoch Sawyer & the ladies, and to Dr. Grigg & lady. Also, my best love to Jamie, Mary, Willy, Lou and Icha. I hope you are all enjoying fine health & spirits. I will write again soon. Be well, dear Mama, the warmest love of

Your devoted son,
Samuel

P.S. Remember me kindly to all the servants.

S.P.

Camp 5th Ala. Reg.
May 28th, 1863

My dear Sister,

Although I do not feel much in the humor for writing this evening, still as I have received several ever dear and welcome letters from you which are yet unanswered I'll try and write. On Thursday last we returned to Camp, but did not do duty for several days as notice of our exchange had not been received by the officers here. I assure you the idea of going to drilling and doing guard and other camp duty again was anything but agreeable. All of the soldiers both North and South are heartily tired of the war, but the abominable Yankee Government seem determined to continue to wage it against us. So there is nothing left for us but to stand up and fight it out to the bitter end. It does seem that whipping the Yankees does very little towards bringing the war to a close, but I hope they will break down after a while and let us enjoy peace once more. Oh! What a blessing it would be, and we would be better able to appreciate it now than ever before. The news from Vicksburg has been very gloomy of late— showing that her condition is critical. I trust tho' that she will not fall into the hands of the Yankees for it would be a very serious loss to us and would give them great encouragement. We are now encamped in a nice piece of woods not more than half a mile from Winter Quarters. Since my return here I have received a most welcome letter from Mama of the 12th inst and one from Louty also. I was very sorry to hear that Mama had been suffering with a bad cold and an attack of rheumatism and also that you and Jamie were not very well. I sincerely hope that you are all now in the enjoyment of perfect health. Mama said that she had heard of my safety but would not feel satisfied until she should receive a letter from me: so I hope my telegram from Richmond and letters to her and Jamie have long since reached home. I wrote from Washington too, but it is rather doubtful whether the letter was sent through. After being taken prisoner I thought that as I was going where there was no blockade & where everything was plentiful I would try and get some little things for Mama and you children, but on getting to Washington soon found that our money was not worth anything. They would not take it at any discount. I had a dollar and ten cents in silver and some of the other boys had a little, but it soon went for something to eat—such as cheese, pies, oranges, apples, dried figs & etc. and I tell you they were nice. A day or two before we came away, though, the Yankee sutlers came around and tried to buy up Confederate money and offered ten cents on the dollar, and afterwards, rose to thirteen and fifteen cents. We knew it was a perfect system of swindling and would not sell them much for we had been told that in the city we could get fifty & at some places seventy five cents on the dollar. I let them have a $5.00 bill for sixty-five cents as I wanted to eat some more fruit before leaving there. I thought of your flower seed and wanted very much to get some but had no opportunities of sending downtown. I had before that sent to Richmond but they could not be had there. You must write me word how the flower garden is coming on. They marched us by the White House in Washington and I tell you the grounds about it were beautiful—the richest, most luxuriant grass and shrubbery you ever saw. It was altogether too nice a place for "Old Abe" to live in.

While running through the woods trying to get out, before I was taken prisoner, I was so hot & broke down that I had to throw away my blankets—that nice pair that Mama dyed for me last Spring. I was very sorry to lose them but it could not be helped. My haversack was lost too, and in it was that cap that you knit for me. I had been sleeping in it ever since I left home and missed it very much at first, but it is warm weather now and will not need anything to sleep in. John had my knapsack and lost my overcoat, shoes and some clothes, but I have plenty left. He lost nearly all of his clothes too. By-the-way John had his likeness taken & got me to send it home by mail some days ago. I directed it to Jamie, and you must tell him to send it to Suky: also $10 which I will enclose in this letter. The other day after getting Mama's letter I wrote to Tom Biscoe and was a little uneasy that he did not answer it; but our officers came up yesterday and Capt Williams told me that Tom was a prisoner and confined in the Old Capitol with him. I was very glad to know that he had come out safely, and hope that I will meet with him soon. Mr. Joe Grigg is now a courier for Genl Rodes. He will have a much easier time now than he had in the ranks. Saml Pickens of the 12th Ala told me to give his love to Mama and all the children.[18] He wrote to Mama after the battles. You must excuse

18. Sam was referring to Colonel Samuel B. Pickens, commander of the Twelfth Alabama Infantry Regiment. Colonel Pickens's family was not related to the Greene County Pickenses. Samuel B. was the son of Thomas Jones Pickens, a native of Charleston, South Carolina. On the Twelfth Alabama, see Park, *Sketch of the Twelfth Alabama Infantry of Battle's Brigade*, 5–9.

this scrawl, for it is a hard matter to write sitting on the ground in a tent with a crowd talking around me. My warmest love to Mama & Jamie, Willie, Lou, Icha and yourself. I enclose some Yankee letters.

Ever your aff brother,
Samuel

———•———

Umbria
June 12th, 1863

My beloved Son,

I have not had the pleasure of writing to you for sometime past, and will now tell you the cause of my silence. A violent attack of liver complaint followed by one of acute rheumatism confined me to my bed for one week, and caused me to endure the greatest agony. I am about again, and feel quite well today. I had been terribly worried of late by the German and his Wife, and things have come to such a pass that they refuse to eat at the table with me & my children. Of course their meals are sent into their room (No. 3) at their request, and constant complaints are sent to me about the fare and cold victuals as though I kept a boardinghouse. I haven't spoken to either of them since yesterday week, as we never chance to meet on the piazza out in the yard. I said I had been in bed a week, but it was only at times that I laid down in the day my suffering having been greater at night. Yesterday week some of the dogs went into the basement room now used as the school room; the teacher requested Willie to turn them out; he was busy at the time and did not move at once to obey him; his German blood rose and he said he would beat them unmercifully. Willie said Mr. S you may whip them, but you must not beat them unmercifully. I will die with my dogs. The teacher arose, took up his books & left the room; but returned immediately and told Willie he was a liar. W. came to me highly incensed and declared he would not allow anyone to call him so, particularly a foreigner. He determined not to go to school again, but I persuaded him not to lose the time, so he followed my advice. Well the teacher sent for me into the parlor, and as Jamie was about to leave. He requested him to stay; he did so, and was quiet, though he said he felt tempted to speak several times, so great was the insolence of the German Divine. He opened the conversation by saying that Willie had called him a liar; that unless Willie apologized to him, he should never enter the school. I replied that Willie had not called him a liar, and should not apologize to him; that he had called W. a liar, and should never do so again; that I had ordered W. to leave the school if such language were ever used again. I said call the scholars and ask them what occurred in the school for really you are in such a passion, you do not know what you said or did. Mary said, Mr. S. you called W. a liar. Fannie Marbury was called & gave the same testimony. He was furious and said if Fannie persisted in saying so, he would not teach her another day. Poor little Lou happened to be at the piano at the time of the fray; but hearing what the children had to say about it, before the teacher called for me, stepped up and said something about it to him. He could have torn her to pieces, and called her a vixen. I said, I do not agree with you that she is one. He seemed ashamed of himself for showing so openly his hatred for Lou and begged my pardon. Soon after his speaking of Lou, I called her vixen, he seemed not to like it. He consulted with Mr. E. Sawyer and Dr. Grigg as to the course he should take. I had seen them and begged them to induce him to leave so both of them advised him to do so; but he will not quit unless I pay the whole salary $600. I am not willing to pay him so handsomely for annoying me a little over 5 months, so he is carrying on the school, though he admitted the last day I conversed with him the scholars might do as they pleased study and improve or otherwise I have never met with such an impertinent & disgusting man and as to his temper! It is the worst I ever saw. It appears that some of my acquaintances (I will not call them friends) know Mr. Ss' peculiar temper, but were not friendly disposed toward me, else they would have stopped me from getting such a man to teach my children. They all hate him cordially, and I wish I had never laid my eyes upon him. The wife—a red-haired vixen herself—instead of being a peacemaker and acting a lady like part, makes war upon the children and persuades her husband to punish them. She is ever listening to what is going on, and when she hears no evil said, her wicked imagination gets her something to awaken her husbands' wrath. My dear Son, you cannot imagine how unhappy these people have made us all. Would that I could be relieved but it seems I am obliged to submit.

Mary received a letter from you a few days since; in it you mentioned the loss of your blankets, overcoat. This last article you must replace by getting another immediately without regard to price. I consider an overcoat indispensably necessary and beg of you to get one though you may have to pay $200 for it. If you are careful in covering yourself whenever you are put on guard . . . your health will be preserved. I have blankets on hand and can easily dye them and send them to you if you say so. Have you the last blankets I sent you; if you have not, I can't see how you will get along, unless you have a friend willing to share his with you. Mary has wool, the sheep having been sheared, and will soon make a cap for you. Twenty or more sheep were sheared & Mr. Lawless sent her 2 lbs. I hear each sheep should yield 2 or 3 pounds so Mr. Lawless is pretty well supplied with wool.

I want to ask you if we should employ Mr. Lawless or get Hardy Burgess who is looking for a situation. . . . (I have heard he is very strict—perhaps more so that we should like. He is however a good manager. You must give your opinion.)

Should you need boots or shoes, Mr. Hamilton will make some for you. Your losses are all trifling and will soon be made up. I feel like the deepest sense of gratitude to our Maker for preserving you unharmed through the battle and sparing your life to us. Oh! if you could return to us now and be with us always. It seems to me ages have passed since we parted and time rolls heavily along. We shall all be so happy once . . . peace is proclaimed and we are all together again. Our hearts will overflow with gratitude to the bountiful giver of all good deeds so our lives, I trust will be dedicated to His service.

The children are all well and in fine spirits. [Despite] their teacher, they manage to make themselves happy together. . . . Mr. Damer is now giving a music lesson to Lou, who will make a splendid performance Sunday. Mary plays remarkably with her, and both do credit to their teacher. We shall have fine times when you come and take part in the concert. You must play the flute and violin. Jamie sometimes favors us and plays delightfully. He is quite busy today in having our wheat threshed out. We have made a fine crop, the servants say the heads are large and heavy. Our corn is as good as any on the road, so you will perceive that Jamie is a good farmer. . . .

John's likeness is an excellent one and Suky was delighted to receive it. She was here on Sunday looking well and requested to give her love to John and her thanks for the likeness. Little John is beginning to cut teeth. I will give Suky the $10 bill soon.

I hope you have seen Biscoe and that you will be together often. Give my warmest love to him. I wish you & he could start for home instantly. We must wait patiently God's appointed time for closing the war. May we be purified by the trials through which we are passing and be more zealous in the performance of our duties hereafter.

———•—•———

Hagerstown, Md
July 12th, 1863
[In his diary he says he started this on
the 7th after arrival in Hagerstown.]

My dear Mama,

I will write you a few lines by the mail that goes off this morning. I hope that if you have not already heard that you soon will hear that through the infinite mercies of a kind Providence I passed safely through the bloody battle of Gettysburg, Pa. On the 7th a list of the casualties in our Co. was sent to Richmond to be telegraphed to Greensboro & at the same time I wrote to you. Our army has fortified itself in a fine position near Hagerstown where it is awaiting an attack of the enemy. Genl Lee is said to be well pleased with the position & confident of success. I saw Tom Biscoe yesterday. He was very well. Joe Grigg & Gilliam are also well. Jack Wynne begged me to mention that he was also & to let his family know it as he will not write today. My dear Mama let me express my heartfelt thanks to you for a kind & affectionate letter read from you a few days since. My thanks to Mary & Lou too, for kind favors from them at the same time. I was truly sorry to hear that you had suffered from liver complaint & hope you will be free from it in future. Oh! What a pest that German & his wife must be to you. I wish you would get rid of them. My dear Mama let me entreat you to ride & walk and take plenty of exercise so as to prevent attacks of liver complaint. Oh! I sincerely hope the war will soon end, & that I may enjoy the inestimable blessing of being once more in the midst of our dear family in peace & happiness. That is my constant prayer & I know it is yours, & also that of all the family. We are on the eve of a great battle & my trust is in the Lord for a safe issue, & a great and decisive victory to our arms. I hope soon to have an opportunity of answering your valued letters in full. I will try & write to Jamie, Mary & all the children soon. Please give my warmest love to them all & accept for yourself the same.

Your affectionate son

Samuel Pickens III
(Doy Leale McCall Rare Book and Manuscript Library,
University of South Alabama)

An 1887 photograph of John, the enslaved man that
Mary Gaillard Pickens sent to serve Sam while he was in the army
(Doy Leale McCall Rare Book and Manuscript Library,
University of South Alabama)

William Pickens, one of Sam's younger brothers
(Doy Leale McCall Rare Book and Manuscript Library,
University of South Alabama)

A front view of Umbria, the Pickens home
(Prints and Photographs Division, Library of Congress)

SIX

◆ • ◆ • ◆

Defeat, Despair, and Renewal

JULY–DECEMBER 1863

In Alabama, people read about the Confederate Army crossing the Potomac on its way north and, according to rumors, approaching the outskirts of Washington, DC. James wrote that he hoped the stories were true but remained skeptical. The day he wrote, however, the *Selma Reporter* published an account of the movements, based in part on northern sources, that seemed to confirm parts of the story James heard. Then, within a week, other reports from the northern press appeared that described a terrific battle with thousands of casualties that ended with Lee's defeated army desperately trying to escape. The news from other fronts was depressing as well. The community thought for a time that General Braxton Bragg's campaign in Tennessee had the Union Army there on the run, only to be disappointed with news of Bragg's retreat from Tullahoma, Tennessee. Even more alarming was bad news coming out of Vicksburg. Reports from the besieged city had also been contradictory, James wrote, though a steady stream of refugees moving slaves and property from the region in late June suggested that the Confederate hold on the city was tenuous. He had only heard rumors that the Confederate garrison in Vicksburg had surrendered.[1]

Disease, death, military reverses, the demands of the Confederate government for men and materiel, continued price inflation, and fears of Union

1. *Selma Morning Reporter,* July 7, 11, 12, 14, 1863.

139

raids intensified war weariness in Greene County and across Alabama. Opponents of the war became more openly assertive in demanding an end to the fighting, though they could not agree on the terms of a peace settlement. Some of the opposition thought an agreement could be reached that would preserve southern independence. Their hopes rested on flawed assumptions about the strength of opposition in the Union states to Lincoln's prosecution of the war and news of war weariness in the North. Others called for peace and restoration of the Union. Discontent fueled the creation of secret "Peace Societies" across the state. In the state gubernatorial election held in early August 1863, Thomas Hill Watts, a former Whig and Confederate attorney general, decisively defeated incumbent John Gill Shorter, with support from voters who resented Shorter's role in enforcing conscription. Combined with the defeat of secessionists such as J. L. M. Curry, some viewed the election as evidence of the political strength of those who called for peace negotiations with the aim of "reconstructing" the Union and preserving slavery.[2] Watts, however, left little doubt that he supported the Confederate war effort, while disagreeing with some government policies. He believed that discontent with the policies of the Confederate government did not translate into widespread opposition to the war itself.[3]

Citizens were organizing mass meetings across Alabama in August and September to reinforce and express popular support for the Confederate cause. Like their neighbors, James and Mary Gaillard complained about the personal and material demands of the war but viewed their sacrifices as necessary in the greater struggle for southern independence. James, wanting to assure Sam that the people at home remained steadfast in their support for the war, sent him a copy of the *Alabama Beacon*, in which there was an account of a mass meeting and barbecue in Greensboro called to demonstrate public support for the war effort. The organizers of the meeting declared that its purpose was to "uphold and strengthen the soldiers abroad, fighting for homes, liberty and property." W. C. Herndon, the chair of the meeting, urged

2. Walthall to Lt. Col. G. W. Lay, August 6, 1863, *OR*, ser. 1, vol. 2: 726–27; McKiven, "Thomas H. Watts, 1863–May 1865," 73–75; McIlwaine, *Civil War Alabama*, 120–25.

3. *Selma Morning Reporter*, July 16, September 27, 1863. The Pickenses subscribed to the *Reporter*. See Mary Gaillard Pickens to Sam Pickens, May 9, 1862. The best current analysis of the election of 1863 in Alabama is Severance, *A War State All Over*, chaps. 2–3.

those in attendance to approve resolutions "indicative of the unfaltering faith of the people of Greene County in the justness and final triumph of our cause." Speakers at the event did not deny the grave threat facing the Confederacy. The Reverend P. P. Neeley warned that "the people must see their true danger and remedy the evil likely to ruin them." It would not be enough, Neeley argued, to punish "speculators, cowards, skulkers, submissionists, the tories, and Judas Iscariots of this second Revolution." These "evils" were but symptoms of a more fundamental problem—the failure of the people to fully commit their cause to God. The "want" of religion, Neeley declared, gave rise to a "selfishness" that posed a greater threat to the "revolution" than the "Abolitionist" armies.[4]

Bad news from the war fronts came at a difficult time for the Pickenses. While they were awaiting news of Sam's condition, an outbreak of disease spread through the household. The first victims of this "bilious fever" were enslaved people, several of whom died. Soon the infection spread to Mary Gaillard and James. James reported that victims either recovered or died very quickly, after days of misery. The epidemic struck when James and Mary Gaillard were marketing the plantation's cotton, replacing an overseer, and trying to find substitutes for overseers subject to conscription and possibly for James, whose substitute had deserted. James either had to find someone to replace Rainsford or he would have to enter the army. Mary Gaillard prayed for an end to the war and the "misery" the war inflicted on everyone.[5]

A battered and demoralized Army of Northern Virginia withdrew from Pennsylvania and returned to its base along the Rappahannock, near Richmond, in early August. If Sam wavered in his commitment to the Confederate cause during this period, as many Confederate soldiers did, he never

4. *Selma Morning Reporter,* September 12, 1863. The effect of the losses at Vicksburg and Gettysburg on Confederate civilian morale continues to be a subject of debate among historians. See Beringer et al., *Why the South Lost the Civil War,* 80–81, 292–93; McPherson, *Battle Cry of Freedom,* 665; Levine, *The Fall of the House of Dixie,* 206–18; Gallagher, *Lee and His Army in Confederate History,* 83–93; Rubin, *A Shattered Nation,* 80–81; Glatthaar, *General Lee's Army,* 302–3.

5. On the response of women to the defeats at Vicksburg and Gettysburg, see Faust, *Mothers of Invention,* 234–39, and "Altars of Sacrifice." Faust argues that women generally turned against the war in the fall of 1863. Usually a reference to bilious remittent fever meant yellow fever.

revealed any doubts in letters home or in his diary. He had learned from soldiers returning to the army from furloughs, and from copies of the *Alabama
Beacon* some brought with them, that the fall of Vicksburg and the failure
at Gettysburg had fostered increased discontent with the war, but he and
his comrades thought stories of civilian opposition were exaggerated. They
knew that, in the state elections of August, "reconstructionists," who called
for a negotiated peace and "reconstruction" of the Union, and other "croakers"
had challenged candidates who supported continuing the war.[6] But, as James
informed Sam, loyal Confederates responded to the peace movement at the
polls and with meetings affirming their commitment to the Confederate war
effort.[7] Visitors to their camp from Alabama also assured them that stories
about civilian opposition were mostly false.[8]

James and his mother hoped Sam would get a furlough to return home
for the winter, but he had to wait while men who had been at the front longer than he had been received furloughs. Sam and Mary Gaillard did allow
John to return home. Sam's comment in his diary about his disappointment
at seeing John leave, while he remained, revealed a conceit that had become
an article of faith for enslavers—that slaves were more free than they were.
"I find myself in very low spirits & home-sick at seeing John start home . . .
when that in expressible pleasure is denied me. Oh! What [would] I give to
be as free to go there as John is!!"[9]

6. *Selma Morning Reporter*, July 16, September 27, 1863; Severance, *A War State All Over*,
chaps. 2–3.

7. *Selma Morning Reporter*, September 12, 1863. On civilian morale in the summer and
fall of 1863, see Beringer et al., *Why the South Lost the Civil War*, 80–81, 292–93; McPherson,
Battle Cry of Freedom, 665; Levine, *The Fall of the House of Dixie*, 206–18; Gallagher, *Lee and
His Army in Confederate History*, 83–93; Rubin, *A Shattered Nation*, 80–81; Glatthaar, *General
Lee's Army*, 302–3.

8. Diary of Samuel Pickens, August 30, 1863; Murray and Hsieh, *A Savage War*, 326.

9. Diary of Samuel Pickens, December 9, 1863. Pickens's comment reflects the influence
of the proslavery argument that, because the paternalistic enslaver assumed the responsibility
of caring for the needs of the enslaved, it was really the enslaved who were free.

Umbria, July 7th 1863

My dear Sam,

Nearly three weeks have glided away since I received your last letter, and how anxiously have I been expecting since then to get another in answer to my two last, but have not yet been favored with any. However, I shall hope on, and continue to weary you with my prosy communications, in hopes of thereby eliciting a reply from you.

All things are the same at Umbria now, that they were when I last wrote, with the exception that the [*writing unclear but referring to the departure of the Staudenmayers*]. They left in the carriage for Newbern, at 11 o'clock, on the night of the 26th June, a very late hour for traveling; but they thought as the weather was warm, that it would be more agreeable. They are certainly a very unfortunate couple, calculated neither to enjoy much happiness themselves, nor to cause those with whom they are thrown to enjoy any. It all proceeds too, in a measure, from his unfortunately sensitive disposition. She, of course, sympathizes with him and together they make themselves miserable. But enough of the Staudenmayers. *Requiescat in pace.*[10]

I suppose you have had detailed accounts from Mary & Louty of the picnic & concert recently had, or rather, of the latter only, as they did not attend the former. However, I will mention a few circumstances connected with both, and will commence with the picnic, which took place at Myers' bluff, below Port Royal, on Tuesday last. It was a very small affair, only a few ladies & gentlemen being present, Ed. Boyd & his two sisters, Thomas Cowin, a Miss [*unclear*] of Tuscaloosa, Miss Kate Waters, a refugee from Mobile now residing in Greensboro, Mrs. Clark [*rest of sentence unclear*]. I thought I would accompany him, tho' it was so excessively warm that I had concluded at first not to go.[11] We had a very hot ride of about 12 miles before getting there, and at first arriving at the place I thought it would be very dull. But I think it was more pleasant than it would have been had there been a

10. May they rest in peace.
11. Thomas Cowin was the younger brother of John Cowin, who had been killed in Confederate service. Thomas later enlisted in Shockley's escort cavalry while a student at the University of Alabama (Muster Rolls of Alabama Civil War Units).

crowd there. We had music on the violin by Mrs. Boyd, & dancing by the ladies & a Mrs. Smith, who seemed to take great delight in the amusements of the day. I was introduced to Miss Horn and Miss Waters, both of whom were very interesting & pleasant ladies. Miss H is well acquainted with Mrs. Tutwiler & family with whom she spent a few weeks just before the close of the session, & was present at some tableaux at the end. Miss Waters is a very lively & agreeable young lady & was the life of the picnic. I have often heard of her fine voice & exquisite singing, but never heard it until the other night at the Concert. She sings very well indeed. We had a very good dinner under some shady trees, and afterwards a game of 'muggins' under a shed, when the party enjoyed another dance & broke up about 5 o'clock in the evening. The concert came off the next evening in town, or rather in the chapel of the Southern University.[12] [*Much of the next two sentences are blotted out. He wrote that the concert was a benefit for families, probably of soldiers, and raised $500.*] We had some of the finest violin music by Prof. Frank, that I ever listened to. Then sometimes a duet on the piano, & sometimes the piano & violin. The singing, generally, was very good indeed. I thought Miss Damer the finest of the singers; next to her, Miss Waters & then Miss Eliza Snow. The Misses Webb, of town, also sang very well. Mr. Damer & his daughter sang—he accompanying her on the piano—a piece, Holy Mother, which brought down rapturous applause.[13] Miss Ida Dorroh & Gayle came up the evening before, spent the night & went with us the next morning. Gayle has been very sociable of late, spending several days with us last week, as week before. Miss Ida was with him & seemed to enjoy her visit very much. She is a very sociable & unaffected young lady & very different from the generality of our neighbors, altho' much farther off than some of them.

Well, I have not told you anything of home. Mama and all the children are & have been quite well. Icha was slightly indisposed this morning caused by eating green fruit, but he is well again this evening. Mr. Enoch & I went to town on Sat. last to find out what the people intended to do

12. Southern University was in Greensboro. In 1918, Southern merged with Birmingham College, forming Birmingham–Southern College in Birmingham. See Yerby, *History of Greensboro*, 85–86.

13. Thomas D. Damer and his daughter Juliet.

under the Governor's late call for 7000 troops, [*unclear*] I detest the idea of being ordered about from camp to camp for six months by Gov. Shorter & think I would rather join you in Virginia than go through with it. I have not determined what to do.

We have all been regarding with the utmost attention & interest, the great movement of Genl. Lee by which he has cleared out Virginia of Hooker's Army & completely outwitted this General. It was reported yesterday tho' no mention of it was made in the paper—that Genl. Lee is menacing Washington City, being within five miles of it. Also that we have taken New Orleans, & that Bragg's pursuing Rosecrans who it is reported is "flying," or in other words retreating very rapidly. As nothing is said of any of these reports in the papers, they are scarcely to be believed but are probably sensation, rumors to make up for the absence of news. However, I hope they are all literally true, particularly those relating to the capture of Washington, & N.O.

We have rec'd several letters from you lately, which we were very glad of indeed, as it had been some length of time since we had heard from you. First, Icha rec'd one, of the 17th ult & then on Thurs. last, Mama recd. two, one dated June 20th, the other March 15th! How the latter could have been delayed on the way so long seems unaccountable & proves the fact which I have often observed before that a very few [*This is unclear but appears to say very few letters reach their destination. There is also a comment about a visit to Canebrake.*] The corn at the Goodrum place was splendid, generally, when I was down there before. Now it must be very much better, as rain was then badly needed & five ones have fallen since. I have not been to the Canebrake since March or April, but intend to go soon, if I can.

We heard this morning quite a different version of the news which I told you of above, to the effect that instead of Bragg's whipping Rosecrans, the latter has whipped Genl. B & was pursuing him.[14] Also, that a bloody battle has been fought in Pennsylvania by Genls. Longstreet & Hill, and a portion of Hooker's army. But the worst of the bad news which we have seen this morning is that the devoted garrison of Vicksburg are reported to have

14. James was referring to the retreat of the Army of Tennessee under the command of General Braxton Bragg before the advancing Union Army of the Cumberland under the command of Major General William S. Rosecrans (Daniel, *Conquered*, chap. 12).

surrendered & the city is said to be in Grant's hands. I trust that this is untrue & that it may yet come off signally triumphant in the end. So many bad reports are calculated to depress ones spirits, and particularly so after hearing of our success in almost every direction, so lately. No one believes the report about the surrender of Vicksburg, which report I hope may be contradicted.

I was glad this morning to receive a letter from you from Greencastle, Penn dated 23rd ult., which is of a later date than either of your other letters. [*Unclear but appears to be a comment on the constant marching Sam was enduring.*] The North ought to be made to feel some of the dispositions & trials & sufferings which they have inflicted on our people.

Well, I have swelled the proportions of this letter to a bulky size. Mama sends her warmest love to you & says she will write to you in a few days. She and the children all join me in kindest love to you. Mr. Enoch says, "always give Sam my warmest love." The Dr always enquires kindly of you.

I will write soon again, & will be most happy to hear from you as often as you can write. I am, as ever

Your affectionate brother, James

July 14th 1863

My beloved Son,

Earnestly are we hoping and looking for a letter from you. Oh! My dear Sam I cannot tell you how painfully anxious I have been about you ever since the battle of Chancellorsville. The same almighty Father who mercifully preserved your life there has, I trust, again watched over you and kept you safe in "the hollow of His hand." If a Mother's prayers have been heard, you have been shielded from every danger, and we shall embrace each other again on Earth. What sad times we are passing through! Oh! When will this cruel, this terrible war be over! "My trust is in Him who governs all things in heaven and Earth." I hope a letter from you will soon come telling of your safety and Biscoe's and giving a full account of your proceedings in Maryland and Pennsylvania. The hand of God! has been with us throughout the war and has I trust guided our Army through the battles you have been in and crowned you all with success. Every one has unlimited confidence in Genl Lee who "with aid from on high will accomplish great works." I pray unceasingly that we may soon be blessed with peace, and you return to the bosom of your family. How truly happy we shall all be then. May God! hasten the day when we shall be folded in each other's arms. Write as soon as possible and relieve our minds about you and Biscoe. I hope all our friends have [*unclear*] unhurt—particularly Mr. Joe. Remember me very kindly to him and all. Dr. Grigg and his family are well. [*Unclear*] has another son.

I have been dreadfully troubled in mind my dear son since I wrote last to you and this is the reason of you not hearing from me for some time. I was kept in such a nervous, worried state, I was unfit for writing and every other duty. But thank God! We have got rid of the German & his wife both of whom we found rude, disgusting and insulting. To get him off, I was obliged to pay the whole year's salary $670 but this was better than keeping the bad-tempered man to annoy the whole family. Without any provocation he called Willie a liar in school before all the scholars and then said Willie must apologize to him before he would teach him again. I told him that W should not apologize to him but should walk out of the school if he ever insulted him again. I think I wrote this before. I am troubled and scarcely know what I have told you. Jamie went to Eutaw today, where all conscripts were obliged to make their appearance. He has been discharged from Confederate service, having put in a substitute but is still liable to militia duty and will be called out on the 25th of this month: I don't wish Jamie to leave us. I think it impolitic to call out all the men from this section and leave the women and children unprotected at home. I don't know what I shall do if Jamie will go; but I trust he will get someone to go in his place. Even if Jamie should stay with us, I feel inclined to go to some town instead of staying here. Our neighbors say they will remain at their homes—some to take care of their property—others because they can't afford to move—among the latter stand our friend, Mr. E. S. [Enoch Sawyer]. He was here this morning and said if he were in my place he would not think of staying at home. But "sufficient unto to the day is the evil thereof."[15] We may not be obliged to move.

The children are enjoying fine health. So far we have had a very healthy

---

15. From the Sermon on the Mount, Matthew 6:34.

summer. I hope it will continue so Mary & Lou continue to take music lessons under Mr. Damer with whom they are quite pleased. He is a truly fine teacher for Mary & Lou have improved [*unclear*] and give promise of being fine performers. Mr. Damer is taking a little holiday now. Willie, and I believe Icha, are actively engaged in making cider today. I wish you could enjoy it with us. We are having an abundant fruit crop. The June apples and our peaches are finer this year than they have ever been before. . . . We had a young soldier with us a few nights since—Mr. Monroe of Eutaw, who was an editor of a paper in that place.[16] Mr. J [*unclear*] Pickens & family are in Mobile at present. I don't know what has taken them there. Henderson was in Vicksburg at the time of the surrender. Considering the state of the country, we have [*unclear*] and to sell all our cotton, and Mr. [*unclear*] is to sample it this week and buy it for the government. I hope you will approve of what we are doing in this and every other matter. Oh! that you were here to take the reins in your hands—how thankfully will I resign them. Let us hope that our trouble will soon be over "through God! We shall do great acts, and it is he that shall tread down our enemies."[17]

Your friends make frequent and kind inquiries about you. Dr. Grigg says I must never write without sending his love to you. Mr. E Sawyer is a warm friend of yours. All of that family always desire their love to be sent to you. Old Uncle Jack is here on a visit and has much to say of "Mas Sammy." He looks well & is the same good old [*unclear*] he has ever been. All the servants are well & send much love to you. We are making large crops at both places. We have been blessed with fine seasons and our deepest gratitude "to the giver of every good and perfect gift." Remember us kindly to John & tell him Suky was here on Sunday looking well. All the children are well she says and

16. William O. Monroe was editor of the *Alabama Whig* and the *Eutaw Whig and Observer*, a merger of the *Alabama Whig* and the *Independent Observer* of Eutaw, the county seat of Greene County. According to his service record, Monroe did not formally muster into service until July 23, when the Seventh Alabama Cavalry Regiment was organized. He was elected a lieutenant. Within a month after entering service, Monroe was on leave suffering from "*Pthisis Pulmonalis*" (tuberculosis). A Confederate surgeon judged his condition to be a complication of his untreated measles that made him unfit for service. The army approved Monroe's resignation in January 1864. See CMSR, Alabama, RG 109.

17. Psalms 108:13.

all send much love to John. I gave her the $10. The children unite with me in warmest love to you, my ever dear, good Son.

May God! bless you and send you to us soon in health and safety is the prayer of your devotedly attached

Mother

———◆·———

Umbria August 22nd 1863

My beloved Son,

Every member of the family, except myself, wrote to you last week, and sent the letters to Mr. Jos Borden, who kindly consented to take them and a bundle for you. He was taken sick and prevented from leaving his home on Monday last. Since then he has met with a heavy affliction in the death of a child 10 years old. I am truly sorry for the parents. The bundle sent to you contains 2 checked shirts. Our friend, Dr. Grigg, was very kind in letting me have the homespun to make them: one pair of shoes & 4 pair of socks for you: a pair of shoes & 3 pair of sock's for Biscoe and 2 pair of socks for John. I would have sent more socks, but could not get them. I hope your shoes will fit; but if they do not, I will get Mr. L to make another pair: your measure came after he had commenced your shoes. If Biscoe's do not fit, he must send us his measure. Do my dear son tell me if you want any clothing and I will endeavor to send on the articles needed. I was sorry to learn that you have again lost some of your clothing. There is some difficulty in buying clothing now but occasionally we can get cloth from Mr. Shackelford, and your friend, Mr. Steinhart, who will soon be our neighbor: he has purchased Mr. Sadler's place at high price. We attended the funeral of Genl Dent yesterday at Col McAlpin's old place near us. The Genl was quite pleasant and genteel and a very good man withal, I believe. He had a congestive chill from which he never rallied.[18] We have seen several cases of chills & fever here—some have been very sick—amongst them

18. She was referring to General Dennis Dent, who lived in Tuscaloosa at the time. He raised a regiment in 1836 to fight the Creek Indians, thus the military rank. As leading Alabama Whig and supporter of Zachary Taylor in 1848, he and Samuel Pickens differed po-

William's wife and child. I think I mentioned in a former letter that Mr. Allan had begged us to let Martha & her 4 children stay here, until they could return home in safety—the Yankees have been within a few miles of his plantation. Icha was sick several days last week with fever. Dr. Grigg was unfortunately sick at the same time with fever, so I was compelled to manage his case. He is well again, but looks thin & pale. The Dr has recovered sufficiently to resume his practice, and indeed I am truly glad he is at his post again, for he was needed by many and much missed. There is much sickness in the country at present. I hope it will not last long. We have had many cases of chills & fever at the Goodrum place and Canebrake also. Robert Marshal was very sick; he is well now. Mr. High sent the letter you wrote to him, to us to read. I think he is very sorry to leave his comfortable home and regrets having said to me that he would not stay with us another year on the same terms—$600 per annum. I am glad he is going, as we have been so fortunate as to engage Mr. Willingham at $900. I am satisfied we shall make twice as much as we did under Mr. High's administration & that the plantations will be put in good order and kept so. We have engaged Mr. Lawless for another year and have to pay $500 to the government because he is a conscript. Mr. L did not wish to go into the army & said if we would keep him that he would pay a part of the $500.[19] We have just finished taking fodder here: the hands will go to the Goodrum place to assist there in the same work. Mr. High has saved a large amount of fodder. Jamie has gone to town today to receive the money for our cotton 153 bales—we shall get $23,089.80 for it. Jamie got $1500 from Mr [?] to pay for a substitute—out of that sum he brought home $400 which we have spent except $200 which I sent to Mr. Borden for you. So Jamie received today 21,589.80. I will pay off all we owe, if I can meet with a safe opportunity to send the money. The balance

---

litically. Dent served in the Alabama House and Senate until 1850. See Garrett, *Reminiscences of Public Men in Alabama*, 159, and the *Independent Monitor* (Tuscaloosa), March 9, 1848. The reference to McAlpin was to Soloman McAlpin, who migrated to Greene County, near Eutaw, in the 1820s (U.S. Census, 1860).

19. Mary Gaillard was referring to the "twenty slave" exemption the family secured for Lawless. The 1863 revision allowed a widow in her situation to obtain an exemption for one man to assist in the supervision of enslaved people. Because James had hired a substitute, Mary Gaillard and James secured an exemption for Lawless. The law required a $500 bond be paid. See Sacher, *Confederate Conscription*, 175–76.

will be a large sum to keep on hand, but I don't know what to do with it in such times as these. I would be afraid to lend it out, without your advice, so you must give it in your next favor. Several very kind letters from you have made us very happy of late. You can't imagine my dear, dear Son what a value we put upon your letters. You have been very kind in writing to us often and we are constantly on the lookout for one of your interesting and affectionate letters. I trust in God! that the happiness of having you with us will soon be granted to us; and that we shall never never part again. Until we meet, I can never feel happy. The melancholy news of the death of Vila Uhlhorn has just reached us by Ross who is on a visit here. She and Gena whom you saw here when we came from N. Carolina went to Choctaw to be with their Sister Mrs. Israel Pickens. Israel & his wife went to Mobile and during their absence Vila was taken sick and died. I was grieved to hear of her death. . . . [*Words missing*] have been ill and almost every one in that neighborhood. Mr. Wright of your company has been to see us several times; he is a modest, clever, sensible young man who we all like.

With the exception of Icha, we have been blessed with health. I endeavor to make the children prudent in keeping out of the Sun and night air, and hope we will continue healthy. Oh! that we may all be spared to meet again and be happy once more. When will the war end? Some say never. I trust in God! it will soon close and we shall soon be together. I ask nothing more. I shall then be perfectly happy.

All are well and send you warmest love. My love to all friends. Remember us kindly to John. Your friends all send love as always. May God! bless you, my dear Son, and keep you safe in the hollow of His hand.

Your Mother

--- • ---

Umbria
Sep. 4th 1863

My dear Sam,

Your long, kind and interesting letter of 24th ult came to hand yesterday and I made haste to reply to it: not that I can promise you anything rare, rich or [*unclear*], but to give you the little news from the family and our neighborhood.

But before doing anything else I must exchange this ink for some a little blacker as I see it doesn't agree with the rough paper. It is ink manufactured by Mr. Russell, in town & has only one recommendation, which is that it is cheaper than the extortioners' ink to be found in the other stores.

To commence, we have the sickliest neighborhood, or country rather, as the sickness is general, that you ever heard of. I feel sorry for the Dr, who is kept quite busy. He says that he does not recollect any two of the sickliest years of his practice which were as bad, in that respect, as the present has been. The cases, too, are quite serious & terminate very suddenly—either recovering or dying. I expect you heard of Gen'l Dent's death week before last, which occurred at his residence (the old McAlpin place). He was taken on Tues. or Wed., I think with a chill & had fever afterwards, but was not regarded as very sickly by the Dr. On Thurs. tho' he had another chill & grew worse 'till about 2 o'clock the next (Frid.) morning, when he died. He was a very pleasant, agreeable & intelligent old gentleman, very courteous & polite in his manners, & was much beloved by the neighborhood. He moved from Mobile last winter with his family, when the city was thought to be in danger from an attack, and intended, then, I believe, making this a permanent residence. I was never more surprised at anything than I was on learning that he was dead, for it was only a week or two before that Mr. Sawyer & I, on our way to town, saw him sitting in the shade of a tree near his place reading a little book. He said he had got tired of the house & had gone out to see the hands gather fodder, but finding that too warm had gone to the tree to rest & cool. He looked then very well, but the sun was too warm for such an old man, & that day's exposure to it was what I think brought on the attack from which he never recovered. Mrs. Torbert, the week after his death, lost a child from an attack of diphtheria & quincy,[20] which was also very sudden. Last week Charlotte at the Goodrum place died & a few days after, Ann's child, Gene or Eugenia, died also. At Present, Mary Ann is quite ill with bilious fever[21] of a very malignant & dangerous type. The Dr was here

20. Acute infection of the tonsils, sometimes resulting in abscesses.
21. This may have been typhus, though yellow fever is a possibility.

yesterday during the crisis in her case, and he said if a change for the better had not taken place when it did (yesterday even'g) that she would certainly have died. To-day she is much better, tho' extremely low, yet. I myself, am just out of a sick bed where I was confined four days with a very bilious attack. I do not recollect of having been sicker before. For a minute I could neither feel nor see & was almost unconscious. I am now much better than I was, altho' a little weak yet.

Our Fast day we intended going to town, as there was to be preaching at Wesley on that day but it being quite warm & town being far away, we did not go, but went to Genl Dent's funeral which took place that morning.

Old Mrs Parr in this neighborhood was at the point of death a day or two ago but is slowly recovering. Mrs. James is very sick also. In fact, there isn't one place, I do not think, which is entirely free from sickness. Tom Biscoe spoke (or wrote rather) in one of his letters of coming on a visit to us, but if you see him say that it is the Dr.'s advice that he should not do so, as he will inevitably be made sick & it would go very hard with him, coming as he would from a cool & healthy region of country to a warm & sickly one. The last of this is 1st of next month, tho' I hope will see an abatement or cessation of the sickness, and a cool & pleasant, healthful & invigorating change in the atmosphere.

Mama was taken soon after I recovered with a bilous attack from which she suffered a good deal; but is much better to-day, altho' not well. I hope, tho,' that she will be, in a short time, quite well again. Truly your cool & pleasant Virginia temperature is enviable at present. It must be delightful in the Valley of Virginia at this season of the year, and if no war were upon us 'twould be very pleasant to travel through it. I constantly hope tho' that it may soon cease & that quiet & peace & happiness may be restored to our country once more.

I am glad to hear that David Barnum has got the appointment in the Navy, altho' I am sorry that such a clever young fellow should have left your mess. I was very much pleased with him when he was here last winter.[22]

22. David Barnum had enlisted in and joined I Company, Fifth Alabama Infantry Regiment, in August 1861. He was subsequently captured during the Battle of Sharpsburg (Antietam) and was paroled in September 1862. In 1863, he mustered into the Confederate Navy

Matt Jones & you must have a solitary time of it, there being only you two in the mess; however, I expect you are with the others when not at meals or during the night. I am glad that you are living better than you were recently. From what Ed Pasteur told us the ordinary fare of the soldiers must be very hard to "stand," for a constancy, tho' he said that he and the others bore it very well and were satisfied with it; preferably, I suppose, because they had become accustomed to it. The papers mention that the Army of Northern Va has recuperated its strength & vigor since the Maryland & Pennsylvania Campaign, its ranks have strengthened and that it reposes in its wanted confidence, strength awaiting the next scheme proposed by the Yankees for the capture of Richmond, in nine attempts for the accomplishment of which enterprise they have most signally failed. It remains to be seen whether their next will meet with any less degree of failure, or whether it, like the rest, will "cave in."

Well, I must close if I would have my letter go by this evening's mails, which I will attempt to do.

I will not close, tho,' without mentioning the gallant defense being made at Charleston against a superior and overwhelming quantity of large guns which are making strenuous efforts to reduce our fortifications & batteries. I sincerely trust that they may not succeed in capturing that city but that it may successfully resist the attacks of the enemy, for I think the moral effect of our successfully withstanding their assault would be great & that such a result would dishearten the Yankees in the war policy.

You will see, by noticing the *Beacon*, which I inclose to you, that there is to be a large mass meeting in town tomorrow, which is to be addressed by prominent speakers for the occasion. A barbecue is also to be given. I expect the invitation is extended to citizens of adjoining counties, that the assembly will be a large one. It is so [*unclear*] to ride to Greensboro in this sultry [*unclear*], and as I have just got out of a sick bed and am still weak, I don't expect to attend.

I have extended the limits of this letter considerably, and must at last close, hoping soon to hear again from you.

Mama is feeling much better this evening, and I trust after the medicine

---

on September 4, 1863. When the war broke out, he had been a midshipman at the U.S. Naval Academy. See CMSR, Alabama, 1861–65, RG 109.

which she has taken has had effect that she will be perfectly well again. She joins me in kindest love to you, as also all the children do.

Ever your affectionate brother,
James

P.S. The Dr. sends his love to you & says he thinks often of you as he rides by the Herndon field which is the old game ground of other times, when you he & Mr. Joe used to hunt there so frequently. He says the field is alive with game now.

We never see Mr. Sawyer now.

Remember me to all our friends, to Mr. Joe, Williams, Tom & Pick, & etc.

All send howd'ye to John

James

———•—•———

Camp near Kelly's Ford
Rappahannock River, Va.
October 21st, 63

My dear Mama,

Your affectionate and welcome letter of the 8th inst. came to hand evening before last and I was extremely sorry to learn that you and Jamie had been sick again, and also, that you had so much to trouble you & disturb your peace of mind. Whilst this terrible war continues it seems that no one can be free from trouble and distress. May the Lord in His infinite mercy send a speedy termination to it and restore this land to peace and happiness. I wonder if Jamie's substitute *has* really deserted. If a man so highly recommended has deserted, there is no reliance to be placed in any substitute. It may be that he was taken prisoner in the battle of Chickamauga. At any rate it will have to be first *proven* that the man has certainly *deserted*, before Jamie can be held responsible. Has Capt. Wright notified Jamie of the fact. He ought to write to the Capt. and if it should be true he will be disposed to favor Jamie, as much as possible. You say that besides this you fear that Jamie will be drawn into State service notwithstanding he has a substitute. Now if the man from Perry Co. whom Jamie employed is now in the service of the state as his substitute certainly Jamie cannot be called out. And, moreover, as long as Jamie, by substitution, shall continue in the State service, even if his substitute in the Confederate service has, deserted, I should think he would not have to take his place. But when his term of State service shall have expired then he may be called on to take the place of the substitute in the Confederate service. I sincerely trust, though, that the Scotchman will prove true to his contract, for I know that you would scarcely be able to get along at all without Jamie's assistance at home.

How to carry on the children's education to the best advantage in such times as these must be very perplexing: the course you have pursued tho' is, no doubt, the only one practicable, and if Dr. Cunningham succeeds in getting a competent & conscientious man for private tutor the children, knowing that they are backward in their education, will certainly of their own accord study diligently & improve themselves as much as possible. Now is their time for getting an education & if they do not avail themselves of it they can never make it up hereafter.

I was sorry to hear of Mr. Spaulding's death. What an uncommonly sickly season the past has been in Ala., and I know you have had a hard time in nursing and attending to the sick in the family and amongst the servants. I hope it is over now & that the country has become perfectly healthy again. I am extremely sorry, my dear Mama, that you have been so uneasy about me. We had an active little campaign & very hard marching, but were spared the awful consequences of a battle. It is true we were exposed several times to the dangers of shot and shell but the casualties in our Regt were very few, & confined to the sharpshooters, who go a little in advance of the line of battle. I am very much obliged to you for the money, shoes etc. which you sent by Lieut. Christian. I have not gotten them yet, for just as Lieut. C came to us we were starting on a march and he deposited the trunks in Orange CH. He says that no letter was given him for me, as I suppose that the letter containing the $200 must be in the bundle. You ask about the condition of my wardrobe. I would like to have a suit of thick, warm clothes if you can get the cloth in the neighborhood & have it made up by the patterns you had last Fall. I have drawn a new jacket from the Quartermaster & can get pants too, but the cloth is very thin & trifling.

The jacket would have to be a little fuller in the breast & the pants enlarged a little. I have no undershorts & but one pair of woolen drawers. Jack Wynne has a suit of outer clothes, woolen drawers, & undershirts of nice knitted stuff all of which were manufactured at home, but I fear that none of our weavers are sufficiently skilled to make such. Maybe it can be bought in the neighborhood; if not, I'll try to supply myself from Richmond. Will not need a blanket as I have that very heavy lined one that you sent me last Winter & another. In a former letter you asked about Burkville, Va as a place of retreat from the Yankees. I suppose it would be a very secure place, but trust that you will never have to leave Umbria to seek safety anywhere. Dr. Grigg could find out all about the place & the chances to get board etc., as he has a brother living there. That is the place you recollect where, in 1859, Willie got separated from us & went to Petersburg while we took the train to Richmond. I don't know how to advise you with regard to selling corn. In cases where soldiers' families are in need of it, I suppose, of course, they must have it.

Since Gen. Lee recrossed, a few days since, to the South side of the Rappahannock we have been uneasy lest we should be sent to Tennessee, for it was rumored that A.P. Hill with two of his divisions & Rodes' Divis of Ewell's Corps would go West, but our fears on that score are allayed as today (Oct 22nd) we moved to the place selected for our Winter Quarters and are to commence building cabins at once: I do hope that all military movements are over for this year & that ere the time for the opening of another campaign we may be blessed with glorious peace.[23] The reason I have never spoken of going home on furlough this Winter is because there is so little chance for it. There are several in the Co who have been out two years & a half & have not yet had furloughs: they will have the preference & then the balance of the Co will draw for furloughs—not more than two or three will be allowed to go from a Co at the same time. I would give anything in the world to be with you, my dear Mama, & the children at home this Winter & if there is any possible chance will go. I had a delightful dream last night of being at home—may it soon be realized!

23. Collins, *Major General Robert E. Rodes*, 316–20. The "hard marching" was in support of operations in response to Union probes in the fall of 1863. Sam feared being sent to reinforce the Army of Tennessee. Jefferson Davis and General Lee decided to send General James Longstreet's corps. See Daniel, *Conquered*, 186–87.

& will try and answer it very soon. Please present my kindest regards to all friends. John begs to be kindly remembered to you & all the family & also to the servants. Give my warmest love to Jamie, Mary, Willie, Lou, & Icha and accept the same from

Your devoted son,
Sam

Umbria
Oct. 31ˢᵗ, 1863

My dear Sam,

I have allowed a longer time to lapse since writing to you than I intended, but hope you will receive this poor scrawl as an apology for my neglect. I will certainly write more punctually in future.

Mama received the first letter which we have had from you for the past three weeks, almost, on yesterday, and we were all gratified to learn from it that you were well. It relieved us from great anxiety in regard to your safety and health. What a long & hard march you have had! It seems to me enough to wear one out to take such a continuous and arduous tramp.

You must have been greatly relieved when it was accomplished, and will doubtless be more so when the last is performed and you are once more ensconced in comfortable quarters for the winter. I trust you will have no more marching to do this winter, or, in fact, again. For, if by wishing I could have the war to close tomorrow and peace to be established, I would most assuredly do so. However, I hope on, and trust to the decree of an all wise Providence for such a result of our difficulties. Next Thursday passed, and it will have been a year since you left us, to undergo the fatigues, hardships and dangers incident to a soldier's life. And what a year it has been to us! Fraught with wars and rumors of wars, with battles and bloodshed, it has gradually passed from month to month, each telling its tale of sorrow, anguish and suffering. But amidst the general confusion & trouble which a cruel and merciless foe has caused wherever his minions have occupied the country, we of this section of the state have great reason to be thankful in that we have so far been free from their cruelty and oppression, and have hardly realized the extent and real nature of the mighty drama which is being enacted on all sides of us.

May God in mercy ever protect this and all other sections of our country from further devastation & distress, is what I sincerely pray.

I suppose you heard of the death of poor uncle Joe,[24] who died very suddenly on 16th inst. Although it was an unexpected event to us, the Dr said he was expecting it to take place at any time since uncle Joe's attack of dropsy last summer. It seems his was dropsical complaint—the throat swelling so much & so rapidly that suffocation ensued, causing his death. Delphine requested that he should be buried by her mother, at the Goodrum place, which was done. We had just finished the sugar-cane business, in which uncle Joe took a part, it being light work and suiting him as he had just got well of his first spell, & could not do much else. The case was such a sudden one that we sent for Dr Sawyer who, on coming and examining the body, said uncle Joe had been dead for some time.

Did I ever write you word that I wrote to Capt. Wright in relation to the treacherous Scotchman Rainsford, whom I heard had deserted? I received a letter soon after from Capt. W, in which he mentioned that the said Rainsford had deserted the company on their march through Cumberland Gap, and from letters which he had received from the wife of R he was convinced beyond a doubt that R had deserted to the enemy with no intention whatever of returning. So, that expense which I was caused was a useless one.

Sun. Nov. 1st. This morning Mama received another long and exceedingly interesting and gratifying letter from you, for which she told me to present her thanks to you and say that she will soon reply to it. Mama has just recovered from an attack of what she thinks was liver complaint, but which I think was brought on by a singular fall which she had the other day. She had her handsfull of bundles & was starting down the steps to get in the carriage. Not being able to hold her dress out of the way of her feet, she tripped & fell

24. Joe was an enslaved person on the Umbria Plantation (Inventory of the Estate of Samuel Pickens Jr., Greene County Probate Court, 1857).

from near the top of the front steps to the bottom & just under the wheels of the carriage. Fortunately tho! the mules did not start & she considered her escape perfect, with the exception of a bruise or two. But on returning from her ride she was taken with severe pains which caused her to return to bed. All this took place whilst I was at the Cane brake where I had gone on We. last. On my return on Frid., Mama was up and was a good deal better, but went to bed early feeling pains from the fall. She took morphia and felt so well to-day that she and I ventured to town, hearing the Bishop would probably preach; but we turned at the old Milton place as Mama did not feel well enough to go farther. This morning (Monday 2nd) she is very well again and I trust she may not have a return of the pains. She has just gone out to Mrs. Burge's to hurry her up with the woolen cloth which Mrs. B is the weave for her.

The children all have been remarkably well during the sickly season which has just closed.

All but Mama & I escaped. I had a second attack of chills & fever of which I think I informed you in a previous letter. The first chill which I had had for several years & which lasted for an hour or more. I have entirely recovered now I trust.

Dr. Sawyer has been at home now about three weeks, on a health furlough. (By the way, I think he looks as well as I ever saw him.) He has got an extension of his furlough for an additional twenty days; so he will be at home for some length of time still. He inquires very kindly after you whenever he comes over & expressed a wish that some one of us might receive a letter from you before he left. So the next time he comes over Mama can tell him the news from you. He has a great deal to say in regard to his patients, the place where he is, or was stationed, Brandon, etc. etc. I think he is now a full Surgeon.

I have twice, during intervals in which I have laid aside my pen, taken the gun & slipped cautiously down to the meadow, back of the horse lot and unsuccessful attempts at killing two large hawks. The first trial was at one of them, on the wing; after firing both barrels to no purpose, I was rather chagrinned by the other, which flew and lit in very good distance upon a tree close by. Had I reserved the second barrel, I would have literally torn it to pieces i.e the hawk—not the barrel. The second attempt I made just now. It was at one of the same hawks which were there before, and which was on a celebrated old poplar tree, not far from the lower end of the horse-lot. Tom (Biscoe) knows something about that old poplar, for 'twas the same one on which several hawks were sitting last winter which we missed almost as often as we shot at them.

I got within pretty good gun-shot of this one just now, but it was rather too far for a load of eight buckshot, which scatter too much for accurate shooting at the distance I was. I might say here, if I had a load of Bb's, I could have torn this one all to pieces, too, or very nearly so. I am certain that you would not have allowed either of them to leave, if you had tried them.

I sincerely trust that you may come home this winter, and that before you return the war may close. Oh, what a joyful sound, that of the close of war, with its attendant sorrows and troubles, and the return of peace & tranquility. Would the change had already taken place and that you were with us, no more to leave! I trust this event may soon take place.

Daddy Simon has just finished the shaft which broke about six weeks, or more, (nearly two months) ago.

He made new band wheels and a new water wheel, as the old timbers were so rotten that it was not worth while putting them to the new shaft. If you recollect, the old wheel had only one long band wheel, which D. Simon changed for two, or one for each jinny, which lightened the shaft slightly.

He says the machines work finely. We ought now to be able to get thread enough for clothing for the three places. Mr. Willingham says he makes, with two jennies worked by hand, a great deal more cloth than is requisite for the negroes at the Herndon place, & has an abundance to sell. Bye-the-by, Mr. W goes to the Canebrake to-day, and Mr. High leaves, I think, at the same time. The wagons from the Canebrake came up on Sat. and have been here since then. Mr. H came to have a final settlement with Mama on Saturday, & all went on quite smoothly until Mama informed him that she would deduct for the value of a mule which was driven to death by Dr. Osborn who went, on business connected with Peyton's substitute, to Demopolis. H vowed and declared that the business was of an entirely different character from what we supposed; that it was solely on our account that he, or rather his deputy, Dr. Osborne went. That, moreover, the mule died, not of over fatigue as we imagined it did, but of blind staggers which it would have had any how; and finally, that there would be no settlement with him, so long as we deducted for the mule. Also wound up by saying that if we did not go to law to recover damages that he would get clear of the business, or something to that effect. He intended dining with us, but after the above circumstances transpired he soon shuffled off in such a towering rage that the could hardly veil his anger with politeness. I hope that Mr. Willingham is not only a better planter, businessman & manager, generally, than High, but that in employing Mr, W., all such unpleasant occurrences may be at an end. I think he has become quite a conceited gentleman since his sojourn at the Canebrake.

I am sorry that my letter closes with such a long rigmarole of stuff instead of a more pleasant theme; but it is unavoidable: I wished to acquaint you with what I consider highhanded conduct. Were you here I could tell you more—let this suffice, since this is a letter and not a conversation.

Well, I'm at length, at an end. Have acquainted you with all the news, etc., afloat. The Dr was here to-day, received your message & desired that we should return you his love.

Jim Brown reached home a fortnight ago, I believe, and looks quite well. He was wounded in the shoulder or back, I think. Joe Brown is also at home. He is in the best spirits for a lame man I ever saw; very lively and cheerful.

Tell Mr. Joe I will believe he is going to write to me when I receive a letter from him.

Mama and the children join me in kindest love to you.

I will write soon again, but in the meantime shall look with anxious expectancy for a letter from you. I presume you did not receive my last letter as you have been moving about repeatedly since I wrote.

Your affectionate brother,
James.

P.S. Mama incloses $500, and sends you a bundle of 2 pair of improvised drawers, paper, pencils, etc. and a bundle or two for Tom.

Hearing that Lieut. Borden would leave in a few days, we send the things by him. Mama sent you $200 in a letter of mine to you, by Lieut. Christian. Hope you will yet receive it. Jas. P.

Umbria, Nov. 10th 1863

My dear Sam,

Knowing that you would not receive my last letter (which will go to you through Lieut. Borden) until I could write another, and it being some time since I have written to you, with the exception I have just alluded to, I thought I would hastily pen you a few lines to inform you of the health of the family & also to solicit a long reply from you.

I wrote you word that Mama had been quite unwell, as I thought by reason of her fall, but the Dr since informed her it was liver complaint. I am glad to say that she is now very well again, and I trust that she may continue to enjoy good health.

The sickness of the neighborhood is greatly diminished and the Dr has a great deal more of leisure than he has lately had. I trust from present appearances that we may have another fall similar to last (or rather winter.) It is exactly the same kind of weather that we generally have in September & October, tho' hardly so cool, and the sky is as clear and bright as crystal. If it remains so as long as it did last year it will be much better for the soldiers since it was very cold last year at this time.

Since writing the above it has cleared off, the wind has changed to the North and it is quite cool, tho' very pleasant. Hope that we may continue to have such pleasant weather, and that it may get no colder.

The children & I attended quite a nice Concert on Wednesday last given by the ladies of Greensboro for benevolent purposes. The singing was done principally by Miss Damer & Miss Smart, both of whom, but more especially the former, performed very well indeed. Miss Damer is by far the sweetest singer I have ever heard. One is almost enchanted by the sweet, clear, full & melodious strains that flow with as much ease & volubility when uttered by her, as light from the sun. She is, at present, spending a few days with Mary again.

She, you recollect, was here about three weeks or more ago, and was so much pleased with her visit that she has tried it again. I know of no young lady more agreeable, pleasant and entertaining than she. She is also quite pretty, I think.

We were invited by the Dorrohs to spend the day yesterday, and complied with their invitation. Gayle has been spending a week or two at home, having got a furlough, and as he was to leave to-day I thought I would take the day, yesterday, to return a visit he paid me a few days since. We had a very pleasant time indeed.

It was very mild when we were going but, before our return in the evening, the wind changed to the north and it became quite cold, tho' riding we did not feel it much.

I hope you are not having colder weather than we are at present, & that it may not be very more so.

We had a Dr. Vaughn with us a few days since, who stopped for the night on account of it being a [?] evening. He is a Surgeon in the 2nd Missouri Brigade, I think, & is very pleasant, lively & interesting gentleman. He is spending some time in Greensboro before returning to duty, but has formed a great many acquaintances in this neighborhood and spends most of his time in the country. He visited Mr. Cowin and several other families around. He is very good looking too.

I suppose Mama has informed you of the visit she had from an old friend of 'lang syne' who used to live in this neighborhood a Mrs. [?]. She, her sister, I believe, Mrs. Mays, and her daughter Miss Mary [?] spent a few days with us last week. I didn't recognize her when I first saw her (as I was only five years old when she was here last) but can recollect of a great many little incidents and events which took place whilst she used to visit us. She is a very genteel good old woman & was as much at home as she was, I suppose, when last she was here. Mama was very glad to meet her. She is on a visit to Dallas and at the same time is anxious to find a place on which to put her negroes until she can make arrangements for moving from Mississippi. Her place there (a farm on the Yazoo R.) is in the lines of the Yankees, & she is desirous of moving to Ala until the war closes. On her return from Dallas she will spend some length of time with us, I expect. Her sons Robert & James are both in the Army. She said I had changed but little since she was here, but she did not know whether it was you or I, at first, to whom she spoke.

We commenced yesterday sowing wheat. Although delaying longer than I intended at first, yet I do not think it will hurt, as it may not be as apt to be killed by frost as it might have been if planted earlier. Mr. Burger fears that his will be killed. His wheat, Mr. Saddler's, I think, and several others,' is up very prettily, much earlier than it was last winter.

I believe I have related all the news of any interest that there is to write.

I trust you will be able to get a long furlough this winter and come home.

We have got no paper from Selma for several days & have therefore heard nothing in the way of army or political news.

Hoping that you are well & that we may soon hear from you. I am, as ever,

Your affectionate brother,
James

P.S. Mama & all the children join me in warmest love to you. Remember me to Mr. Joe, Gilliam & all other friends. Jas. P Tell John howdye for all.

———•··———

Sunday Morning
November 22, 1863

My beloved Son,

Jamie wrote to you a few days since, and doubtless told you anything that was interesting in this part of the world; but a letter of later date, telling you that all at home are well will I know be acceptable. We have had several frosts, and the country has become healthy and almost everyone is enjoying the inestimable blessing of health. If we could have peace now, how happy we should all be. Last night for the first time since you left us, I dreamed of you—you had returned home and were standing in the hall, putting down the good things with which you were laden and remarking that you had come in unobserved. I was truly happy whilst the dream lasted; but alas! how great was my disappointment on awakening to find you were still far away. What a state of misery has this cruel war brought upon us. I trust that God! in His great mercy to us will soon restore peace to our country and you my dear Son to us. I have felt great uneasiness about you, since I heard you had lost your clothing. Dr. Grigg informed me that Mr. Joe had given an overcoat to you. I felt much relieved when I heard it, for I consider it an all-important matter that you should have one to guard against pneumonia. Give my love to Mr. Joe, and tell him I am under great obligation to him for his kindness to you. Take care of the coat and don't let a Yankee get it, though you may find the one to whom it belongs. I hope to have some nice grey jeans soon but how can I cut it for you, when you have out grown your patterns. Do you remember how the tailor worried about your coat? Well, I am afraid I should do the same thing if I attempt to cut for you at a distance. If you succeed in getting a furlough about a month hence, and come home, we can rig you from head to foot if fortune favors us. I will not indulge a hope of seeing you until the close of the war, lest I be sadly disappointed. Hope buoys me up, and I feel constantly that the war will soon close.

Monday

Jamie saw Lieut Hobson in Town not long since. He complimented you highly and said he was admiring you for your bravery just before he rec'd a shot. He intends visiting us as soon as his wound will admit of his taking such a long ride.

I have at last paid Tartt Stewart & Co. Dr. G said they made a gentleman pay commissions on his cotton which was pledged to them (as ours was) but which he sold himself, as we did. T.S. & Co acknowledged the receipt of the money I sent by Mr. Burge and said they had not charged commissions as they supposed I still hold the cotton which was promised to them. I wrote them a polite letter, telling the various times under which I had sold the cotton. They wrote a genteel letter and were satisfied without commissions. I have paid everyone in Mobile to whom we were indebted except Mr. Ross, who refused to be paid. He wishes a C. States bond, bearing 8 pct. I have always thought him a mean man—he should be sent to Yankee hands.

We have succeeded in buying a buggy with good harness at $400: it has not been used much & is quite a bargain. I have engaged a carriage from A. Johnson of Greensborough at $700. Another bargain if he does not cheat me. Potter asks $1500 & $2000. I gave $120 yesterday for 3 gallons of peach brandy which formerly cost about $1 per gallon. I gave $75 for a pair of cotton cards, which were only 37½ cents per pair before the war. Our quinine cost us this

Summer near $400. I rec'd a very kind letter from Dr. Cunningham saying he could not find a teacher and advising me to write to Genl Smith of Lexington Va. Jamie wrote immediately and we are anxiously awaiting his reply. I am very desirous to have the children under a good tutor, one who will not refuse to explain as Mr. Staudenmayer did. I have asked Dr. Wadsworth to assist me in getting a teacher and he kindly said he would. Mary speaks of going to Raleigh in Jan but her going will depend on circumstances. Of course she will not go if the enemy be near that place. I fear Mary will not consider her education complete unless she finish at St. Mary's under Dr. Smedes. Fannie Marbury goes to the Greensboro Academy, but does not like it. She has been there only two weeks, and would gladly stop now; she lives in the hope that we shall have tutor in our family soon. I am anxious to have the children at their studies and yet I dread the thought of having another private teacher. Not one of the three we have had pleased me.

A letter was received today from Biscoe, and I felt greatly relieved and truly thankful that no accident befell him in the last battle in Va. He was not in the battle, but was engaged in a Court Martial. Perhaps you and Biscoe can come home at Christmas.

A young soldier has just come in out of the rain—he is one of Genl Polk's staff. Mary and Jamie's with Miss Damer, who has been here nearly 3 weeks, are entertaining him. Miss D sings delightfully and I have often thought how charmed you would be with her voice. She is rather pretty and very lady like. You have never told me how you like the girls of Va, those of Hanover C.H for instance. I was sorry to hear that Charley & Theodore Uhlhorn were both wounded—only slightly but Charley may lose one of his thumbs. They will miss their Mother & friends now more than ever. Do you remember my old friend, Mrs. McCurry, who left Greensboro for Mississippi when Mary was only 3 days old. Well she, her daughter [*unclear*] have paid us a visit lately. I was much pleased to see her the pleasure was so unexpected. She has gone to Dallas & promises to come & stay here if she cannot get back to Mississippi.

Your friends are all well & inquire kindly about you and send much love. Dr. G will soon be a near neighbor at the Lyle place. He is busily engaged in fixing up the place. Rev. Mr. [*unclear*], whom I like very much always makes particular inquiry about you. The children send warmest love to you. The servants at both places are getting better. Uncle [*unclear*] is still here sick but he is [*unclear*] better. Give my love to all friends, particularly to Biscoe. May God! Bless you my dear, good Son.

Your Mother

Remember us kindly to John. Suky & all are well [?]

———————•—•———————

Umbria, Dec. 20th 1863

My dear Sam,

I have taken my chair, pen & paper in order to scribble you a few lines which I hope may pass for a letter, but do not promise you much in its perusal. I suppose you have been informed of the melancholy occurrence on Friday evening or Thursday night two weeks ago—the death of Mrs. Sawyer. I believe I mentioned it to you in my last letter, but presume you did not receive it. Mr. Enoch I feel sorry for. Was over there on Thursday last to see him and Dr. S, who has been quite sick, by the way, and Mr. E told me of all the trouble which he has seen foreshadowed on his mind for years, which would result to him on the death of his mother, and which have crowded upon him like an avalanche since its occurrence. The place will be sold as soon as legal arrangements can be made to do so. Charley Stickney is the Administrator, I think, of the Estate, and says it will soon be sold. He is disposed to act by the letter of the law, so that when the negroes which have been left Mr. Enoch have been put under the guardianship of some one for him, the money put away for his children & the house in which he lives sold, I do not know what he will do for support. And all those things that I have mentioned Mr. Stickney proposes doing. Now Mr. Enoch expects Mama to purchase the land for him—which will be sold for several thousand dollars. Mr. E wishes Mama to become purchaser for him and in case he never pays, the land will fall to Mama's possession. I think, considering the precarious & complicated state of Mama's monetary affairs & the unsettled state of the country that such a request is rather unreasonable. If all unite to lend him a helping hand then, of course, Mama could and would contribute cheerfully to his assistance, but I do not think that she should share all the expenses.

We were all quite surprised to see John, who arrived by stage from Greensboro about five o'clock this evening, and were very glad to hear that he had left you quite well. But oh what disappointment to us that you were not with him. I sincerely trust that you may be able to visit home this winter, notwithstanding you think there is not much chance for your doing so. It is, as you say, thirteen long months since your departure, which has seemed as ten times the length of time to me. We must all do as you say tho "hope for the better time coming; which I trust that God [*unclear.*] Oh, what troubles what injustices, how much sorrow and distress will have ceased when this terrible scourge shall have been swept from our country, and peace and happiness been restored to us once more. Before that time arrives tho it is thought that every male citizen between the ages of 18 & 45 will have been called into the service; those who have furnished substitutes as well as the others. I will again ask of you your opinion in regard to my joining you. I do not care to go any where else than with you. So if I must go, I will go to Virginia as soon as I can fix & get everything ready for so doing. I notice that the substitute law has been repealed, but do not know whether it is retroactive in its provisions or not. I do not think Congress has the power to pass an ex post facto law unless the plea of military necessity authorizes the act. This of course out weighs every other power, and of the necessities of the country requires its available force, it is right that all should lend a hand in the cause.

Well, I have written three pages and have said nothing about home. Few changes have taken place in its appearance generally since you left it, but your departure forms the chief & principal change which has occurred to detract from its gaiety & happiness.

Mama & all the children are quite well and desire their love to be given you.

Accept the same from your affectionate

Brother James

P.S. Please excuse all mistakes, errors, blunders, blotches, etc which are too numerous to mention & which have caused me to become disgusted with the appearance of this letter; but as I wrote in a hurry and in the midst of a conversation between the children & Mr. Hughes, the young man who is staying with us, I could not avoid making them.

I had almost forgot that Christmas will soon be upon us, and that in a few more days the former season of mirth and merriment will have arrived. 'Tis the second time that all of us have not been together. God grant it may be the last! How different does it now seem compared with the animation, pleasure, excitement etc., which its presence in other times afforded, especially to the children. Now they seem to regard it as older people do & speak of it always in a comparative sense, i.e. that it is nothing like what Christmas used to be.

I believe they anticipate a little pleasure in some concerts, consisting of Tableaux and Charades, which the ladies of Greensboro and its vicinity propose giving for the benefit of the soldiers a few days after Christmas.

I would like you much to be present on the occasion if you only heard Miss Damer sing. I know you would be charmed by it for 'tis the sweetest music that I have ever heard. I suppose you think I mention this enough, but really I'm enthusiastic on the subject. I hope you may soon have the pleasure of listening to her fine singing. Well, I must close, hoping soon to hear from you. Adieu my dear brother.

J.P.

SEVEN

The Government Demands More

JANUARY–MAY 1864

On January 1, 1864, Sam wrote in his diary: "This is the birthday of another year—the 4th one of the War; & God grant that it may be the last. May the weather to-day which is bright & sunny—a pleasant change from the last ones of the past year, be typical of a happy improvement in our national affairs." After the retreat from Gettysburg, defeatism had spread throughout the army, but morale had improved since. In his letter of February 8, Sam described an army that remained confident that the new year would bring victory. Already the troops had repulsed two Union movements against Richmond. One was a crossing of the Rapidan on February 6 by Hays's Third Division, intended to divert Confederate attention from a larger crossing of the Chickahominy and an advance on Richmond. The first brigade of the Third Division to cross the Rapidan met little resistance and advanced to within a mile of the Confederate line. General Alexander Hays then sent the remainder of the division across, hoping to advance further, but encountered stiff Confederate opposition and withdrew. The official purpose of these operations was to create distractions to cover the escape of 109 prisoners from Libby and Belle Isle prisons in Richmond. However, the discovery of a set of orders on the body of Colonel Ulric Dahlgren, who had been killed during the abortive raid, revealed what the southern press trumpeted as the real purpose of the raid—the kidnapping and execution of Jefferson Davis and his cabinet and the burning of Richmond—as evidence of the evil the "invaders," as Sam called them, were capable of. The Fifth never saw any action, so the movement to Richmond became a welcome break from the monotony of camp life.[1]

In Greene County the mood was as dark, stormy, and cold as the weather there. In February, west Alabama faced another scare from the Union Army, when General William Tecumseh Sherman left Vicksburg with about twenty thousand troops headed southeast, in the direction of Meridian, Mississippi, where he intended to destroy the railroad junction. At the time, people living in east Mississippi and west Alabama had no idea where Sherman might go. Newspaper speculation and rumors about the goals of the Union campaign, and the response of the Confederate Army, fueled fears of Union occupation of the region. Sherman did not, however, continue into Alabama.[2]

It was not the threat of invasion that was most on Mary Gaillard's mind that January and February, though. The Confederate Congress in December 1863 had passed a law that made men who had hired substitutes eligible for the draft, and as Sam mentioned in his February 12 letter, James had been "mustered in." The Pickenses had already used the "twenty slave" exemption in 1863 for the overseer, William Lawless. As he had always done when the subject of James's status arose, Sam suggested alternatives that would either keep James out of the army or would limit his exposure to the rigors of the combat soldier. Sam advised James to go to Pollard, Alabama, and join the cavalry, "as it is a much easier & more pleasant branch of the service than Infantry." But the letter never reached James and, on January 29, Sam received news that James would soon be traveling with Captain Williams from Alabama to join Company D. For Sam and his mother, the departure of James was deeply troubling, to say the least. Back in 1862, when Sam was preparing to leave for Virginia, he had reassured his mother, and himself, that James would be there to assist her in the management of the plantations and the younger children. James's departure, he wrote, "is like breaking up our

1. Diary of Samuel Pickens, January 1, 1864. Cavalry Brigadier General H. Judson Kilpatrick planned the raid, which began on February 28. See Eicher, *The Longest Night*, 641–43.

2. Linden and Linden, *Disunion, War, Defeat, and Recovery in Alabama*, 113–14; Eicher, *The Longest Night*, 634–37.

home, as Mama will be poorly able to spare him & says she cannot remain at home without him." James was unsuited to military service, Sam wrote. His "constitution is delicate"; he would not be able to "endure the rough & arduous service that we have out here."[3]

Mary Gaillard again struggled with depression as she reckoned with the impending departure of James and the news that Sam would not be allowed to return home that winter. Sam explained that, though he could get a furlough, he had decided to remain in camp to help James adjust to life in the army. He was also assisting James in trying to secure a medical exemption from a combat unit provided for in the current conscription law.[4]

As Sam and Mary Gaillard expected, James struggled to adapt to life in the army. James, along with other new conscripts that winter, did not have the benefit of a transition period in a camp of instruction where he could at least learn the basics of army routine.[5] Instead, he left a relatively safe and comfortable life as a civilian in a region still untouched by the violence of battle and, two weeks later, was in the Army of Northern Virginia's winter camp where he witnessed, for the first time, as he wrote to his mother, the "desolation & ruin which are the consequences of this war." He wrote his mother of his admiration for the men in the army, who he believed would ultimately prevail. Yet he knew that he was unfit for service in a combat unit.

3. Diary of Samuel Pickens, January 29, 1864. Pickens's distress about the conscription of James appears to contradict his disdain for men who did not serve. But, as Reid Mitchell explains, soldiers believed that families with men in the army should not be forced to send their brothers to war as well (*Civil War Soldiers*, 84–85).

4. The law allowed conscripts to appeal to government officials for assignment to non-combat government agencies. On the December law's provision regarding details, see Sacher, *Confederate Conscription*, 239–42.

5. According to Sacher, conscripts such as James who decided to join a particular unit rather than be assigned by the government often skipped camps of instruction (*Confederate Conscription*, 245).

Near Richmond,
Febr. 8th, 1864.

My dear Mama,

You will doubtful be surprised to find us at this season of the year suddenly transferred from our Winter Quarters near Orange C.H. to the field in the vicinity of our Capitol. I will tell you the cause of it. Last Wednesday night the 5th as unexpectantly as anything in the world would have been [unclear] for us to be ready to march at half past six o'clock the next morning. We were sorely disappointed & distressed at having to quit our snug cabins in mid winter and go to marching and lying out in the weather, especially as we expected to enjoy a quiet, peaceful time there for three months longer; however we [unclear] & got ready and the next morning the [unclear] us up before day & soon after we started. Marched by Orange C.H. to Gordonsville sixteen miles and as we had not marched much for some time & were loaded down with baggage, which always accumulates on our hands in Winter quarters, and were very much fatigued by it. Late in the evening we took the cars & went to Hanover Junction. Our brigade & [Robert D.] Johnston's under Genl Rodes were the only troops sent & we thought our destination was eastern N.C. to reinforce Gen. [George] Pickett who was making an expedition against it to try and recapture it, but it turned out that we had come to take the place of Pickett's Div which had been stationed there. We went to the houses that they had occupied & went to work repairing them, for there was no telling how long we might remain. But we were not destined to be quiet long, and after sleeping in them two nights we left an hour before day yesterday morning and marched two miles to the railroad. A dispatch was read stating that the Yankees had crossed the Rapidan & were pressing Genl Lee & that they were advancing on Richmond from the [unclear] had driven in the pickets at Bottom's bridge & were within fifteen miles of the city and Gen Battle was ordered to hurry there with one Brigade. We filled three very long trains, & after some delay, proceeded to this city. The alarm bells were ringing, the militia was turned out, and there was a good deal of excitement amongst the citizens, who were, no doubt, much relieved to see some of Lee's veterans come to their assistance. While marching through town we had a good deal of [unclear] as the men were in the highest spirits

& delighted at the novelty of the scenery and were jeering & laughing at the men they saw along the streets who ought to be in the army or at least should be under arms at such a time as this, when their city is threatened by the invaders. We came out to the fortifications—bivouacked two miles from town & have been quiet since. It seems from the morning paper that the Yankees crossed the Chickahominy and formed a line of battle yesterday morning but our troops threw a few shells at them & they [*unclear*] back [*unclear*] on the Rapidan [*unclear*] at Morton's Ford, but were whipped back by Gen. Ed. Johnston's Division. So things were not half as bad as was first reported.[6]

I hope everything will relapse into the usual state of quietude, that we will soon get back to our Winter-quarters. I owe Jamie a letter but suppose he will be on here soon, as Col. Hall recd a notice the other day that he had been mustered in.[7] I have had very few letters for some times past & the last one was from Willie, dated 21st ult. I hope all are quite well at home. Excuse this letter as it is very cold & I can scarcely write now, but will write again very soon if we remain quiet.

Please present my kind regards to all friends & warmest love to all the family & accept the same also from

Your ever affectionate son,
Samuel.

———•—•———

Umbria, Ala.
Feb. 23rd, 1864

My beloved Son,

I am indebted to you for two kind, affectionate and ever welcomed letters, which I will now answer. I was quite surprised to learn you were in Richmond, and very glad an opportunity was afforded for you to visit our good Dentist

---

6. *Daily Richmond Enquirer,* February 15, 1864; Baltimore *Sun,* February 9, 10, 1864; Charleston *Mercury,* February 16, 1864; Collins, *Major General Robert E. Rodes,* 338–40; Eicher, *The Longest Night,* 634; Salmon, "Morton's Ford," 260–62. Cullen Battle was the commander of the Third Alabama Infantry Regiment.

7. Josephus Hall had recently been promoted to regimental lieutenant colonel.

and to enjoy yourself at the Theatre and other places of amusement. Dr. Pleasants is quite genteel in manners. I wish we could all pay him a visit now. I advise you to let him examine your teeth again before you return home. You see I am looking forward to a speedy termination of the War. I know not why it is but hope buoys me up and I am led to believe that our troubles will soon be at an end. God! grant it may be so. But whilst I am cheered with the hope that we shall soon be blessed with peace, I have some heavy and sore trials to bear until that happy period shall arrive—a separation from you my dear, good Son, and from my dear Jamie. I have been so much troubled in mind that I could not write to you as I desired, and I have just recovered from a very severe attack of liver complaint. I would not send for the Dr because I know how to treat that disease. I am now better than I have been for many weeks past. I was very sorry to hear of you having had a chill, and trust you will never be troubled with another. I have a great dread of chills. I suppose yours was occasioned by exposure—living in the open air in such a climate as Va. This was the day determined upon for Jamie to leave us, but Capt. Williams deferred going until the 29th of this month. I dread the day. Biscoe arrived here a week ago and is in fine health and spirits.[8] He has only a short time to stay with us and wishes Jamie to have his furlough lengthened so that they may travel to Va in company with each other. If Capt. Williams will consent, Jamie can stay at home until about the 15th of March. What would I not have given if you could have come with B. We could enjoy ourselves so much better if you were amongst us and then you & he & Jamie could travel back to Va so pleasantly together. But I will not dwell on this any longer. I cannot see you until the war is over, I suppose, so I will never cease to offer up my feeble prayers that this terrible war will soon come to a close.

John wishes to remain here until Jamie goes on but I am afraid you miss him very much. He has enjoyed his furlough very much & has had the use of a mule or horse all the time. Poor old [*unclear.*] death has made me feel quite sad. She was a good, faithful servant to the end of her days on Earth.

Jamie's fine mare—Kil I believe is her name—was taken by the impressing officers from the Canebrake a few days since. They allowed only $600 for

8. Biscoe had received a thirty-day leave so he could spend time with Mary before the spring campaign began (CMSR, Louisiana, RG 109).

her. The poorest, meanest horses are selling at $700 to 8 or 9 hundred. The officers arrived here today, but went off without taking any of our horses. I was much afraid that poor old Tom or some other [*unclear*] would be taken.

Enoch Sawyer spent last evening with us. He is in better spirits now than he has been in for some time past. He has rented the place for one year and bought some old mules so he must "put his shoulder to the wheel" and try to get his helpless family along. I am sorry for him but it is not in my power to help him. Dr. Sawyer is at home making great efforts to get Fannie Marbury to her friends in Georgetown D.C. She is anxious to go, particularly so since our enemies have come near to us. Mrs. Torbert will be married next week to Ed Bayoll. She has been a gay & extravagant widow.

I can't give you any news for I never go out. I am waiting for you to escort me about. The weather is spring-like. I have all my doors & windows open. Your friends make constant inquiries about you & send much love always. [*Sentence unclear.*] Col. Pickens has not visited us yet. The children are all well & desire to be affectionately remembered to you. May God! bless you, my dear Son and send you home very soon to your Mother.

Umbria, Mar. 5th 1864

My dear brother,

According to a promise which I made you in my last letter, I will again write you a few lines to inform you of the health of the inmates of Umbria & to acquaint you with the little news of this neighborhood.

Since the slight attack of liver complaint which Mama had not long since (of which I informed you) she has been quite well, and the children are all very well also. I hope she will continue to enjoy good health. Now that our new carriage is completed she can take a long & pleasant ride in it every day, which would be of great benefit to her.

While I am speaking of this article I will give you a short description of it. It is something like one of those carriages which we saw in Mobile, tho much smaller and by no means as good looking, has four seats, two behind, and two in front which can be turned at pleasure to face either the back or the fore part of the carriage. Altho' it is not the kind of vehicle which Mama ordered and which she would have preferred, still as it is in every respect more desirable than the old carriage we did not return it. Johnson was more cunning in his trade than you can imagine. For instance, when he had almost completed the carriage he led us to believe that Wiley Tunstall had a slight prior claim to it and that W. intended to have it if he had to pay more for it than we were to give. He also said that Wiley had agreed to pay $600 and three hundred pounds of lard (which, as it now sells would have increased the cost of the carriage by at least $450 or $500.) He said he did not wish W. to have it and if we would give him four hundred and fifty lbs. of lard we might call the carriage ours. Mind, this was said after he had agreed to our bargain, which did not mention lard, at all. It was only a ruse of his to obtain a little lard. I have not the slightest idea that Wiley Tunstall wished the carriage, after hearing that we had engaged it, if at all.

I suppose you have heard that a wagon, four mules and a driver were impressed from us by order of Genl. Polk, for hauling Government or Army supplies from Meridian, or probably some nearer point.[9] They were kept a week. Some impressing officers (so-called, tho' in reality they had no authority whatever to impress) stopped at the Canebrake, and places in that neighborhood, and took a good many horses. They took my little filly, which Mr. Willingham was having broke, and left a certificate from Genl Lee, a cavalry officer who is in the rear of the enemy, for $600, their valuation of the horse. I have since heard that these men (ten in number & armed cap-a-pie [*head to foot*]) had not the slightest authority to touch a horse this side of the Warrior river. They have disappeared from this neighborhood and can not be found. I requested Mr. Willingham, who was going to Demopolis with the wagon team, to make enquiries concerning the men, their authority etc., & to ascertain if there was any hope of my getting my horse back. He told me that he went to Genl Polk's Headquarters and was told by the General that the men were perfectly unauthorized to impress horses & that he (Genl P.) had sent a detail of cavalry in pursuit of the lawless gang; with what prospect of getting up with them I do not know; but very little, I think. I was extremely

9. Leonidas Polk was in command of Confederate forces, Army of Mississippi, around Meridian (Eicher, *The Longest Night*, 635).

sorry to hear that they had taken the little filly, as I would have given Di in place of it, sooner, I believe.

All that excitement in regard to the advance of the two columns of Yankee troops, from Vicksburg & Memphis respectively, has died away, and no more apprehensions are entertained of their ability to penetrate this state. For, the column under the command of Genl Sherman, which advanced to Meridian & destroyed the depot & rail-road from that place to Jackson, retreated to the latter place; and the other column which was to have formed a junction with Sherman's at Meridian, was met by Genl Forrest, decidedly our best cavalry officer, was badly whipped by him, and have retreated to Memphis again. Genl F. had a brother (Col. Forrest) killed in this engagement.[10] The Yankees seem to be trying the metal of Fort Powell, below Mobile, as it is stated that they fired five hundred shots at it in one day. It is feared that if Ft. P. falls the enemy will meet with little difficulty in reaching the city with their gun boats. I trust, however, that that Fort will hold out as nobly as Ft. Sumter has and that they will find the taking of Mobile as hard a nut to crack as that of Charleston seems to be.

Willie received a letter from you day before yesterday, I believe and from it we were glad to learn that you are quite well again. I hope you may not have a return of chills, as they are very enervating and unpleasant visitants.

Tom is quite well and sends his love to you. I said "well," but he is not, or rather has not been. He took a very bad cold whilst traveling, and has been very much annoyed with it ever since his arrival. Sometimes he was compelled to take medicine. Now, however, he is much better. He has written on for an extension of his furlough (which expires on the tenth inst.) to the 20th. I hope he will be able to obtain it, tho' he fears he will not, as there has been some movement on the part of the Yankees on the Rapidan, lately; however, I notice by this morning's paper that the report of their crossing at German's ford was false, & that all is quiet along the front. We may probably leave on the 15th inst., for Va. I dislike the idea of leaving Mama more on her account and the childrens' than my own, as there are a great many things which require some one to help her, & which would either be sadly neglected without

10. Nathan Bedford Forrest's cavalry defeated Union cavalry under the command of General Sooy Smith at West Point and Okolona, Mississippi, in late February (Eicher, *The Longest Night*, 636).

some one, or imperfectly done by an agent. Such for instance, as the paying the tithe & other taxes, and other things. However, Willie is growing in years and will have to learn a little of business, so as to help her.

I must close as it will soon be time to mail my letter, and I wish it to go this evening. If I have time to do so, I will write again to you before I leave.

Miss J. Damer has been on a visit to Mary for two or three weeks; consequently, we have enjoyed some delicious music. I wish you could hear it. Her father has gone to Tuscaloosa to teach in the female institution in that place, so Mary & Louty have no teacher at present. Mr. D. will stay until May or June.

Mama & the children all join me in kindest love to you. Write soon, & Believe me, ever,

> Your affectionate brother,
> James

P.S. John and all the other servants said their "best respects" to you. John has been complaining for two or three days with rheumatism & feeling otherwise badly. His wife, Suky, is quite sick with pneumonia.

Mr. Enoch was here last evening. He inquires kindly regarding you and sends his love to you. I've not seen the Dr. for several days.

> Jas. P.

———•———

> Umbria, Ala.
> March 7th, 1864

My ever dear Son,

I wrote to you about ten days since, and determined then that I would write to you more frequently than I had done of late; but household affairs, low spirits and rheumatism in my right hand have all combined to make me defer the pleasure of writing until now.

Willie rec'd a letter from you two days since, and it afforded us all the greatest pleasure to read it and hear that you were well. I am glad you missed a second chill, for nothing undermines the constitution so soon as chills do.

Take good care of yourself my good Son and may a kind and gracious Providence grant that we may be permitted to see each other again on Earth. I was delighted to hear how much you had enjoyed yourself in Richmond, and of the liberty enjoyed by you and the rest of our brave soldiers. What a treat it must have been to walk about and to enjoy the good things of city life. Would that the pleasure had lasted longer, and that you would have come from Richmond to your dear native state. But I must wait with patience God's appointed time for the war to close, and for you to return to us. May we all be benefitted and made better by the trials and sorrows and privations which we have been called upon to endure in this terrible war and may we dedicate ourselves to our Heavenly Father for the remainder of our days on Earth.

We attended the Episcopal church in Greensboro yesterday & Jamie, Miss Juliet, Damer, Biscoe, Mary, Wille, and myself all went to hear Dr. Cobbs preach.[11] It was communion Sunday, and I am always glad to embrace every opportunity of going on such occasions. Capt. Williams' bride sat near us, but I did not notice her sufficiently to pronounce upon her beauty. Most persons say she is very handsome. Ed Bayol's bride was there also; she looked quite pretty. We are delighted at having Biscoe with us and regret exceedingly that the time for his departure is near at hand—he expects to leave us on the 13th of this month. We shall miss him & Jamie so much. I can't tell what will become of us. May a kind Providence watch over us and guard us from every evil. John's wife has been ill with pneumonia but I hope she will be well by the time Jamie starts so that John will be ready & willing to leave. We had the most delightful weather in Feb that was ever felt in that month—how different from the climate of Va—whilst we had spring like weather you were almost frozen. We had a remarkably dry winter and some persons are predicting a wet spring, which is generally followed by a sickly summer. But I hope this will not be the case. Let us not indulge in gloomy anticipations. "Sufficient unto the day is the evil thereof."[12] Dr. Grigg paid us a short visit yesterday afternoon and sent his kindest regards to you. He and all of the

11. The Reverend Hooker Cobbs became the rector at St. Paul's Episcopal Church, Greensboro, in 1861 (Galhunter, "History of St. Paul's Episcopal Church").

12. Matthew 6:34 from the Sermon on the Mount. "Take therefore no thought for the morrow; for the morrow shall take thought for the things of itself. Sufficient unto the day is the evil thereof."

family are well. The Dr has improved the Lyle place very much, and will in the course of another year make it very comfortable. When the war is over, I think he will get a place of his own. Dr. Sawyer spent last evening with us. He still casts his eyes to the ceiling whenever he relates a story, some of which were so long last night that everyone present was completely wearied out long before he left. He and Markie started today for Georgetown. Of course he will only go as far as Richmond, and from that place one of her Marbury uncles will escort her to her place of destination. She came over this morning to say farewell. I felt sorry to part with her for I think it highly probably that we shall never meet again. Her attachment to her native state is however very strong, and she says it is her intention to return to it at some future period. We shall miss Markie much, altho' we have not been so much together since the old lady's death as we were in former years. If you were now in Richmond, you would undoubtedly have the pleasure of seeing Fannie & her uncle. Mr. Enoch visits us occasionally, and always speaks very kindly of you. He is industriously engaged in farming and will no doubt make every effort to support his family and succeed, if he does not fall into his old bad habit. Mr. E was displeased with his old friends for not standing security for his [*unclear*] management of the property left his children by the grandmother. I was afraid of involving myself in difficulties and did not offer my name altho' many hints were thrown out. After suffering much anxiety on the subject, and being almost in despair, he got Mr. Sadler and Richard Randolph to stand security for him. Whenever he sees me, he inquires about you, and sends his love. On the 15th of March our taxes are to be paid. I fear Jamie will be off before then. What shall I do without him. I know the Dr or Enoch would assist me at any time, but I should feel some hesitation in calling upon them, as their time is fully occupied. The children are all well, and as happy as larks. I regret not having succeeded in getting a teacher: precious time is lost, which can never be recalled. I will leave Umbria in a few days after the close of the war and go where good schools are to be found. Jamie and Mary have written to you within the last week. I am afraid that many of our letters are lost on the way. I feel great anxiety about Jamie's entering the army, because I think he is unfit for the service. I wish he could obtain an easy situation & one in which he could serve his country without the risk of losing his health. The servants desire to be kindly remembered to you. Frank at the Canebrake has been very low but is now better. The children unite with me in warmest love to you, my dear Son. May God! bless you

Your Mother

Remember be kindly to all friends. Destroy this, I pray you. Such a pen, paper & ink were never used. ½ past ten o'clock, so good night my good son.

———•———

Montgomery, March 19th 1864

My dear Mama,

As Tom and I will be in this place for several hours this morning, I will have time to write a few lines to you telling you of our journey hither after leaving home. We reached Newbern at 7 o'clock, I believe, and rested for the night at the hotel in that place, leaving the next day about 6½ and arriving at Selma at 11.

Before proceeding farther, I must notice the reception at Greensboro of my cap sent me by Mary with a note, also, and must return her a thousand thanks for it. It is very pretty & very comfortable and will prove of inestimable value to me. Whenever I wear it I will think of my dear sister & of the sympathetic expressions of her kind & affectionate note to me.

To continue, we lay over in Selma from 11 A.M., 'till 11 P.M., exactly 12 hours, & you cannot imagine the fatigue & inconvenience which this delay caused us. At the hint of every whistle which we heard we would start & ask if that were the Montgomery boat, but would be soon set off by being informed that it was the foundry whistle. Finally, however, we ascertained that our boat was lying at the wharf; so gathering up our baggage we went down in order to go aboard but had to [*unclear*] for several hours in the cold, as the boat was freighting at a wharf some distance above us & did not come down 'till 11, when we got only 'deck-passage,' i.e. had either to sit up, or lie down on the floor of the boat all night as every stateroom & booth was full. We preferred this, tho,' to remaining in Selma, and taking it soldier style, (wrapping in our overcoats & lying on the floor) we managed to spend the night tolerably well, and after 13 ½ hours travel reached this place, where we will be until 9 ½ o'clock tonight. The boats & cars are literally crowded with soldiers returning some to their homes & others to their several commands. By the way, I saw yesterday & traveled last night with our friend who took dinner with us the other day & who was so very anxious that he should reward you for it. He recognized me as Tom & I were endeavoring to get passports & transportation, in Selma, and I knew him as soon as I had seen him. I also saw Mr. Wynne [*unclear*] & Mr. Frank Brown there.

Thus far, as we have got on very well. Have not been annoyed by guards or passport officers, etc., but I fear we will have enough of them to encounter on the remaining portion of our route; I trust not tho! We have had delightful weather for traveling, it being neither too cold nor too warm.

As dinner is ready & we wish to mail our letters this evening I must come to a close; promising, if I have time to do so, to write again from Richmond to you.

My dear mother you cannot imagine how I miss you and the children [*unclear*] already. If so much so now, what will not be the degree henceforward!

God grant this terrible war may soon cease, that peace with all its attendant blessings may again bless us & that soon we may all be together once more in tranquility & happiness, is the warmest prayer & wish of your

Affectionate son,
James.

P.S. Tom joins me in love to you & all the children Louty & Icha

———•———

Columbia, So. Car.,
March 21st, 1864.

My dear Mama,

After a fatiguing travel of several days in the cars Tom and I find ourselves at this place, free, for the night at least, from that hurry, bustle and confusion attendant on one's journey by the cars, and at leisure to pen a few lines to you. After writing you at Montgomery, I met Davy, cousin Corry's servant formerly, who seemed glad to see me and who said that Julia Pickens expected me to go and see her before I left the place. So I went to her house & spent a few minutes with her & very pleasantly, too. She has grown in height a little (not much) since we saw her last, has become a good deal stouter & more healthy in appearance since then, and altogether, has improved very much. However, I do not think she is quite as pretty as she used to be. She played very pretty accompaniments to several songs which she [*unclear*] indeed. I was informed by her that Dr. Sample has again married; this time to a Miss (or Mrs.) White, of Montgomery whom Julia knew very well & of whom she spoke very highly. I made her promise to visit you and the children, tho' whether she will keep her promise or not is a question, as I expect she rarely visits out of the city.

Tom, John & I have so far, got along very well, managing to get good seats in the cars on every train, instead of having to stand up as a great many, not as successful as ourselves, are compelled to do. Today, however, we have met with a little delay, owing to some accident which happened to the cars on the Wilmington road. We intended going that route, but on learning of the accident, we did not change trains at Kingsville but proceeded on to this place, where we will have to stay 'till 9 o'clock tomorrow morning, as we missed the evening train for Charlotte today. We got here in time for supper if we had had any to eat, but as they gave us only some hard biscuits and very bad rye coffee, we had little. We depend, during the day, on our baskets which have been faithful companions of ours since leaving Montgomery, and we have found nothing on our way to equal their contents. Besides, they will be amply sufficient to last us to Richmond. The good weather of which I spoke, ceased the very night on which we left Montgomery, and it commenced to rain so we set out on foot for the cars & has rained almost incessantly ever since.

I am glad to hear of the resumption of the cartel for the exchange of prisoners. It seems the Yankees are beginning to pay much more respect to our authorities than they have formerly done. They have appointed another agent of exchange in Butler's place, and more, are giving two of our men held by them for one of theirs held by us.[13] Tom met, today on their way home on furlough, two or three members of his Regt., who had just been exchanged.

13. Benjamin F. Butler was negotiating a resumption of exchanges. During this negotiation, exchanges took place until, in April, General U. S. Grant again suspended exchange. Butler had not been replaced at that time (Hesseltine, *Civil War Prisons*, 217–20).

Well, I'm compelled to close as I have a short candle & little fire. So I will bid you, my dear mother, good night. Give my love to Mary, Willie, Louty & Icha, & tell Mary I shall write to her next.

Remember me kindly to Dr. Grigg & Mr. Enoch when you see them & to all other friends. Tom sends his love to all.

Ever your affectionate son,
James

P.S. John sends howd'ye to all and desires that his love be given Suky & inquires after her health.

Jas. P.

Mama I would have those certificates attended to by someone before 1st [*unclear Latin phrase*]

J.P.

——— • ———

Raleigh, N.C.
March 24th, 1864

My dear Mama,

From this place I will commence another letter, as we left Columbia in much haste on last Tuesday morning that we had no time to mail the letters which we wrote the night previously. We awoke on that morning bright & early, of our own accord. (I believe we might have slept 'till that night & would not have been molested by the servants of the Congaree hotel.) After dressing we proceeded to the depot and were much disappointed in hearing that the regular passenger train had left about ½ an hour before. However, we made the best of it, and determined to take passage on board of a freight train which left only a few minutes after we had got on board. I will say that it turned very cold on Monday night and sleeted; so that on awakening the next morning the ground had the appearance of a recent fall of snow. So you can imagine our situation—in a baggage car, on board of a freight train, with no fire & seats made of sacks of corn. We, however, got permission of the conductor to spread a coating of moist sand in the middle of the car & build a fire on it, which relieved more than half of our sufferings; for we could stand all our other privations much better than we could [?] of a comfortable fire. In this situation we rode very slowly, for freight trains are always much slower than the passenger trains) during the whole of Tuesday & the following night, & until 1 o'clock on Wed. (yesterday.) It turned much warmer, tho' on yesterday morning we were quite comfortable when we arrived at Charlotte. By the way, on Tues. it commenced to snow & by evening it was between 3 & 4 inches deep. The trees presented a most magnificent picture, as they were laden with frozen snow & contrasted beautifully with their green leaves. The sight was quite unexpected to Tom & myself, as we had left home during a most delightful spring temperature of weather.

We arrived at this place this morning at 10 o'clock having traveled all night & since 6½ yesterday evening, from Charlotte, N.C. Raleigh looks quite natural indeed. I was forcibly reminded to day as we drove from the depot to the hotel, of the day Sam & I arrived & proceeded thither to meet our dear Mother, sisters & brothers. But alas, they are now far away. God grant that we may soon meet again, when the war shall have ended & peace been proclaimed. I must now close as Tom & I have to mail our letters, if possible for the evening's mail.

Your affectionate son,
James

———•—•———

Umbria, Ala.
March 24, 1864.

My dear son,

My dear Jamie and Biscoe left us a week ago and will probably reach Richmond tomorrow and camp the next day, so that ere this reaches you, Jamie & you will have had a happy meeting. I cannot tell you how sorry I was that Jamie was obliged to leave us, or how sad I have felt ever since. Yet I know that duty called him away and that when the war is over both he and I will rejoice to think that he had acted well his part in it. Hope sustains me now and whispers in my ear that my dear sons will soon return to me unharmed and in honor.

I had the pleasure of receiving two kind and welcome favors from you lately—one dated 20th and the other the 10th of this month. The latter by Mr. Childress came after Jamie had gone which I regretted as you told him to exchange his money in Richmond for $5 bills. I hope however that he heard of it from some other source and got rid of the "bills" as his are not current. We have had some days of pleasant weather after Jamie left and then a cold rain set in which lasted 2 ½ days. Yesterday & today have been clear and cold. We have had heavy frost and it is feared our fruit has been killed. I am sorry as fruit is missed in such a hot climate as this is. I will have a large crop of melons planted which, I trust, will be enjoyed by you, Jamie & Biscoe. Many persons are of opinion that the war will close this year and some that it will end by July. If so, you will all be with us in time to eat melons, figs & etc. Willie rode to Greensboro two days last week to pay our taxes for this year, Col. Kerr having told Jamie that he would receive it at any time, if we would give him the amount due: this I did, but he put Willie off by saying that he hadn't time, as many were waiting upon him, who had not paid last year's taxes. I determined then to have our money funded, which will be rec'd for taxes at any future period. I rode over to see Dr. G yesterday afternoon, thinking he would tell me of someone going to Selma or Mobile. He said Mr. Sadler spoke of going and advised me to send to him. I thought it best to go, so I carried the money last evening to Mr. S who kindly said he would attend to it—$3000 including $100 belonging to John & $30 I got from Mary & one of the servants to make up that sum. I mentioned to Mr. S that I had two checks for cotton to be sold to the Government which I would like to convert into bonds. Early this morning before starting for Selma, he rode here to get the checks & he said he thought I might find some difficulty in having it done, and that it would afford him pleasure to attend to it for me. I appreciate Mr. Sadler's kindness very highly, and know it will be a relief to Jamie to hear that the business will be attended to before the 1st of April. I intended to send Willie to Selma with Mr. Enoch, who will be obliged to go there on business for himself. Tell Jamie I have just rec'd from Mr. Willingham the number of bushels of corn raised last year and will soon make a return to Mr. Snedecor. 16,000 bushels of corn were raised at the Canebrake, and 7,900 bushels at the Goodrum place. 500 lbs of meat were sold to the Government on Saturday last for which I rec'd $1000. Some of the meat from the Canebrake is also to be taken.

The children are all well. Mary & Icha have gone to visit the Dorroh's and may not return until tomorrow. Icha is on Racador & thinks he can ride any horse in the country. Willie is busily engaged in having the land prepared for sugar cane and Lou is busied about hens & eggs. I make her practice music every day and feel assured that she will be a proficient by the time she is grown up provided she has good teachers. I wish more and more every day that I could procure a good tutor for all. Can't you send me a crippled soldier—one who can no longer serve his country, and is qualified to teach. Mr. Perry wrote to the Sawyers that there were many in Va, who could be got as teachers and to know if Enoch wished one. Mrs. S said they would like to get a lady to teach in their family. What folly! I fear they will mismanage their affairs and come to want. Mr. Enoch is busily occupied in farming. I wish him success. He & the Dr often speak of you and send their love. Mr. Willingham says he is getting on very well in planting corn. He has no cotton seed to plant, all of it having been put up in a large bulk green has rotted. No seed can be purchased, and he requested me to ascertain if any can be got from the G. Place. I presume it can, as Mr. L was here on Saturday & said he would plant 20 or 30 acres of poor land, such as would not bring cotton. The steam engine is out of order & requires an engineer. There would be no use to send for one as white lead & India rubber would be wanted but cannot be got. I fear Mr. W will not remain with us after the first year expiration as his daughters dislike the Canebrake and are quite dissatisfied I am told. I think Mr. L has been with us long enough. If you agree with me, I will make an effort to get another. Dr. G says any other man would do better than L. I hope you & Jamie will be here to find overseers and install them. Wheat at the G.P. has all been killed. I have not heard of the wheat crop at the Canebrake. Ours is backward but looks well. I hope it will turn out well. My ink is so bad. I can scarcely write. All unite in warmest love to you & Jamie. May God bless & protect you both my dear sons, is my constant prayer.

Yr Mother

Remember us kindly to John. All the servants send how'dye.

Camp "290" near
Orange C.H., Va.
March 28th, 1864.

My dear Mama,

I will drop you a few lines this evening just to tell you that James has arrived here safely, and is very well, with the exception of a cold, a necessary consequence of a trip on the cars. I found him looking hearty and altered but very little except that his beard had grown a good deal since I saw him last. Tom did not come by as I hoped he would but went directly to his Regt as his furlough had expired. He and Jamie had a disagreeable time coming on, as the weather was cold—raining and snowing part of the time, and then they missed connections and had to lie over along the way, where you meet with the very meanest accommodations now. Jamie got here yesterday evening just a short while after I finished and mailed my letter to Mary, in which I stated that he had not come. I am delighted to see Jamie but would have been much happier to have met him at home in the midst of our beloved family. By an order from Gen. Lee, I can get a furlough now in consequence of Jamie's having come here as a recruit and although it will be a flying visit, still I feel anxious to go as I would have the inexpressible happiness of embracing once more my dear mother, sisters and brothers & of enjoying your sweet society though for a brief season. I think too, that I may be able to give you some assistance in business matters etc. I shall not go, though, until Jamie settles down & becomes accustomed to things here. He seems very well satisfied & says he finds us much more comfortably situated than he expected to see. He has several old acquaintances & school mates in the Co. Jamie will write you tomorrow. I must close and send this over to Division Hd-qrs in order that it will go off in the morning. Joe Grigg & Gilliam have come over to see Jamie. Please thank the Dr for his letter to me by Jamie. John sends howd'ye to all. Jamie unites with me in warmest love to you, my dear Mama and Mary, Willy, Lou and Icha. Adieu

Your affectionate son,
Sam

P.S. My letter blew in the fire just now, and came near getting burnt up.

S.P.

———•———

Umbria April 11th 64

My beloved Brother,

Your kind, interesting & welcome letter reached me on Saturday last & I will now endeavor to give you a short reply—altho' I am trying to write on this mean paper, but as it is Confederate, I cannot grumble. I as well as Mama, the children & servants are delighted at the thought of having you with us once more. How I wish dear Jemmie was to come with you. I miss him terribly & Mama is constantly sighing & wishing you both back. I went with Lou & Willie to Flat Woods church yesterday & heard Mr. Armstrong. Miss Iola Dorroh sat with me & I told her you were coming home. She said she was delighted to hear it & begged me to let her know when you arrived—which of course I promised to do. She says she misses Jemmie very much. Mr. Gayle Dorroh returned to the University of Ala on Thursday in the steamer "Sumpter." He says he will write to Jemmie as soon as he reaches Tuscaloosa. Mr. Dorroh paid Mama her first visit last Saturday week & altho' she was in a hurry Mama entertained her as agreeably that she staid much longer than she expected to. Tell Jemmie I have not returned Mrs. Bayol's visit yet. I wish I had him to go with me; but I expect to wait until you come. I have no doubt you are fond of visiting the ladies now, as you have been deprived of that pleasure so long.

Mama & I are going to Greensboro to-morrow & I intend to drop this letter in the P. Office there. I have not much opinion of the Hollow Square office now. Mr. Frank Robinson (Miss Eliza's brother) keeps it now & I hear does not attend to his duties faithfully.

Mat Sawyer, Icha & I took a very pleasant ride up the Hollow Square road this evening. I have not been well for two or three days & Mama says it is because I do not take exercise enough, so I intend getting up early to-morrow morning to walk. Mama has been wanting to visit the Canebrake for several months, but has put it off until the roads improve. I don't suppose she will go for some time now, as there are mumps on the place. Two concerts are to be given in Greensboro on the nights of the 15th & 16th. I wish you & Jemmie were here to attend them.

I am very sorry to hear how badly off for shoes you are so I hope you can get a pair to travel home in. We have a nice pair of boots for you & also a pair for cousin Tom. Do if you see him tell him that we have a pair for him or he will buy a pair before these reach him.

Did you get your box? I hope you did for I know you will enjoy eatables from dear old "Umbria."

Did you ever read "David Copperfield"? I have almost finished it & like it very much.

Mama is getting ready to go to bed so I must close.

Mama & all the children join me in warmest & dearest love to you, dear brother Sam & also to dear Jemmie. The servants send howdye to you, Jemmie & John. In the hopes of seeing you soon. I remain as ever my dear Brother your devoted sister.

Mary

P.S. Do brother Sam when you pass through Raleigh inquire about Dr. Smede's school. If it is good now & Mr. Handson & Miss Overton are still teaching. I must go somewhere to school & I prefer Dr. Smedes. Don't forget to inquire.

Your truly devoted sister

———◆··———

Camp 5th Ala., Regt
Near Orange C.H. Va.,
April 11, 1864

My dear Mother,

Since writing my last letter to you, which I mailed whilst at Raleigh, I have reached camp, and seen a little of the life of a soldier. In traveling I took a bad cold which annoyed me very much (being attended with a disagreeable cough) but from which I have almost recovered. I hope soon to be entirely relieved of it. We had a very fatiguing & disagreeable trip from Columbia to Richmond, & in fact, as far as Orange C.H., as the cars were very much crowded and we missed connections at every place, after leaving Columbia. From the latter place our only means of traveling was by a freight train, and consequently we made up [*unclear*] to going very slowly, as these trains never injure a track, seriously, by fast traveling. It snowed on the morning we left & turned very cold, but as there was no such thing as a stove aboard, we had to endure it. However, about mid day it grew so intensely cold that endurance proved no virtue, & necessity compelled us to seek some means of warming. Getting permission from the conductor, who by the way, was an exception to his class, to build a fire, we spread some moist sand in the middle of the car (a boxcar) and on this built a very comfortable fire. But having avoided Sylla, we came in contact with Charybdis. For after getting relieved of cold, we had to endure a regular smoking. If bacon had been in the car in which we rode, it would have been cured in that day's ride. It took us till that evening (Tues. 22nd ult.) to reach Chester, S.C. when we should have arrived at 12 o'clock that day. At this place we had to lay over all night and slept on board of the car 'till 8 o'clock the next morning. We, however, had plenty of time to wash the smoke & cinders from our faces & take a very good breakfast (the best we had had since leaving home) before proceeding on our way. We had, also, time to view the village of Chester, which is a very pretty little place indeed, as seen from the cars. The snow lay very thickly on the ground, & the tops of houses, branches of trees, etc. were covered with it also. The sun shining over the whole scene made a beautiful picture indeed. From Petersburg to Richmond we rode in a car crowded to overflowing with soldiers, & had no seats save for myself my carpetbag, & Tom his valise. Having no backs to our seats, we were very much fatigued on getting to Richmond, & part of the time had to stand in order to get rested. On getting to Orange we took it afoot on the plank road & were soon at our respective camps. I informed Mary of our trip from Richmond hither, so will not fatigue you with another recital of it.

By the time I had reached camp I was perfectly relieved as the fatigue & annoyances of travel were ended and there was some prospect of having a little rest. The Regt. was on picket when I got to camp, but Sam, Jack Wynne & others of our mess had been excused from picket duty and were in the cabin when I came. Sam was taken by surprise when he saw me as he was not expecting me so soon. He looked just as he did when he left home, altho' somewhat stouter & more robust. The breaches and vest which I brought on are a little too large for him, which inclined him to think that Mr. Joe's tale in regard to his size had produced an impression upon our minds at home & that we had imagined he was enormous. As I had a bad cold when I arrived at camp & the weather was cold & rainy, I got excused from duty until to-day, when I thought I would commence upon the duties of camp. So I went on guard & stood for two hours. I have been relieved for that time & at its expiration will have to go again for four hours, & so on tonight till tomorrow morning. It falls to each man's lot about once every week, to perform guard duty. There is really little use in it, at present, the army being in Winter quarters; but it is a formality which has to be observed in military organizations.

I saw the other day the father of our generals & the great old chieftain of our gallant & heroic army, the venerable Genl Robt E. Lee. He is a very fine looking & able old man & is beloved by the whole army & highly respected. He was riding down the plank road by himself & unattended by his usual retinue of staff officers & escort. I was much gratified & pleased on Frid. evening last, on seeing two letters one from Mary dated 27th & 28th & one from Louty, dated 23rd ult. From them we learned that all at Umbria were well. I hope that you & the children will continue to enjoy good health.

Sam requests me to say that he is much obliged to you for the kind letter which came to hand yesterday, dated 24th ult and will answer it very soon. Please tell Mary & Louty that I will answer them very soon, also.

Friday last, the 8th inst, was generally recognized by the soldiers as Fast-day & observed as such. Our mess observed the fast 'till the evening. We attended a prayer meeting held by Rev. Mr. [W. G.] Curry, Chaplain of this Regt, which was attended by a large crowd of soldiers. Mr Joe came up from headquarters and went with us. He desired me when I wrote to remember him kindly to you and all the children. I have been introduced to & have lately seen Col. Sam Pickens & his brother, Capt. Miles P and was very much pleased with both. They are very pleasant, gentlemanly & kind & seem to be warm friends of Sam's.

I shall anxiously await an answer to this letter, & we will constantly expect to hear from home as this will be our greatest & chiefest pleasure.

Sam joins me in warmest love to you Mary, Willie, Louty & Icha.

Accept, my dear Mother,
The love of your affectionate son,
James

P.S. John sends how d'ye to all.

P.S I was very glad to hear that an opportunity afforded for you to send your money before 1ˢᵗ April. Mr. S., is indeed very kind.

————————

On Picket at Cow's ford,
Rapidan River, Va.
April 22ⁿᵈ 1864

My dear Mama,

Your welcome & exceedingly interesting epistle came to hand on 13ᵗʰ inst., whilst I was in winter Quarters, and I would have answered it immediately on its reception, but having to move down to this place with the Regt, which was going on picket, was prevented from doing so.

We were roused at 6 o'clock on Wed. morning last, 20ᵗʰ inst, by reveille, and after roll call & breakfast, were marched down to this place, to relieve Genl. [Stephen Dodson] Ramseur's Brigade, which was doing picket duty here. It is about 11 miles from our Camp in Winter Quarters to this place & this was the first march of that distance that I have yet taken. However, it was comparatively easy, as the men were stopped three times on the way, to rest, which lightened the fatigue considerably.

Immediately on our arrival here, we struck our tents, built fires & made preparations for spending the night, thinking we would have to act only as reserves & that we could not be called on for duty until the next day, but on this we were mistaken, for we had no sooner commenced our preparations, than an order was recd for Battle's Brigade to relieve Ramseur's at once. So we were marched about a mile farther & details were made of men from the Regt to go on picket that evening. The detail only took eight from our Co., so I was left with Sam & Jack Wynne. We set to work & cleaned out a brush harbor, under which we were to sleep. It consists of two forks stuck in the ground, with a pole in the forks. On this, other poles are placed, with one end resting on the ground. On these poles brush is thickly laid, and after strewing the ground with the same & digging a trench around, the harbor is finished. We were quite tired after our march, particularly myself, who am not used to marching; and after a hearty supper, we spread our blankets & had quite a good night's rest. Last night was the second that I've spent in Camp sleeping almost on the ground. I am detailed this morning to do picket duty on post, which is on a high bluff commanding a view of the Rapidan (about 150 yds. below) and also of a valley on the other side of the river, & of the Blue Ridge Mts., in the distance. The valley is just beginning to look green & the general appearance of the country reminds me very much of the scenery around Charlottesville in the spring of 1860, when we were there. The Yankee videttes, riding from post to post over the river can be seen in the distance, and also their pickets, stationed at regular distances from each other. Very friendly relations used to exist between our pickets and those of the Yankees last year, & they would frequently meet & exchange papers & coffee & sugar, for tobacco & other things, but this has been prohibited by both parties & now our pickets never go across the river.

It is mournful to contemplate the news of desolation & ruin which are the consequences of this war. Just over the river may be seen a rich & fertile valley with green fields and meadows around and beautiful pastures, crowned here & there by stately dwellings, once the abodes of opulence & peaceful serenity & prosperity. Now, these residences are deserted & only await the hand of time to crumble to ruin; no longer are to be seen around them the faces of happy & contented inmates & to be heard the merry shout of joyous children, nor are the fields now filled with lowing herds & crops of grain & other cereals. All have departed! and now are only [*word unclear*] the marks of ruthless war! But this picture might be amplified & extended so as to fill volumes. It is needless to pursue it further. God grant that we may soon be visited with a speedy, just and an honorable peace & that we may soon enjoy again the blessings of prosperity & happiness, of which we were almost entirely [*unclear*] before this war. Heartily do we unite with you in the prayer that soon the war may close, and that we may all again be united together. You cannot imagine my dear mother how much I miss you & my dear sisters & brothers, nor how often I earnestly desire to be with you. If peace were declared & we were all together again, no pleasure would be greater to us no [*unclear*] on earth so dear. I trust that that pleasure may soon be enjoyed by us. If the news which we have just heard yesterday & today be true, and it is not probable that it is false, as it comes in an authentic form, we never have had greater cause for encouragement & hopes of a speedy end of the war. It is reported by Genl. Lee to Genl. Ewell, that Genl. Hoke in N.C. attacked some Yankee fortifications, capturing a Brigadier general, [*number unclear*] prisoners & twenty-five pieces of artillery.[14] This is very favorable to our cause. Also, the news this morning is that Genl. Banks (Yankee) has been again defeated in Louisiana, and [*number unclear*] prisoners captured from him. I trust is also true, but it needs confirmation.[15] Then we have Genl Forrest's successful attack on Ft. Pillow, with an unprecedented slaughter of its garrison, who at first refused to surrender.[16] He then carried it by assault, & it is stated that, out of the garrison, consisting of 700 men, 600 were killed. Every engagement in this campaign, so far, has resulted in decided favor & advantage to us, & in perfect discomfiture & defeat of the Yankee hordes. Surely the God of battles is with us & he is sending victory to our arms. May we not hope confidently that He will continue with us until the last; when the last battle shall have been fought, and that He will crown our cause & our arms with success? Our armies are better clothed, better fed, better equipped at present than they have ever been before. Moreover, they have been greatly augmented by the laws recently enacted by Congress. All have submitted (except in a few instances here & there) to the decrees calling them forth to battle & have entered the ranks cheerfully and in spirits. The morale of the Army is good, its discipline becoming more & more perfect, & with its

14. He was referring to the Battle of Plymouth, North Carolina. Under the command of Brigadier General Robert F. Hoke, a Confederate expedition against Union forces occupying Plymouth. See Durrill, *War of Another Kind*, 194–210.

15. James was probably referring to the Battle of Pleasant Hill in Louisiana, April 9–10, 1864, where Confederate forces more or less ended Nathaniel Banks's 1864 Red River campaign (Eicher, *The Longest Night*, 655–49, 657).

16. James did not mention that many of the troops killed had surrendered and were Black (McPherson, *Battle Cry of Freedom*, 748–49; Woodward, *Marching Masters*, 144–45).

prestige, gained in the past over many fields of glory [*word unclear*] added to the undaunted courage & bravery which animate it for the future, it may justly be called the greatest Army of modern times. Its leaders, too, are acknowledged by the world to be men of superior intellect & of fine military qualifications. Well may the Yankees approach it cautiously & take pains in placing before it their best Generals. Well may they make good their calculations; for here, at least, they are opposed by one of the greatest military tacticians of the age; the noble old General, Robert E. Lee, and by one of the most invincible armies of which the world can boast. We have every reason to be hopeful and encouraged that our cause will eventually triumph; and none why the most despondent should not take courage & cease to complain. It is the opinion of some of our wisest men, that if the coming campaign result in our favor, that the defeat of Lincoln as President for another term will be certain; and if this take place that an armistice and a truce of peace will be the result. In fact so general has this opinion become that there is not a soldier in the service who does not anticipate a peace by next fall.

God grant that none are wrong in this belief and that this year may see it verified! Oh, what happiness to [*unclear*] would it not produce, & what a day of general rejoicing will that be which ushers in peace! I anxiously long and ardently hope for it.

Sam is quite well & is at camp whilst I'm on post. He is now 1st Corporal of Co. D, & has only to post guards, has no post duty to perform. I learn that Henry Childress has just arrived at our camp (which is about ½ of a mile from our picket post), so I expect Sam is engaged in conversation with him & the others who are there.

He joins me in warmest love to you, my dear Mother, & to my dear sisters & brothers. He wrote to you on the 19th, last Tuesday. We are anxiously expecting letters from home telling us news of the health etc. of its dear inmates. We will write as often as circumstances will permit us.

I must close, as the mail will soon leave.

Ever your affectionate son,
James.

P.S. [*Unclear*] our kind regards to Dr. Grigg & family, to Mr. Enoch & family

& to all inquiring friends. I saw Mr. Joe & Gilliam James the other day, who are both quite well.

Tell the servants all how d'ye for us. John sends howd'ye to all.

———•—◆—•———

Camp 5th Ala. Regt.
Near Orange C.H.
April 30th '64

My dear Mary,

After spending a week on picket on the Rapidan, our Brigade returned to Winter Quarters three days ago. When we left here we did not expect to come back, as it was getting late in the season, the weather good, the roads dry, and nothing apparently to prevent military operations. We did receive orders one day while down there to be ready to move as the enemy was advancing on Germanna Ford. This proved a mistake, however, and we had no further excitement, but passed the time very pleasantly. Some would go fishing and occasionally catch a good size perch or a string of little cats and perch, but as a general thing it didn't pay for the trouble. We had a cannon ball there that we would throw for exercise, and also pitched quoits, jumped etc. Sometimes we'd go and hunt wild onions, which were pretty good when cooked up, or even eaten raw as shallots; but the objection to them is that they make the breath so very offensive that you can't bear to be in a tent with men who have been eating them. On that account I was glad to get away from the wild onion region, though they are very wholesome and the soldiers who live on meat & bread alone require some vegetable diet of the kind. Some of the boys, too, would amuse themselves with the rather cruel sport of hunting and killing field mice or rats. I don't know by what name they are called. There are none of them in Ala. They are larger than mice, are covered with a thick coat of fine, soft fur, have short legs and tails, large head, and look a good deal like a mole. They burrow in the ground, though not deep, and with bayonets the boys dug up a number of them. They are spiteful, brave little things & the boys would bring them to their tents & make them fight by holding them together and pinching their tails. Wasn't it mean. If you would turn one loose & run after him, he would rear up, show his teeth and snap at you; showing how brave & independent they are, but it seemed ridiculous to see such a diminutive little animal showing fight when attacks by such a monster, comparatively speaking, as a man.

Spring was just beginning to show itself in the beautiful valley of the Rapidan. The fields were becoming green with grass & clover, the fruit trees blooming, and other trees budding & unfolding their tender leaves to the balmy breezes & general sunshine. In Ala. you saw all this a month ago, no doubt although the Spring has been very late there. We had a very hot march of ten miles back to camp & were much fatigue and exhausted by it. Jamie stood the march very well, but was sore & stiff a day or two afterwards. We were all glad to get back here where we could take a bath & put on clean clothes, sleep in our straw bunks and have warm meals to eat twice a day. So we are doing finely now, tho' I wish our long expected box would come that we might have more meat, and all the other nice things that Mama & you & Lou fixed up at home for us. I'd never send anything by Express again.

You asked me if I had read David Copperfield—I have not, but would like to do so, as I am told it is very good. We get hold of very few books here, but I have read several interesting ones since we have been in Winter Quarters such as "Washington & his Generals," "Edge-hill," "No Name," "Aurora Floyd," "Romantic Passages in Southwestern history" by Judge A.B. Meek, of Ala., & that is about all.[17]

I'll not have the opportunity of making enquiries you desired concerning St. Mary's school. It is a great pity that you are not at some good school, but I do not think it would be prudent for you to go to Raleigh, for it might fall into the hands of the enemy. Mary, please tell Mama that I received a letter from her last evening & was very much obliged to her for it & will answer

17. *Edge-Hill, Or, The Family of the Fitzroyals: A Novel* was published in 1828 by a Virginian named James Ewell Heath. On Heath, see Tracy, *In the Master's Eye,* 49–50. *Aurora Floyd* by Mary Elizabeth Braddon and *No Name* by Wilkie Collins are both mid-nineteenth-century English sensation novels. *Washington and His Generals: Legends of the Revolution,* by George Lippard, was first published in 1847 and then reprinted as part of the hundred-year celebration of the Declaration of Independence. *Romantic Passages in Southwestern History* was published in Mobile by S. H. Goetzel in 1857.

it soon. Dr. Grigg's certificate was enclosed in it. We are much indebted to the Dr for sending it. Let me tell you of a sad spectacle we were called out to witness day before yesterday. It was the execution of three deserters from a Co. in the 4th No. Car. Regt. They were made to kneel down & were tied to stakes, blindfolded and then shot to death with musketry. 'Twas an awful sight, indeed, but it is astonishing what little effect it seemed to have upon most of those who beheld it. A few more years of war would give the soldiers hearts of stone. Well I must bring this to a close. Jamie says tell Mama he rec'd her letter of the 15th & will reply to it in a few days. He joins me in best love to dear Mama, Willy, Lou, John & yourself. Give my kind regards to all friends & remember me to all the servants. John sends howd'ye to all the family. He is very anxious to hear from Suky. Write very soon again to

Your affectionate brother,
Saml Pickens.

———— • ————

Camp 5th Ala. Regt.,
Near Orange C.H., Va.,
May 2nd 1864

My dear Mama,

Your last long, affectionate & highly interesting letter was handed me the other day just as we reached this place on our return from picket duty near the Rapidan R. You cannot imagine, my dear mother, how much gratification and pleasure the perusal of your letter afforded me, telling as it did, of the health of our dear mother, sisters & brothers, & conveying the latest news from home & the dear ones there.

We were exceedingly tired after the fatiguing march of ten miles from the Rapidan, & only felt partially relieved & more comfortable after we had taken a bath & put on clean clothes. As I was not used to such a long walk, I felt very sore in my joints & limbs for several days afterwards. Sam did not suffer in this way, but complained of sore feet, as the shoes which he wore were a pair of those which Tood Cowin brought on, & being of Stickney's make & quite rough, they galled his feet very much.

The day after our return to camp we were called upon to witness a very heart-sickening & melancholy sight—the execution of three deserters from some No. Ca. Regt (the 4th, I think). There were present on the occasion ten regiments, armed & drawn up in lines around three sides of a square space, about 200 or 300 yds in area. After the troops had all been thus arranged, two ambulances, strongly guarded, came slowly up with a band of music in front playing the "Dead march," a very solemn part of the ceremony. They were halted on the open side of the above square, the unfortunate men lead out, (their arms tied behind them), to three stakes. They then knelt for a few minutes, in prayer with a minister, ere their souls were launched into an unknown eternity. Oh what must have been their thoughts at this moment, when about to leave forever on earth, the sight of friends, home & a spring adorned world!

After this, an officer of the provost guard stepped forward, & tied, each to a stake, the three men as they knelt by them. He then blind folded them & gave separately, the commands, "Ready!" "Aim!" "Fire!" and in a few seconds more the whole that remained of three animate beings on earth, was their lifeless, ball-riddled bodies, whilst their souls were wafted into an unknown eternity & into the presence of their maker! 'Twas a sight entirely novel to me, & surpasses in the awful aspect of its nature, the gallows. I felt a mixed sensation of sickness & horror, after the volley of musketry was fired, & was glad when we formed into line & marched away from the scene of the unpleasant occurrence. General Ramseur, who, I think, commands the Regt to which these men belonged, was, it is said, much affected by the sight. He shed tears & made an earnest appeal to his Brigade never again for any of them to suffer himself thus to be shot. He hoped never again to see one of his brave men perish in this ignoble and ignominious manner.

It seems singular that after hearing or seeing such a sight that one could have the face to desert, & yet it is so. It is a stern law that compels so summary & terrible a punishment, & yet it is necessary, in the discipline & morale of the army.[18]

18. For a discussion of the evolution of Confederate policy regarding desertion see Carmichael, *The War for the Common Soldier*, chap. 5.

The letter which you wrote me previous to your last, & which you thought had not reached me, I received & wrote a reply to it, but suppose you have never received it, as such great irregularity prevails in the management of the mails.

Sam received your last letter to him, dated 30ᵗʰ ult., which contained the Dr's certificate of my health, etc. Please tell the Dr that I am much obliged to him for sending it. If we make no movement soon I will make an application, through Dr. Hill (our surgeon) for a detail. We are now under marching orders. A report came this morning saying that Burnside with 25,000 men (of which 8,000 are negroes) has reinforced Grant, and an order was received from Genl Battle to the Brigade for them to be ready to march at a moments warning. Where we will go when we leave here, I have no idea; but it is presumable that we will go to Raccoon or Morton's Fords.

I sincerely trust, notwithstanding, that I may succeed in getting a detail, & that soon I may be again with you all, to render to you the poor assistance, that I may possess, in your business affairs. I was extremely sorry, my dear mother, that I was compelled to leave you, as I knew how disagreeable it always was to you, to attend to business; and if I had had any reasonable length of time in which to act would have made endeavors to have secured a detail to attend to it for you. But I had to act precipitately, & furthermore, knew nothing in regard to the nature or specifications of the several exemptions which were passed sub sequent to the enrollment of the men who had before been exempted on account of substitution. I now see that I could easily have obtained the detail or exemption by waiting but the day on which I went to Eutaw I was perfectly ignorant of the fact. Sam contemplated paying you all a visit, when I first came on, but hearing that the furlough would only be for 30 days & that at least fifteen days of this time would be devoted to traveling, allowing only a few days for him to remain at home, he concluded that it would be better to wait. I know what a great pleasure it would be to him to visit our dear Mother, sisters & brothers again & be welcomed by them to our dear home, the most blessed spot on earth to us; but the short, fleeting period which the time spent there would seem to him, even were it to consume months, would soon fly by & then the sorrow & pain of again parting would rise as a great barrier in the way of his joy & happiness.

I humbly trust in God that I may be able to be with you very soon again, and Sam also; but if I should not succeed I trust to Him to grant us deliverance out of all the dangers through which we may pass, & eventually a reunion with our dear Mother sisters & brothers, in peace & happiness!

I must now close as the mail is soon to leave & I fear my letters may not go with it. Excuse all mistakes, as I wrote in a great hurry & very carelessly.

EIGHT

The Shadow
of Death

MAY–DECEMBER 1864

During the night of May 5, Company D received orders to pack and be ready to move at dawn the next day. Early on the morning of May 4, the Confederate Army began to shift east to defend against what Lee believed would be a Union assault on his right flank. The Union Army, then under the command of General U. S. Grant, had begun to cross the Rapidan late on May 3 but had paused near the Wilderness Tavern to allow supply trains to close up. Getting into the Wilderness ahead of Grant was essential, for Lee planned to take advantage of the dense woods there to offset the Union Army's advantages in men and firepower. After a day of hard marching, the Fifth stopped for the night near Locust Grove, along Wilderness Run.[1]

The next day the movement continued to the northeast, along the Orange Turnpike. Rodes and General Jubal Early's division followed General Edward "Allegheny" Johnson's toward the Wilderness Tavern with orders to avoid battle until General James Longstreet's corps joined them. James wrote in his diary that the column moved slowly and stopped frequently until forming a line of battle between 1:00 and 2:00 o'clock to support John M.

1. Captain J. W. Williams, "Pen Sketches of the Greensboro Guards, Co. D, of Fifth, Alabama, C.S.A," originally appeared in the *Greensboro Record,* June–July, 1903. Copy of the series of articles can be seen in "History of the Fifth Alabama Infantry Regiment," Confederate Regimental History Files, Alabama Dept. of Archives and History. Collins, *Major General Robert E. Rodes,* 344–46.

Jones's brigade, which had unexpectedly encountered the Union Fifth Corps. Rodes placed Battle's brigade behind Jones, whose line soon collapsed. Battle's brigade attempted to fill the gap in the confusion created by Jones's fleeing troops. But Battle's men soon gave way as well and, James wrote in his diary, he "retreated & with them I returned, being almost exhausted." The brigade soon regrouped and joined a counterattack that restored the Confederate line. Terrified and physically ill, about an hour later, James returned to Company D and nervously awaited another Union assault.[2]

There was little fighting along the Fifth Alabama's sector on the 6th and 7th, a welcome respite, Sam wrote his mother, after the fierce fighting in the Wilderness. Expecting orders to move, and alarmed by James's mental and physical condition, Sam secured a permit for his brother to go to a field hospital about two miles behind the Confederate breastworks, where James reported to Dr. Thomas Hill.[3] According to James, the doctor was "surprised" that he had gone into battle and "advised" him to remain with him. James described symptoms that at the time suggested that he suffered from a form of homesickness called "nostalgia" then classified in medical literature as a "mental disorder." DeWitt C. Peters, a U.S. Army doctor, described the condition in 1868 as "a species of melancholy, or a mild type of insanity, caused by disappointment and a continuous longing for home." The symptoms, he wrote, included "great mental dejection, loss of appetite, indifference to external influences, irregular action of the bowels, and slight hectic fever."[4]

2. Collins, *Major General Robert E. Rodes*, 344–46.

3. Thomas C. Hill, the regimental surgeon (National Park Service, *Civil War Soldiers and Sailors System*).

4. Peters, "Remarks on the Evils of Youthful Enlistments and Nostalgia," 75–76; Bartholow, "The Various Influences Affecting the Physical Endurance." There was debate about the relationship between physical and psychological symptoms. Some argued that the depressed mental state of the soldier caused behaviors that led to physical symptoms, while others believed that dysentery, typhoid, and other camp diseases, in most cases, exacerbated soldiers' psychological distress. For the history of nostalgia as a disease, see Starobinski, "The Idea of Nostalgia," 81–103; O'Sullivan, "The Time and Place of Nostalgia," 626–49; Lande, *Psychological Consequences of the American Civil War*, 14–16; Anderson and Anderson, "Nostalgia and Malingering in the Military During the Civil War," 156–60; Anderson, "Dying of Nostalgia," 247–82; Matt, *Homesickness*, 90–97; Sommerville, "'A Burden Too Heavy to Bear,'" 465–67, and *Aberration of Mind*, 33–36; Dean, *Shook over Hell*, 129–30; Clarke, "So Lonesome I Could Die," 253–54.

James was transferred to Howard Grove Hospital in Richmond. The hospital, he wrote in his diary and his letter to his mother, was located about a mile from the city, on a hill, shaded by large oaks and pines. He described the ward he occupied as clean and orderly, and none of the men there suffered from serious physical wounds. Judging from James's description, the treatment he and the others in the ward received was what the medical literature of the day prescribed for sufferers of "nostalgia." Medical staff attempted to create a peaceful, relaxing environment evoking the home "nostalgics" longed for.[5]

On the morning of May 8, the Fifth broke camp and began moving toward Spotsylvania Courthouse to counter Grant's renewed attempt to flank Lee. The Fifth advanced to join General Richard Anderson's division, then fighting off an assault by the Union Third Division, V Corps, a position on the left leg of a bulge in the Confederate line called the Mule Shoe. Grant, after withdrawing from the Wilderness, had moved southeast in an attempt to place the Union Army between the Army of Northern Virginia and Richmond, north of Spotsylvania Courthouse. On May 10, Grant ordered an attack on the left of the Mule Shoe, believing that was the most vulnerable part of the Confederate line. Leading the Union attack was a brigade of the Union Sixth Corps led by Colonel Emory Upton. Upton's plan was to strike a sector defended by Brigadier General George Pickens. Upton's attack broke through the Confederate line, but after a series of counterattacks, including one by the Fifth Alabama, the Confederates closed the gap and turned back multiple Union assaults the next day. During the battle, Sam contracted a severe case of diarrhea. When James found Sam at the hospital, he was shocked by the extent of Sam's physical deterioration during what Sam described as the most intense fighting of the war.[6]

Mary Gaillard and the family again anxiously waited for news from James, Sam, and Tom Biscoe, knowing that the fighting in Virginia had re-

5. Walsh, "Cowardice Weakness or Infirmity," 492–526; Linderman, *Embattled Courage,* 166–67; McPherson, *For Cause and Comrades,* 76–81.

6. Diary of James Pickens, May 6–10, 1864; General Ewell's report, *OR,* ser. 1, vol. 36, pt. 1: 1070; *Greensboro Record,* August 6, 1903; Hubbs, *Guarding Greensboro,* 180–85; Collins, *Major General Robert E. Rodes,* 352–57; Rhea, *The Battles for Spotsylvania Court House and the Road to Yellow Tavern,* 161–75.

sumed and was, according to accounts they read in the newspaper, the worst of the war. As Sam had indicated, mail service had been disrupted, so for weeks all the family knew was that the Confederate Army had repeatedly repulsed determined Union assaults against Confederate defenses. Reports from the front were not reassuring, though, for the cost to both armies in men killed and wounded seemed greater than in other campaigns. Because the letters that Mary Gaillard and her children wrote to Sam and James during this period did not survive, it is not clear when the family learned they were safe and in the hospital. We do know from James's diary that the family learned about the death of Tom Biscoe at the Wilderness on May 5 from men in his company. Neither Sam nor James knew of Tom's fate, it appears, before June 12, when two men from Tom's unit brought them the news and gave them the obituary that was to be published the next day in the *Richmond Examiner.* Biscoe had been killed in fighting north of Saunders Field during the afternoon of the first day of the Battle of the Wilderness.[7]

As Mary and her mother described in their letters to Sam, Mary fell into a deep depression, struggling to come to terms with Tom's death. A few days after learning of Tom's fate, Sam wrote a condolence letter to Mary. In it he sought to ease her suffering the only way he knew, by assuring her that, though she suffered, she must not doubt that Tom's loss was the will of God and part of his providential plan, and to offer guidance about how she should understand her loss and move on from it. Tom had died honorably, he wrote, fighting for a good cause, "gallantly" leading his men, among whom he was "beloved." With the relics he sent—a lock of hair, a Bible that Mary had given to Tom, and Tom's obituary—Sam observed a practice at the time intended, as historian Drew Faust argues, "to make tangible a loss known only through the abstractions of language."[8]

Sam's letters between June and September outlined the movements of Company D during Early's raid into Maryland and subsequent campaign to clear the Union Army under the command of General Philip Sheridan from the Shenandoah Valley. Rodes's division engaged Union troops

7. Biscoe's death, CMSR, Louisiana, RG 109, roll 0148.

8. Faust, *This Republic of Suffering*, 28–29; Mays, "'If Heart Speaks not to Heart,'" 377–400. In the letter, Pickens carefully followed the rules for the condolence letter described by Faust and Mays.

probing Confederate lines near Bunker Hill, Berryville, Shepherdstown, and Martinsburg. Sam admitted that the constant marching and skirmishing in miserable weather wore soldiers down but that was just life in the army, he assured his mother, and he was well. He did not mention the shortages of food, clothing, and shoes that had also become typical of the life of Confederate soldiers. Yet, as Sam had suggested in his letter, morale remained high, when, on September 18, Rodes's division moved to Stephenson's Depot, after several days spent pursuing Union crews allegedly repairing a nearby railroad line. The next day, Sheridan, seeing that Early's command was divided and outnumbered, ordered an attack all along the Confederate front across the Berryville Pike, held by General Stephen Ramseur's division. The Union assault soon threatened to turn the left of the Confederate line. Rodes's and General John Gordon's divisions rushed to the front to block the Federal advance. Battle's brigade led a counterattack and temporarily pushed Union forces back. But renewed Union attacks on Battle's flanks forced the Confederates to withdraw and, that afternoon, Union cavalry successfully turned the Confederate left. Once they heard firing in their rear, Early reported, the Confederate line collapsed in confusion. Soon thereafter, the Confederates retreated through Winchester and would regroup the next day at Fisher's Hill.[9] For Sam, however, the Valley Campaign was over. During the intense fighting of this third Battle of Winchester, a piece of shrapnel struck him in the head. After reaching Fisher's Hill, Colonel Samuel Pickens took Sam to a "country" house, where he awaited transportation back to Howard's Grove Hospital.[10]

Soon after writing this letter, Sam's request for a furlough so he could recuperate at home was approved. He left for Alabama sometime during the first week or two of October and stayed until mid-November. James had

9. Early's Report, *OR,* ser. 1, vol. 43, pt. 1: 554–55; *Memoirs of Henry Beck, 1864–1865,* typescript in the Atlanta History Center Collection; Diary of Captain R. E. Park, 25–26; Glatthaar, *General Lee's Army,* 430–31; Collins, *Major General Robert E. Rodes,* 401–2; Eicher, *The Longest Night,* 746–48; 407–10; Murray and Hsieh, *A Savage War,* 407–10. For a detailed account of the third battle of Winchester and the Confederate retreat, see Patchan, *The Last Battle of Winchester,* chaps. 15–20.

10. Patchan, *The Last Battle of Winchester,* chaps. 15–20. Robert Rodes was killed in the fighting on the 19th. Cullen Battle took command of the division, and Colonel Samuel Pickens replaced Battle as brigade commander.

returned earlier on a medical leave, so for a month, the family was whole again. For Mary Gaillard, the time was like a dream she had a year earlier about Sam's return and ended the same sorrowful way, with Sam leaving. She wrote of a war that had broken up her family and longed for it to end, even if it meant she had to sacrifice all her "worldly" possessions. She was trapped in a nearly incapacitating emotional dilemma, for the war to defend the life her family had always enjoyed threatened to destroy it. As always, she sought comfort in her faith that God controlled events and prayed that his plan would bring "independence" to the Confederacy and the end of the war. But, as she and James wrote, they assumed the war would continue for some time to come and began planning a move to Tuscaloosa, where they would be safer from the diseases that afflicted Greene County every summer and where the younger children could attend school.

‖‖‖

Richmond, Va.,
May 17th 1864

My dear Mother:

A few days since I wrote you a letter, just before the late battles, I think, and fearing that you may not have received it, and also knowing your anxiety since that exist on Sam's & my own account, I hasten to pen a few lines to you to impart to you the latest news from us.

Sam, I am thankful to the watchful providence of our heavenly Father, has passed thro' all the recent dangers on the Rapidan, and is unhurt. He was very well, when I last heard from him, tho' a good deal fatigued from the hard work which had to be performed such as throwing up breastworks, felling & sharpening timber for abattis, etc., etc. (I do not remember if this last word is spelt with one or two b's.) I was so much exhausted after our long march from Winter Quarters that I only took part in the opening of the fight, as I before mentioned. We marched at least twenty miles on Wednesday the 4th inst., and encountered the enemy the next day, after a march of some five or six miles farther, at Locust Grove, where the Thursday evening's battle was fought. I was never more fatigued in my life before. The long & continuous marching that we had undergone was more than I was able to bear, and although I endeavored to keep in ranks when the charge on the Yankees was ordered, after Jones' Brigade was driven back, I found it impossible to do so; moreover I was quite unwell. So I fell back to the rear and remained with the guard 'till I happened to meet Mr. Joe Grigg, who kindly invited me to spend the night on a part of his blanket which I did. We bivouacked at Genl. Rodes Hd. Quars until six o'clock the next (Frid.) morning, when I proceeded to our field hospital & remained with our Surgeon, Dr. Hill, and have been with him up to the time I left for this place. Last Friday, the 13th inst., Dr. H made arrangements to send off the sick & wounded to local hospitals, and on Sat morning we arrived at Guinea's Station. We were sent from the field to Guinea's in wagons. We remained at this station 'till 1 or 2 o'clock in the evening, when the train from Richmond arrived. We then took passage on a freight car (similar in some respects to the one in which Tom Biscoe and I rode from Columbia) and got to Richmond at 4 o'clock on Sun morning, 13th inst. We were taken from the train to the receiving & distributing hospital & remained there 'till six o'clock when we were sent to this place, Howard Grove hospital. It is situated on a commanding hill in the suburbs of the city, & is built under large & shady oaks & pines. The wards are layed off in rows & at regular distances from each other, are neatly built, whitewashed & plainly tho' nicely furnished. Everything in & around the houses is kept in the best order & cleanliness prevails everywhere. It is, upon the whole, a great treat to get from where everything is just the reverse, especially when one is not very well, and enjoy a little relaxation & ease. I am afraid that the Dr's prediction will be fulfilled. It has only been a short time since I commenced the arduous duties of soldiering & I'm already in a hospital. I feel perfectly confident of my utter incapacity to perform the said duties & consider one of the most foolish acts of my life that of having entered the service. Dr. Hill advised me not to try the hardships of military service any longer, as he said he did not think I could undergo them; but I can do nothing else, unless I can procure a detail, and this is impossible whilst an active campaign is in progress. He told me I had better come to this place and rest. But there is no use to complain—I will try and see what I can do in order to better my situation. It is astonishing how much fatigue and exposure Sam endures. I do not know how he does to keep up under it. After the fatigues & hardships of Thursday & Friday at Locust grove they marched at least twenty miles on Frid night & Sat to a point farther down to our right [*Rest of letter is missing.*]

In line of battle near
Mine Run, Virginia
May 7th 1864

My beloved Mother,

Our Brigade was in the battle of the 5th inst. and thank God Jamie and I both came out safely. A most merciful and beneficent Providence in answer to the constant fervent prayers of our dear good Mother watched over us and shielded us from all harm. We were under a heavy and dangerous fire, though not long, and our loss was not severe. In the Regt there were five men killed, twenty eight wounded and forty eight missing; and in our Co none killed, four wounded—Bayley, Bridges, Farrier & Hairsman; and three missing—Sergt. Thomas Ward, Martin & Youngblood. None of your acquaintances have been hurt or captured. I have not heard from Tom Biscoe yet, but hope that he is safe. We left our Winter quarters on the morning of the 4th and marched all day & being very warm it fatigued & worried Jamie exceedingly. On the 5th we were in the battle and that night as Jamie was completely exhausted and had been unwell all day he was sent back to the hospital. I can't express to you how much anxiety and uneasiness I felt at Jamie's going into battle with me; nor how much relieved I was at his going back to the hospital that night. Yesterday we lay behind our breastworks which we constructed the night before & there was no fighting on our part of the line, though skirmishing was kept up all day. On the right and left there was hard fighting most of the day & it is said Gen. Longstreet drove the enemy some distance & captured a number of prisoners. To-day the enemy have made frequent demonstrations in our front, and we have been expecting to be attacked all the while. Since I have been writing this short and hurried letter I have been several times interrupted by having to jump into our works on account of our skirmishers being driven back & the Yankees threatening to charge upon us. We have a good position along here & have strengthed our fortifications again to-day, so it is not probable that they will try this point. Our loss in Generals, I hear, is heavy. Heth (Maj. Gen) & Brig. Gens Jones & Pegram are reported killed and Lt. Gen. Longstreet & Brig. Gens. Stafford & Jenkins wounded.[11] I hope Gen. L will recover for his death would be a serious loss to us. Col. Brown, Chief of Artillery in Ewell's Corps, was killed while standing in our Regt yesterday.[12] The enemy have suffered so that I hope they will give it up & retire very soon, & that this terrible battle will be over & that it may be the last of the war. God grant it may be so, and that Jamie & I may soon return in safety & be reunited with our dear Mother, sisters & brothers. I'll try and write again soon & will tell you more of these stirring scenes through which we are passing. Joe Grigg sends his kindest regards to you all. He & Gilliam James are very well—also Jack Wynne. I suppose Jamie has written or will write to you by the first mail. I don't know that my letter will go off to-day. Please give my warmest love to all the children & accept for yourself the same. Give my kind regards to all friends, & write to me very soon. Hoping that you are all well & happy.

I am as ever,
Your truly devoted son,
Saml Pickens

---

11. Here Sam was writing about the Battle of the Wilderness. He was referring to Major General Henry Heth; Brigadier General Leroy Augustus Stafford, commander of the Second Brigade of General Edward "Allegheny" Johnson's division; Brigadier General John Pegram, a brigade commander in Early's division; Brigadier General Micah Jenkins; and Brigadier General John M. Jones, also a brigade commander in Early's division. Of the three rumored to have been killed, only Jones died. Longstreet, Pegram, and Jenkins were wounded. Jenkins later died from his wounds. See Eicher, *The Longest Night*, 665–70.

12. Colonel John Thompson Brown.

In line of battle near Spotsylvania C.H.
May 16th 1864

My dear Mama,

I will take advantage of the little rest and quiet that we are enjoying today, and write you a few lines just to inform you of my safety. Yes, by the infinite blessings of Almighty God I have been shielded from all harm during the series of desperate battles through which we have passed from the 5th inst to the present time. This has been the battle of the war. In duration and in the stubborn, terrible fighting, and the awful carnage, it has far exceeded all previous battles.[13] I trust it is over now and that the enemy will recross the river. Beauregard has been fighting them near Richmond & has, I hope, driven them away. We have been blessed with signal success in all quarters—Price over Steele,[14] Kirby Smith over Banks,[15] Imboden and Breckenridge in the Valley of Va—and now I trust that Grant has suffered sufficiently and will retire, and that the war will come to a close.[16] God grant it may be so! And that Jamie and I ere long in peace and the independence of our country may be restored to our beloved Mother, sisters and brothers at our dear old homestead. I wrote to you on the 7th after our first battle, and suppose that Jamie has written frequently since, but I fear that you have not been able to hear from us. Telegraphic dispatches have been sent to Greensboro after every fight giving the casualties in the Co but it is probable that none went through, for it is said that the railroad & telegraph between here and Richmond & below Richmond were out & in the possession of the enemy for some length of time. So I am afraid that you have suffered great anxiety on our account. Jamie went to the field hospital the night after the first engagement on the 5th and remained there till the 14th, when he, Capt. Williams and others were sent to General Hospital at Charlottesville, I think. Our C has been very fortunate indeed—none killed, three

13. Rhea, *The Battles for Spotsylvania Court House and the Road to Yellow Tavern*, 161–75.

14. Sam may have been referring to General Sterling Price's repulse of an advance by Union General Frederick Steele in Arkansas. Price was the commander of the District of Arkansas. See McPherson, *Battle Cry of Freedom*, 722–23.

15. McPherson, *Battle Cry of Freedom*, 722–23. General Kirby Smith turned back Nathaniel Banks's Red River campaign.

16. Major General John C. Breckinridge defeated a Union force commanded by Franz Sigel at the Battle of New Market, May 15, 1864. General John D. Imboden was a cavalry commander at the battle. See Williamson and Hsieh, *A Savage War*, 426–28.

severely wounded, seven slightly wounded and four missing. Col. Hall lost his right arm & Lt. Col. Hobson wounded in thigh. William James received a pretty severe [*unclear*]. Joe Grigg is unhurt & very well. Col. Pickens was wounded in the shoulder—not seriously, though. I have not heard from Tom Biscoe, but am in hopes that he is safe. Our loss in General & field officers has been very heavy. We have had a trying time but I trust it is almost at an end, and may the Lord continue to bless us with success so that our enemy, having failed at all points in this its grandest effort to subjugate us, may see the folly & wickedness of his ways, and be willing to let us alone and make peace with us. I did not finish my letter yesterday and continue to scribble to May 17th thinking that I would write it over, but it is doubtful now when we will get an opportunity to send a mail off, & much more doubtful whether it will ever go through, so I will let it stand as it is, humbly trusting that the war will soon be over and that we may be all spared to have a joyful reunion.

I remain as ever,
Your truly devoted son
Sam.

Remember me kindly to all friends & give my warmest love to my dear sisters and brothers, & accept for yourself the same

———•———

Richmond, Va.
May 25th 64

My dear Mama,

I will [be] able to drop you only a few lines tonight to inform you where & how I am, as there is a Mr. Broadnax who is going to start in the morning for Eutaw, Ala & will take letters for us. I arrived here late this evening & am very comfortably situated at the Ala. Soldiers' Home. I will report to Howard Grove Hospital tomorrow morning where Jamie is staying & we will have the pleasure of being together.[17] I have been very unwell with diarrhea for a week

17. It is not clear what the Alabama Soldier's Home was. Around Richmond there were medical facilities dedicated to the care of soldiers from specific regiments and states. How-

but was sent to the Hospital at Hanover only day before yesterday after we had marched to that place. I recd no attention whatever there; they gave me no medicine & nothing in the way of diet, so I did not improve of course. The surgeon came around this morning examining us & sent me & a few others out of our Department (convalescents) to this city. We were put on the train early in the day, etc. but did not get here till just before night. Capt. Williams & Lt. Chas. Pegues are at this establishment, Ala. Sol. Home, & Capt. W says Jamie was here to see him today, & is getting on very well.[18] I brought John down with me today & our carpet bag with Jamie's & my clean clothes. I had a good bath & changed clothes the first thing after getting here—am in a comfortable room with good bed & gas light & feel a thousand per cent better already. I expect to be with Jamie tomorrow & we will write to you regularly. Jamie has done so, I've no doubt, all the time, & also sent several telegraphic dispatches—all of which I hope reached you & spared you all anxiety on our account. I am very anxious to hear from home—have had only one letter from there since this long campaign opened—& that was recd 2 days since from Willie & was dated away back in April. Joe Grigg, Gil. James & Jack Wynne left quite well yesterday. I think I will improve rapidly now that I can obtain proper diet & medicine & will be comfortably situated. Earnestly trusting that you, my dear Mama, & Mary, Willie, Lou & Icha are all enjoying food health, & begging that you will all accept my warmest affections, I am as ever

Your devoted son,
Sam

———————•◆•———————

ard's Grove had been established near a picnic area and park around 1862 ("Howard's Grove Hospital," *Civil War Richmond*).

18. Charles Pegues was from Dallas County and was the adjutant for the Fifth Alabama. He was admitted to Howard's Grove on May 16, apparently for treatment of a wound he received at Malvern Hill nearly two years earlier that caused him, according to his medical record, "constant pain." Later in 1864, near Fisher's Hill during the Valley Campaign, he was wounded again. Subsequently a medical board ruled him unfit for field service. See CMSR, Alabama, RG 109.

Howard Grove Hospital
Near Richmond, Va.,
May 29th 64

My dear Mother,

I wrote a few lines to Louty and mailed the letter day before yesterday; today I will endeavor to inform you, in a few lines, of events as they have transpired since then. On the morning of that day, after breakfast and whilst I was lying on my little bed (about the size of a cot) reading, Capt. Williams, who had walked over from the city with Mr. Paul Lavender to see me & some others of our Co. who are at this place, conveyed the pleasing intelligence to me that Sam arrived at the house in which the Capt too was staying the night before. So immediately after the Capt. & Mr. L had finished their visit at the Hospital & set out to return to the city, I went with them. I found Sam looking much thinner than when I had last seen him, & a good deal worsted & exhausted from continuous working & marching, not to mention hard fighting, which he had gone through during the series of battles which have lately taken place in the Army of No. Va. I was extremely glad that Sam came to rest & to recuperate, as I feared that he would try to endure more than physically he could stand, in his weak state. He came over with me to this Hospital & is near the ward in which I stay, in a tent, but up amongst a number of others for the accommodation of the sick & wounded when the wards are full. I was very sorry that my ward was full & that Sam could not get in it, as it would be so much more pleasant for both of us, to be together; but after making inquiries of the two Surgeons who attended on us, as to getting Sam transferred & receiving no satisfaction, I had to wait 'till this evening to make another attempt & was disappointed then in finding that another man had taken the only vacant bed in this ward. So we will have to wait 'till another change is made & another vacancy occurs, when I hope we may be able to stay here together. Sam is better than he was when he first arrived in the city, but is still weak. I wish he would make an attempt to get a furlough, and recuperate at home, where there are so many little delicacies & luxuries to be had suitable for weak and exhausted nature. And then the pleasure of being at home, having been absent for so long a time, & then separated from dear mother, sisters and brothers, with the change of air, scenery etc. etc., would have a re-energizing, strengthening, soothing effect and he would soon improve under those stimulants.

The constant excitement, added to the other sources of fatigue & exhaustion, which the mind passes through during an active campaign, should, I think, tend as much to relax one's energy & physical powers, as bodily labor; and consequently, a change such as I have mentioned above, to a place of such entirely different scenes and occupations would revivify and strengthen that energy & those powers & restore them to their natural capacity much sooner. How I wish we could both visit our dear Mother, sisters & brothers, and remain at dear home until perfectly recovered! What pleasure and happiness would this not afford us! God grant, tho' that, if we do not succeed in going there, soon peace may be concluded with us for all generations, and that that joy, happiness, independence, & national prosperity which we used to enjoy so bountifully they again bless us. Then, when the marshaled hosts shall have been disbanded and sent with joyful hearts to enjoy the peace their heroic sacrifices & stalwart arms have gained, through God's favor & guidance, may we be united together again and return to our dear home no more to be separated! I earnestly trust that the time is not far distant when the hearts of our enemies shall be changed towards us, and when in the language of a beautiful prayer, "men shall learn war no more," and shall cease this cruel strife, &, recognizing in the signal defeats of all their spasmodic and Herculean efforts & plans to subjugate us, the hand of God in our affairs, be at length compelled to render to us the rights and acknowledgements to which we are so justly entitled. From the great defeat which the Northern soldiery have met with at our hands in all parts of our Confederacy where they have joined issue in battle this spring, & the great hopes which we can reasonably entertain in regard to their next presidential contest, added to the bankrupt state of their financial affairs, from all these & many other causes, we may strongly hope and firmly believe that this campaign is the last of their various futile attempts, if we are favored of Heaven in the future as we most certainly have been at all times in the past, & resist successfully this last gigantic effort of a base & wicked nation, then speedy, just and glorious peace with all its attributes waits in the future. May God be with us in all the dangers & trials which may rise in subsequent enactments of this great drama, and finally crown our arms with signal triumph & success & bless our country with a glorious and heavenly peace as a reward for all of the hardships & sacrifices which we have now endured for a space of three years.

We have had lately several spring showers & once a severe thunderstorm, which cooled the atmosphere considerably & made it very pleasant. The weather which we have in the middle of the day tho' is as warm as summer &, if anything, fully as warm as our July weather in Ala.

There have been crowds of wounded soldiers here lately, so that our hospital was full, but they have been sending them off some on furloughs to visit their homes others to different hospital points farther South; but again they are coming in, and it bids to be as full in a few days as ever before. It is distressing to see so many wounded men & to hear their cries & moaning; so much so that I dislike a hospital, or rather being in one, on that account. However in our ward there are few who are otherwise than slightly wounded & none very sick, save one or two. The others are lively and cheerful and pass time away in conversation, reading, etc. We receive the daily city papers from which we get the latest information from the different seats of war, have good fare, considering the scarcity of provisions in the country & the difficulty of transportation, at this time particularly, receive very good medical attention, & are cleanly & comfortably fixed, and upon the whole could not fare better, unless at home. My dear Mother you must give yourself no uneasiness on our account. We are doing very well indeed & I trust may soon be better. Sam I think looks better even since his arrival here, and as for me, I am like a new creature compared to my feelings on Sun. 15th inst, when I arrived here. I will write very often to you & the children & will inform you correctly of our true state & condition. I trust you & the children enjoy & may continue to enjoy good health. Tell them they must write often to us. I have written several times to one or other of them and am anxious for a reply. I hope soon also, my dear Mother, to receive some letters from you. I hope you received the dispatch I sent you on 20th inst. I was in hopes of receiving a letter on yesterday evening, but was disappointed.

Sam desires me to say that he recd Willie's letter the other day. Also that I must give his warmest love to our dear Mama, Mary, Willie, Louty & Icha, in which I must sincerely join him. Tell them all to write to us & dear Mama write often yourself as it has been a long time since we have heard from you. Communication with home seems to have been cut off.

Well, it is so dark I can scarcely see to write, so I must close.

Believe me your affectionate son,

James

P.S. Give our love to Dr. Grigg, Mr. Enoch Sawyer, our kindest regards to their families & remember us to all our friends. John sends kind regards to you & all the children & howd'ye to all the servants.

———•—•———

Howard's Grove Hospital
Richmond, Va.
June 16th 1864

My dearly beloved Sister,

I received yesterday a letter from Mama inclosing one also from you. The sad and painful news contained in those letters was just learned positively by Jamie & myself in the day before from Capt. Frank Moore whom Jamie met in the city. My dear, dear Mary I cannot express my deep and heart felt sympathy for you in this your great and sad bereavement.[19] You have indeed sustained an irreparable loss. Almighty God in the all wise but mysterious dispensation of his providence has seen fit to visit you with the heaviest affliction—to rob you of the idol of your heart; but I earnestly pray that the same all-merciful Father will pour into your dear, lacerated and bleeding heart the soothing oil of consolation and enable you to bear it with Christian fortitude and resignation. Let us bow in humble submission to the decree of Him "who doeth all things well" and try and say truly and sincerely "Thy will be done." We all sympathize with you, my dear sister, most deeply and share with you this sore calamity. I feel that I have lost a brother whom I loved much. Our dear Tom was the most noble, generous, high minded, whole souled, gallant youth that ever lived.

19. Captain Frank L. Moore, Company D, Fifth Louisiana Infantry Regiment (CMSR, RG109).

'Twas a pleasure and a privilege to know him and to know him was to love and admire him for the many and rare virtues which he possessed. While we feel most sensibly our great bereavement and deeply mourn his loss, it is a source of great consolation to know that our dear Tom fell, Major of his Regiment, gallantly fighting in a just and glorious cause. In his Brigade Tom was universally beloved and esteemed for his pure moral character and for his excellent qualities as an officer. The assistant adjutant General of the Brigade, Capt. Wm Seymour, has prepared an obituary which was published this morning and Charley Uhlhorn has written to Mama enclosing several copies of it.[20] Charley will send a lock of Tom's hair to his afflicted mother and one to you, also to you, a bible in which is written "A token of affection from your loving friend Mary." I will enclose in this, as a little relic, a piece of lead pencil which was taken out of the pocket of your beloved Tom. My *dear, dear* sister Jamie & I would give the world to be with you and offer you heartfelt sympathy and consolation, but you have our dear Mama with you—the dearest, most affectionate and best mother on earth & a meek & humble Christian. Accept the solace & comfort that she can point out to you contained in the Holy word of God. And I trust that you will not give way to feelings of grief and despair, but consider that though a heavy blow has fallen upon us, nevertheless it is the will of God, and that our dear friend has been taken from a world of sin and sorrow to one of endless bliss. It was ordained for some wise and good purpose and may it prove the means of bringing us all nearer to God and of making us sheep of his fold & that by His blessings we may be guided and directed, and enabled so to live that when called upon to die, we too, shall be borne to that "house not made with hands, eternal in heavens," and there be united with all the dear ones who have preceded us, never more to be separated. My darling sister I am so glad that you wrote to me as you did telling me of your distress, and was so happy to see that you recognized in it the hand of God, and trusted & prayed

20. Charles Uhlhorn, Biscoe's and the Pickens brothers' cousin, was a private in the Louisiana Guard Artillery (CMSR, Louisiana, RG 109). William J. Seymour was the assistant adjutant of Henry Hay's first brigade. According to Seymour's memoir, Biscoe was acting major at the time of his death. Seymour also stated that the obituary was published in the *Richmond Examiner*. Despite multiple searches, I have not been able to locate it, but it is reproduced in the memoir. See Jones, ed., *The Civil War Memoirs of Captain William J. Seymour*, xi, 84.

to him to bless you and unite you with our dear and [*unclear*] Tom in a better and [*unclear*] world. I hope this letter will soon reach you and afford you some consolation & assure you that you have the *full* and *sincere sympathy* of your affectionate & devoted brothers. I will try and write a few lines to Mama also now, and send it off with yours. Jamie joins me in warmest & most affectionate love to you, dear Mary, and to our dear Mama, Willie, Lou and Icha

And now for the present [*unclear*] and may God in His infinite mercy watch over, guide and protect you all and sustain, comfort and soothe you in your sorrowful bereavement. Write as often as you can, it will be great happiness to me to hear from you. I will write again soon, & Jamie will also.

Your devoted brother,
Sam

————•—•————

Umbria July 7th '64

Dear Juliet,[21]

You will oblige me greatly if you will find out if any mourning goods have arrived in Greensboro. If there are any do write soon & tell me about them.

I am quite sick, in bed. I have been sick ever since you were here. I don't know if I will ever be well again.

We heard from our dear boys a few days ago. They are back in a hospital. Brother Sam has been very ill & is very weak & thin. Poor fellows, how we long to be with them to soothe & comfort them in their sickness. I trust in my Heavenly Father that they well be spared to us. To lose them would be a great, great trial to me. Oh! I wish as I lie down on my sick bed & think of my once happy future I can scarcely realize that the Darling of my heart has gone, but the truth forces itself upon me. I am indeed without him & will never see him on Earth again. In a lonely & dark grave, far away from dear friends, lies my own Darling. The noble, kind & affectionate Tom Biscoe. Oh! my God, my future looks dark & dreary. My Darling has gone. Have I not had my dear good Mother during this, my time of sorrow & affliction,

21. Juliet Damer.

222

I would, at times, have almost prayed for death to come & release me from any troubles here below & unite me with my darling Tom.

I would ask you out but cannot be as selfish as to ask you to visit so sad a place. Our pleasures are few, very few. Write me a long letter, Juliet.

All join me in love to you, Mary & Flora. Remember me to your Father & brother.

I remain your true friend.

Mary

———————•————————

Berryville, Virginia

July 18th, 1864

My dearest Mama,

I wrote you a hasty letter from Staunton on the 28th ult. Telling you that I had left the hospital & rejoined my command etc., & have not had an opportunity of writing since. One mail was sent back from Harper's Ferry, but I did not know of it till it was too late to write. I will have time to write only a short letter this morning, but will try and give you the outlines of our movements so far this very active campaign. Our corps, after a forced march from Richmond via Charlottesville & Lynchburg as far as Salem in South-western Va in pursuit of Hunter, returned through Lexington to Staunton. Here I joined it on the 28th June & that evening we took up the line of march down the Valley to Winchester. Notwithstanding the very hot & dry weather & dusty roads we did the hardest marching that has been done during the war. We have been on the go almost every day & usually start in the morning at 45 minutes after 3 o'clock, march 15 miles by 12 o'clock, then rest an hour & march five or six miles further, when we go into camp for the night. On several occasions we have made 27 or 28 miles a day, & that is terrible march-ing in crowded ranks, with a cloud of dust about us & a scorching July sun darting his fiery rays upon us. But to resume—from Winchester we went to Smithfield & Charlestown & thence to Harper's Ferry. This was on the 4th July & we met the Yankees 4 miles from H.F., drove them before us, captured the town & a large camp with some prisoners & a considerable quantity of stores.[22] Our Brigade got a good deal of plunder & something good to eat & drink. Gen. Early did not attempt to dislodge the enemy from his apparently impregnable position on the Bolivar & Maryland Heights.[23] So after resting a day & a half, we marched to Shepherdstown where we waded the Potomac & invaded Maryland. Passed through Sharpsburg & saw the field on which the battle was fought in the fall of 1862. Camped the first night 6th July on Antietam Creek. Thence thro' Rohersville & Jefferson to Frederick City. Here on the 9th inst we met the Yankees.[24] Our Brig. was put in line of battle but only the sharpshooters were engaged, while Gen. Gordon with his Division made a flank movement & whipped the Yankees handsomely—taking several hundred prisoners & leaving their dead pretty thickly strown upon the field. Next day we waded the Monocacy river, marched about 25 ms. & camped near the town of Rockville. On the 11th we appeared before the fortifications of Washington City, D.C., four miles from the city, & began to skirmish with the enemy. What a surprise it must have been to them & what alarm & consternation no doubt reigned in the capital of the U.S. during the two days we threatened it. We expected nothing else than to have to storm the fortifications & try & capture the city, but 'twas only a feint, I suppose, to draw troops from Virginia, & in this was doubtless perfectly successful, for

22. Here Pickens was describing the role of Major General Robert Rodes's division in Early's attack on Union troops at Martinsburg under the command of Franz Sigel. Breck-inridge's division would attack Martinsburg while Rodes's and Stephen Ramseur's division cut off Sigel's escape route at Harpers Ferry. Rodes and Ramseur arrived too late on July 3 to prevent Sigel's escape across the Potomac. But, as Pickens wrote, the Confederates did capture Harpers Ferry and the supplies he described. See Collins, *Major General Robert E. Rodes*, 379–80.

23. Collins, *Major General Robert E. Rodes*, 379–80. Federal forces abandoned both places on the night of July 4.

24. A Union force of fifty-eight hundred men under the command of Lew Wallace had taken up defensive positions along the Monocacy River, a tributary of the Potomac east of Frederick, Maryland. Ramseur's division attacked Wallace's position, forcing Wallace to retreat, thanks to, as Pickens wrote, Gordon's successful flanking movement. Rodes's division, which had been employed as a diversion during Ramseur's initial attack, chased Wallace's force and fought the brief skirmish Pickens described with elements of it southeast of Frederick. See Collins, *Major General Robert E. Rodes*, 381–86.

all night we could hear the trains coming in & the whistles of transports; & could even hear their officers giving commands in marching the troops out to the fortifications, & the cheering that went up from the lines as re-inforcements would arrive. Washington is strongly fortified indeed. There are forts at intervals around the city filled with cannon of the largest caliber & longest range; our Regt was sent out in support of the sharpshooters & late in the evening of the 12th inst the Yankees discovered that our forces were retiring & made a vigorous attack driving back the sharpshooters in front of us. We hurried forward & had a sharp engagement which lasted till night, & held the enemy in check. After dark all our troops were withdrawn & began the march back to the Potomac. The residences of the two Blairs—Frank P. the Postmaster Genl & Montgomery Blair—noted abolitionists, were left in flames: tho' it was not by authority of our Generals. The house of the Gov. of Md., however, was burnt, near Baltimore, in retaliation for that of Gov. Letcher at Lexington.[25] We recrossed the Potomac on the 14th, came thro' Leesburg, crossed the mountains at Snicker's Gap & are now near Berryville, where we stopped yesterday. We have just got marching orders & I must close. I'll finish my letter as soon as another opportunity offers, but will send this now. I'm very anxious to hear from home, as I have not had a word from there since early in June. Got a letter from Jamie night before last, in which he expressed the hope of getting a furlough. I trust he has gotten one & gone home. Give my kind regards to all friends & warmest love to my dear Sisters & brothers, & please accept the same, my beloved Mother, from

Your affectionate son,
Sam

P.S. Write soon for I'm very anxious to hear from you. I trust you are all well.

S.P.

———•—•———

25. He was referring to the burning of Governor John Letcher's home in Lexington by Union troops under the command of General David Hunter (McPherson, *Battle Cry of Freedom*, 738–39).

In camp near
Strasburg, Va.
July 23rd, 1864

My dear Mama,

On the 18th I wrote to you from Berryville & that very evening we were carried quite unexpectedly into a battle. We marched 3 or four miles from Camp & found the Yankees, who had crossed the Shenandoah at a ford & formed their line in a very strong & naturally fortified position near the river. Our Brigade was splendidly handled by Col. Pickens & made an impetuous charge & drove the enemy before us at first, but they had a very strong position on the bank of the river where they had a flank fire on us from an island & there fought stubbornly. Only our Divis was engaged, & all along the line we drove the enemy into the river & shot them as they crossed. By night they were all on the opposite side, & after collecting all of our dead & wounded and arms etc. we came back a little distance & camped in line of battle & waited all the next day to see if the Yankees would attempt another crossing, but they did not.[26]

We suffered a good deal in the fight, for a small one. There were six or seven men in our Regt killed & mortally wounded & fifteen others wounded; & in our Co. Lt. Jno. Christian & Sergt. Britton were wounded & Lt. Jones & Private Rinke were taken prisoners.[27] I was with Lt. Jones & was firing at

26. The Union Army was chasing Early and, at about 2:00 p.m. on July 18, a Union force under the command of Colonel Joseph Thoburn crossed the Shenandoah River at Island Ford. Thoburn's mission was to then march south and clear out what Commanding General Crook thought was a small Confederate rear guard defending Castleman's Ferry, where Crook planned a larger-scale crossing by the Army of West Virginia in pursuit of Jubal Early's corps. The Fifth Alabama and the rest of Rodes's division was camped east of Cool Spring, Virginia. Thoburn's crossing surprised the Confederate command, but General Early responded quickly, moving Battle's brigade to a position on the right flank of Thoburn's force. The "flank fire" to which Pickens refers may have been Union artillery on the east bank of the river, or a combination of fire from Island Ford and the east bank. For a detailed account of the Battle of Cool Spring, see Patchan, *Shenandoah Summer*, 70–77, and *Reports of Colonel Joseph Thoburn, First West Virginia Infantry, OR*, ser. 1, vol. 37, pt. 1: 290–91.

27. The men Sam identified were John F. Christian, William Britton, Edwin Pompey Jones, and Jacob Rinke (or "Rencke"). Christian, Britton, and Jones had enlisted at Greensboro. Rinke enlisted at Grace Church, Virginia, in March 1863. See Hubbs, ed., *Voices from Company D*, 397, 399, 408, 417.

the enemy in front when J called my attention to the fact that some Yankees had slipped along the river bank & were almost upon us. He threw himself down in the grass, hoping, no doubt, that the Yankees would not observe him, or that some of our men a little further back would fire upon & drive them off—while I sprang to a rock fence, jumped over & made my escape. It was a very dangerous thing & at the risk of my life, but thank God, through His all merciful guidance & protection I came out safely. I bruised & sprained my foot, tho,' & have been riding in a wagon whenever we moved since, & staying with Maj. Webster, & have had a very pleasant time. This evening I returned to the Co. tho,' as I will be able to march now. We have followed up thus far by the Yankees, but stopped here & offered them battle which they declined & have moved back. We have been threshing wheat & getting a supply of flour & will start in the morning—it is said—back into Maryland & Pennsylvania. I dread the idea of all that marching again. A letter came the other day for Jamie & I read it, & was most happy to learn that you were all well. The date was the 27th of June. I hope to receive more very soon. We hear rumors of unfavorable news from our army in Ga viz. that Johnston had retreated to Atlanta, & had been relieved of his command etc. I hope it may not be true, but fear it is. I am writing by a miserable fire light & must close. Mary said she was unwell when she wrote: I hope she & all are well now. Please give my warmest love to all my dear sisters & brothers & accept the same from

Your devoted son,
Sam

P.S. Have not heard from Jamie since 4th inst. Will write again as soon as an opportunity offers. Do write to me often. Excuse this scrawl. S.P. Kind regards to all friends. Joe & Gilliam are well.

S.P.

———◆—◆———

Martinsburg, Va.
July 27th, 1864

My dear Sister Mary,

It has been a long time since I have had the pleasure of receiving one of your ever affectionate & welcome letters, & still longer since I have written to you; for your last favor came to hand just after we started out on this Valley campaign, and we have been so constantly on the march that I have been able only to scribble a hurried note to Mama occasionally to let you all know where I was and that I was well. In the first place I will give you an account of our movement & of events that have transpired since my last letter to Mama from Strasburg on 23rd. The next morning early we marched through Strasburg, Middletown, Newtown & just before getting to Kearnstown came up with the Yankees. Gen. Breckenridge, Gordon's & Ramseur's Divisions were ahead that day—our Divis being in rear and when we came up we found Gen. B fighting them in front, while Gordon & Ramseur were taking them on the flank. We formed in line of battle to support Breckenridge, but the Yankees were soon driven from their position & completely routed—so our Divis was not engaged, except the sharpshooters. We did a great deal of rapid marching tho' in pursuit of the enemy and a large portion of the distance we were in line of battle going through fields & marshes & over stone fences & rail fences etc. just the most fatiguing marching in the world. The Yankees passed through Winchester in a perfect stampede with our men at their heels firing into them. Some of them tried to make a stand a high fortified hill beyond the town, but seeing that they would be flanked & cut off, they made a short tarry. Our Divis was pushed on to try & capture a wagon train but was a little too late. We had a hard chase after some of their rear guard, but we had marched so far & were so broken down that we could not overtake them although we were in sight. They burnt commissary & ordinance wagons all along the road at least fifty I suppose and we found others that were very slightly injured. We captured some prisoners & artillery too, tho' I don't know the number. You will know the fruits of the victory by the papers probably before we will, for we rarely ever see a paper up here, except Yankee papers. We camped four miles on this side of Winchester having marched (by the road) 26 miles, but in all of our maneuvering we must have some 30 miles. Now don't you think that was a pretty good day's march? Especially in the month of July & over very dusty roads. Was it not a strange way of spending the Sabbath & a most unpleasant one; but there is no Sunday in the army. That night it rained & continued till 10 o'clock next [*Ends here.*]

Joe & Gilliam are well.

———— · ● · ————

Umbria August 10, 1864

My dear darling Brother,

I have been so very sick lately, that I have not been able to write to you & Jimmie. I assure you dear brother Sam 'tis a pleasure to write to both of you & I have missed the pleasure now for some time. I was taken sick on the 4th of July & have been sick ever since. The Doctor is still attending me. I am now much better than I have been; but still very [*unclear*] indeed.

Juliet Damer came out with Mama from Church last Sunday. She is well & very lively. Her company has benefitted me some; for I had become very sad & did not care to see anyone except the family & a few friends. I am glad she is with me. I hope I will one day be well again. I never expect to be perfectly happy again. My loss has caused a void in my heart which can never be filled. Oh! Brother Sam, I sit sometimes alone in the gallery & think of you & dear Jimmie. Many prayers ascend to the Throne of God at these times, beseeching Him to guard & protect you both from the many dangers to which you are exposed & to return you to us.

Brother Sam, you know not how much I love you & Jimmie, to see & be with you both again, is my constant prayer, God grant that it will be answered. I have felt so sick at times lately that I have been almost willing to die, but I want to live now to see my dear good brothers back. What a bright future I had three weeks ago. Alas! It is now dark & obscure. How I wish you & Jimmie were with us now. I would feel happy again. It has been more than two months since I have felt happy. Oh! my if my prayers could only be answered, I would yet see my dear, dear Tom. I pray that the news of his death is untrue. God grant it may be. I ought not to write now for I feel so sad I am calculated to make the recipients of my letters sad also, but I know you would think strangely of me, were I not to write so I will continue. I am so very anxious to hear from you & dear Jimmie. We are all anxious, very, very anxious. It has been more than a week since we heard from Jimmie, & a much longer time since we have received one line from you. I trust you are well my dear Brother.

We have had a great deal of rain lately more than I ever [*unclear*] fall in the same length of time.

We received bad news from Mobile this morning. Fort Gaines, the principal fort has surrendered.[28] Oh! I trust the Yankees will not be able to take Mobile. I fear if that city falls we will soon have the Yankees with us. Mama seems determined not to stay to meet them. If Mobile falls we will move away somewhere, God alone knows where.

When will this cruel war cease & when oh when will we again meet! These questions I ask myself very, very often. These are indeed "times that try men's souls." I wish the summer was over, for you & Jimmie would then stand a chance to come home if only to stay a short time. It will soon be two years since you left us. A long, long time for loved ones to be away. Jimmie has been away near five months. Dear Jimmie, how sad & lonely he must be in a hospital with no kind friend to soothe & comfort him. I feel very sad. Please write soon dear bro' Sam. I want to hear from you so much. I must now close, as it is near dark. All join me in warmest & dearest love to you dear, dear bro' Sam & to dear, dear Jimmie, if he is with you.

I am dear bro' Sam your truly
Devoted Sister Mary.

———•——

Bunker's Hill
August 20th, '64

My dear Mama,

As we have evidence now that mail communications are again opened with the South, I am encouraged to write again. A large mail from Ala was recd by our Brigade yesterday evening, and was heartily welcomed I assure

28. The Confederate garrison had surrendered two days earlier to a Union Army landing force under the command of General Gordon Granger during the Battle of Mobile Bay. See Bergeron, *Confederate Mobile*, 146–47.

you, for it had been a long time since we had had one. I cannot express to you how very anxious I was, my dear Mama, to hear from all, nor how truly delighted was I last evening when in distributing the mail two letters were called out for me. One was from Louty dated July 17th and the other from Mary dated the 26th ult. These are the very first letters that I have received from home since the 24th of June when I left Richmond. Now was not that a painfully long time to be cut off from communion with the dearly beloved ones far away at our Southern home? The difficulty about the mails at first was that the R. Roads in Va. Were cut by the enemy; then that the roads in Ga. & Ala were cut and since the damage done to those roads was repaired and communication opened to Richmond a further difficulty arose to prevent our getting the mail which was a disagreement between the Post Master Genl and the contractor of the Central Va. R.R. in regard to the transportation of it from Richmond to Staunton. This has been all settled, though, and I sincerely trust that in the future no interruptions will occur.

From Mary's letter I was very sorry to learn that she had been suffering with a long spell of sickness and earnestly trust that by the time she has entirely recovered her health. It distresses me too, to hear her speak as she does & write in such low spirits. I hope to have the inexpressible happiness of visiting home sometime during the coming Winter at least, and trust that I shall find Mary & all enjoying fine health and looking rosy and well—so that you can all have your likenesses taken for me. Mama, you must take plenty of outdoor exercise regularly & get Mary to accompany you. She ought by all means to ride on horseback with Willie, Lou & Icha, and with her friends who come to visit her.

I have not heard from Jamie since the 28th of last month. He was then at a Hospital in Lynchburg, & was much better pleased with it than with Howard's Grove. He has had a hard time of it, & I hope has recd a furlough & gone home where he ought to have been all this time.

I will now tell you something of our movements since the date of my last letter of the 8th inst written from this place. We fell back to Strasburg, whither the Yankees followed us, and there formed our line of battle & threw up breastworks. The enemy, after remaining in our front & skirmishing for four or five days, disappeared on the night of the 16th, having discovered that reinforcements from Richmond were about to join us. These were 2 Divisions of Longstreet's corps—Field's & Kershaw's, & Fitzhugh Lee's Division of Cavalry. Gen. Early immediately pursued the Yankees and on the evening of the 17th near Winchester, a position of our forces had a skirmish with them & captured upwards of 400 prisoners. Yesterday we arrived at our same old camp here—a favorite stopping place with Gen. Early—& remained today. Tho' this morning we were put under arms & marched out of camp, as the enemy's cavalry made some demonstration; we soon returned, however. Orders to move in the morning have come around, tho' we do not know in what direction.[29] It is now dark, so I must close with kind regards to all friends & warmest love to you, my dear Mama, & to my dear sisters & brothers.

Ever Your devoted son,
Sam

P.S. John sends love to his family, & to you all. He is very anxious to hear from his family. I will try and answer Mary's & Louty's letters as soon as we stop again in camp. We are having plenty of apples & some roasting ears in the Valley now.

Yrs. Aff.
Saml

Write soon & write often

—————•—————

29. Since Sam's last letter, Rodes's division had withdrawn from Maryland on August 6 to join the rest of Early's corps near Winchester. The Union's recently constituted Army of the Shenandoah, under the command of General Philip Sheridan, was attempting to trap the Confederates in Winchester, but Early escaped and retreated, first to Newtown, then to Fisher's Hill near Strasburg. As Sam described it, Union forces probed Confederate lines for a few days and then fell back, having learned that Confederate reinforcements from Virginia were arriving. After a sharp "skirmish" near Kernstown, Early reoccupied Winchester. Rodes's division took up a position on the Berryville road, east of Winchester on August 18. See Collins, *Major General Robert E. Rodes*, 390–93.

General Hosp. Lynchburg, Va.
Tues. Aug. 16th 1864.

My dear Sam,

A few days after writing to you I received from you a welcome and interesting reply to a letter which I wrote you before leaving Richmond. I had begun to despair of my letter reaching you at all or of my being able to hear from you. Judge then of the great pleasure and satisfaction which your letter caused me, as I had grown exceedingly anxious to hear from you. And as I have not heard from you now for several weeks, my anxiety is again increasing. I hope soon, tho,' that a long letter will come telling of your health and safety.

I was extremely glad to hear that you escaped from danger when you ran such a great risk from the enemies' missils. God's hand protected you and to Him I am truly thankful for your great deliverance & pray that He will continue to guard and protect you, my dear brother, through all further dangers and deliver you in safety after all shall have ended in peace and happiness.

I have been quite unwell again, since writing to you which is the reason why I have not answered your letters sooner. Another spell of bilious remittent fever for about two weeks has weakened and reduced me more than I have been since the long attack which I had at the University in 1860.

Well I have been recommended by the Dr in charge of our ward to go before the Board for a furlough and have been anxiously awaiting its (the Board) meeting for a week past. But every day we who were to go before it would be disappointed, as it did not meet for this Hospital at all last week. However, today it did meet and we went before it. I am glad to say that I got a furlough for forty days and, God willing, will leave for home tomorrow. The man who I told you was desirous of getting a furlough & who would travel nearly all the way home with me, also got furloughed. I am quite weak and feel a little dubious as to my being able to travel; but I trust I will meet with no trouble in reaching dear "sweet home." Would that you too, my dear brother, were going with me! How happy I would be. It would be so much more agreeable traveling and would be affording you, too, an opportunity of visiting home with me. I sincerely trust to a merciful heavenly Father that soon we may all be assembled together at our dear home with our dear Mother, sisters & brothers, in peace, contentment & happiness, no more to separate while life lasts! When that day arrives we will all be perfectly happy if that is to be found on Earth. I know we will be as much so as creatures can be.

I have been anxiously expecting to hear from you, but have been disappointed. In writing before I made a great omission in failing to write you my address. However, you know it now (Hol. Sq.) [Hollow Square.]

I sincerely trust that you are safe & quite well and that I may soon hear from you.

It is growing late and becoming so dark that I can scarcely write, so must close.

Believe me ever,
Your affectionate brother,
James.

P.S. Remember me kindly to all our friends & tell John how d'ye.

Jas. P.

Write soon & write often

——————•—•——————

Camp near Bunker's Hill
August 30th, 1864

My dearly beloved Sister,

I have had the pleasure recently of receiving two very kind and most affectionate letters from you, and I assure you that they were truly acceptable and highly prized. To the soldiers far away from the loved ones at home, letters are the source of his greatest happiness, and they are received and read with the utmost avidity and delight. My dear Mary you have had a long spell of sickness this Summer, but I am so glad to learn that you are now much better. Let me beg of you to take plenty of outdoor exercise: ride on horseback every evening and break in little Violette again for no doubt she is a little spoiled by so long a holiday. I am very sorry to see you in such low spirits. We have indeed sustained a sad loss, but we must bear in mind that it was the will of an all wise and merciful God "who doeth all things well" and for our eternal good.

Therefore be resigned, and do not give way to grief, but cheer up. I was truly happy to hear from Mama that you are to be confirmed by Bishop Wilmer as soon as your health will admit of your taking the ride to church. Three days ago I recd a kind letter from Jamie, and from the news it contained I hope that today your hearts are all gladdened by having him with you again. Yes after a great deal of anxiety about Jamie, as it had been a month since I had heard from him, I was greatly relieved and very happy to see that he had obtained a forty day's furlough and was to have started home on the 17th. Oh! What a delightful change for Jamie from a life in the hospital to our dear old home where he will be surrounded by a kind and affectionate Mother and sisters and brothers. What would I not give to be there too? It would be the happiest time of my life. I live in the hope that it will not be very long ere I shall be reunited with you all at home once more. The Northern Democratic Convention met at Chicago yesterday & I hope they will unite in nominating a *Peace candidate* who may be elected and put an end to this bloody war. Tell Jamie that while he is at home if he have an opportunity he must go before a medical board & try and get a certificate of disability: he could first get one from Dr. Grigg if he has lost the one which the Dr sent him last Spring. Should Jamie succeed in getting a certificate from a board he could send it to Mr. Lyon, who would procure his detail from the Assistant Sec. of War.[30] I hope he will have his furlough extended at any rate for there would be no use in his coming here, where he would not be able to stand the hard marching which we have to perform.[31] Please say to Mama that day before yesterday her most affectionate and welcome letter of 13th inst. reached me, & one also from Willie. I will try and answer both very soon. I am very much obliged to Mama for sending money for us: she sent a great deal more than is necessary, however, it is in good safe hands and we can draw it as we need it. I shall not need any boots

30. Francis Strother Lyon of Demopolis served two terms in the Confederate Congress. He was elected as a Whig to two terms in the U.S. House of Representatives ("LYON, Francis Strother, 1800–1882," *Biographical Directory of the United States Congress*).

31. For several days before Sam wrote this letter, the Confederates had been demonstrating near the Potomac River, evidently hoping to force Sheridan to send forces north of the river to defend against another Confederate crossing into Maryland and/or Pennsylvania. On August 27, Early returned to camp near Bunker Hill, West Virginia. See Wert, *From Winchester to Cedar Creek*, 6–7, 38–39.

till next winter. Tell Mama it would be useless to send a box while we are in the Valley as it would be impossible [*The rest of this letter from Sam is missing.*]

————•———

Umbria, August 24ᵗʰ, '64

My beloved Sam,

Yesterday morning at an early hour, we were most delightfully surprised to hear of the arrival of our dear Jamie. He arrived at Umbria at half past two o'clock in the morning and laid in the front [*unclear word*] until morning, when William went up to him and said "good morning." Jamie answered: "You are a soldier." Jamie said "I am." "How did you get home—did the stage bring you?" Yes—why William don't you know me? Jamie had hardly covered his face with his blade & we and William did not recognize him. As soon as we heard that Jamie had come we sprang out of bed and were soon ready to receive him in my room. It was a very delightful surprise to us all, for we had given up all hope of seeing him until the war was over. I was shocked to see Jamie looking so emaciated—so much like a shadow: he has lost fifty pounds of flesh and weighs only 105 lbs. He left Lynchburg on the 17ᵗʰ and got here on 23ʳᵈ. His furlough is for 40 days, but I have no idea that he will be fit for service at the expiration of that time. Of course, he will endeavor to have his furlough extended and I hope he will succeed. I think coming home and being with us will soon make Jamie look & feel better: already he has improved, although he has been with us only a day and a half. I am sure if Jamie had remained in a hospital two weeks longer, he would have died: he says he believes he would have lost his mind. How ignorant we are of what is forever good. I was truly sorry when I heard that he had brain fever from the hospital in Richmond to one in Lynchburg; but how fortunate it was that he was sent from that hard-hearted Dr. P who would never have granted him a furlough to come home; but would rather have ordered him to go into ranks. Oh! My dear Sam I dread Jamie's going back into the Army: he is totally unfit for service, and I feel confident that he would lose his life if he attempted it again. I think he had better try to get a detail to manage the servants on this place. If we have 20 hands, he can get one, I presume.

Jamie says he will be compelled to return to Va in order to get a detail. He is rather despondent about it, knowing how difficult it is to get out of the Army. It is cruel to rec from a man more in service, when he has proved himself incompetent to serve. The first question I asked Jamie was "have you come to stay!" And so it will really seem—how soon will 20th of Sept come.

Dr. Grigg is coming over this evening to take Jamie's case into consideration & to prescribe for him. I trust he will soon relieve him of the wasting disease, which he has had for some time. God! grant that my dear, beloved Jamie may soon be restored to health & happiness. What would I give to have you my dear, dear Son at home with us. All my worldly goods "would I cheerfully" give up to have the war ended, and you & Jamie with me never again to part. I would ask no greater blessing than this. My trust is in One, who is able to help us in this our hour of great trouble and suffering. May His Almighty arm be interposed between us & our enemies, and may we be a free & independent people with hearts full of love to Him and zeal in His service for the remainder of our days on Earth. Heaven grant an answer to my prayers and let me have all my dear children around me very soon. I hope you have regained your strength my dear son and can perform your arduous duties as you did before you were taken sick. I feel anxiety about you all the time, but put my whole trust in God always. If you need any clothing, shoes or anything else, write immediately, and I can send some things by Jamie or someone else. I heard lately that you were without and nearly bare footed. Now it is not right that you should be so. Will the measure you left with us, answer now, or has your foot spread with the heavy marching you have gone through? I can easily have shoes made for you. I have wished thousands of times that you were near enough to me to get supplies from home and yet I would prefer your being in the Va army because I think it is an honor to be there. If I had the wings of a dove, how often would I have been at your side!

Mary's health is improving. I am truly thankful for it, and feel how blessed we have been. Jamie's coming home has benefited her very much. She has just finished a pair of strong gloves for you. Willie is well and busily engaged in making molasses. I fear he is exposing himself too much to sun and night air. I tell him of the danger, but can't make him take care of himself. Louty is fat & hearty—full of life and joking. She keeps our spirits up and enlivens the house. She is seated near the sofa, keeping the flies off Jamie, whilst he is taking a nap. Icha is well and enjoys life finely. I wish I could get a tutor for them all. There is an advertisement in the Selma paper from a gentleman well qualified to teach. I think I will write to him this evening. Mary Ann is very ill, but I hope will recover. Dr. G attends her. There is much sickness about the country, but we have had only two cases. [*Unclear word*] is just getting about. The servants at the plantations are generally well. The weather is hot and more settled, so we may hope to save our fodder. The corn crops are fine. I presume Mr. Wright has reached Richmond and delivered a letter to Dr. Cunningham containing $1000—one thousand dollars. When you want it, you can get it from him. Jamie owes Dr. Pleasants $100 for which he gave his note.

All unite with me in warmest love to you, my beloved Son. That we may soon be together & never again part is the earnest prayer of your devotedly attached Mother.

Remember us kindly to John. I will let him know how Suky is in my next letter. God! Bless you.

———•———

Camp 8ms. North of
Winchester, Va.
Sept. 7th, 1864

My dearest Mama,

Yesterday morning I had the heartfelt pleasure of receiving from you another long, interesting & most affectionate letter saying that all were well at home, and also containing the good news that Jamie had reached home safely. He must really have been looking emaciated & very badly, as William did not recognize him at first. I am truly happy to hear that he is now with you at home, where he will receive the best of nursing & every kind attention. Oh! what a miserable time he has spent all the Summer confined by severe sickness to a Hospital crowded with sick & wounded. I am sure Jamie will begin to recuperate immediately, but it will be a long time before he will be able to return. In fact he never ought to come to the Army again; he never was able to stand the service and I hope he will be able to get a detail. He ought to go before a board of Surgeons somewhere near home, & take with him Dr. Grigg's &

Dr. Hill's certificate in regard to his health, and I hope he will be successful. This is the first day we have been still for a week, and I have been anxious to write you a long letter in reply to several most highly prized favors received from you; but we were on picket till late this evening & I was unable to get paper, pen & ink, as John had my portfolio at Camp and those articles are very scarce with the soldiers just now. Since I wrote to you, we have been down at Charlestown & then to Shephersdstown & Bunker Hill & Martinsburg & back to B-Hill. Then on last Sunday we marched down to Berryville, where we met the Yankees & lay in line of battle, skirmishing with them all day. They then moved to the right, & day before yesterday (Monday) we marched up here in front of them & drove them till after night—in a cold, drenching rain. We lay all night in our wet clothes, & yesterday were marching about in a drizzling rain & through the mud, which was very disagreeable indeed. Though this is what we have to do very often in the army. Today the weather has been as clear as a bell and as cool & bracing as October. It really felt like frost. We have just heard gloomy news from Atlanta—that it has at last fallen into the hands of the Yankees—after all the hard fighting & the thousands of lives sacrificed in its defense. It is indeed a serious loss. I trust tho,' that the enemy will not get Macon or any point on that R. Road, & thereby cut off communications with our homes in Ala. Every soldier here is wishing that we could be sent to Georgia. If Ge. Early's little army could only be sent there now, I think Sherman's career would come to a speedy & inglorious end. I hope reinforcements will be sent there & save the balance of Ga and Ala.

You must not be at all uneasy about me dear Mama, for I'm in good health and stand the service finely. I have written in a great hurry, & you will please excuse my letter until I have an opportunity of writing a more lengthy one. Please send me some cotton socks by the first one coming on. I do hope you will succeed in getting a good teacher for the children.

Present my kind regards to all friends, and my warmest love to Jamie, Mary, Willie, Lou and Icha; and accept for yourself the same. That we may soon be reunited in peace & happiness is my earnest prayer. Adieu, for the present, my dear, dear, Mama.

Ever Your affectionate son,
Sam

Umbria, Sept. 10th 1864

My dear Sam,

We were all much gratified and highly delighted the other morning on receiving intelligence of your whereabouts and safety and also of your good health. Louty recd a letter from you dated at Bunker's hill, 8th Aug., which altho' not of late date yet was more recent than any news we had had from you. I sincerely trust that you are still in the enjoyment of health and that you are having a good rest after the fatigues and hardships which you have undergone since 28th June. I do not see how you could have done all that severe marching, in the hottest summer weather, & so continuously, too, without being almost exhausted. It has certainly been the hardest campaign of the war, in Va.

I hope that ere you get this you may have recd the letters which we wrote you by Capt. Williams, who was to have left for the Co. a week ago. It is so difficult for letters to reach their destination when sent by the mail that I suppose not one in five which we send in that way get to you. So, to be sure of a few going safely, we take advantage of the opportunities afforded of men who are going directly to, or in the neighborhood of the Regt., to send letters on to you.

Since I wrote my last letter Mama and the children have all been as well as usual & no one sick until yesterday, when Mama had a slight chill which was followed by fever. Today, however, I am glad to say she is much better, and I trust by tomorrow, may be restored to health. Mary was sick also, yesterday, but is better today. Mama and Mary both need exercise everyday which I prevail on them to take but it is seldom that either does. Mary, since her great bereavement, has felt little like taking either exercise or her regular meals; but of late her spirits have become much better and she now rides out with me in the carriage, which has improved her health very much. Her appetite is improving and she looks much better than when I first arrived at home. I humbly & sincerely trust that both her health and Mama's may improve and that, ere cool weather has fairly set in, they may be in good health again.

By that time, may God grant to us a cessation of hostilities, a speedy, just, an honorable & a lasting peace and independence & happiness to our country once more! Great boon! how many thousands will be made happy by it!

Some of the papers, amongst them the *Reporter,* seem to regard the result of the Chicago nomination favorably, whilst others think the two nominees, McClellan & [Pendleton] no better [for us] than the present incumbent— the Ape & Hamblin.[32] *Nous verrons.*[33] I hope "little Mac" will carry out a confession, or rather an assertion, that he made soon after he was relieved of his command of the Army of the Potomac, which was, that "if he were in chief command & the government would agree to it, he would have peace with the rebels in less than sixty days," or a speech to that effect. What a great diplomatist he would be considered by both hostile parties & by the world generally, if, on "succeeding to the throne," soon to be vacated by the fiend Lincoln, he would arrange preliminaries for an armistice & succeed in concluding a lasting and an honorable peace with the South. But I think that in our great & good President they would find one equal not only to the great & difficult task of the conduct & government of a large nation, its armies etc., but also to the no less difficult one of adjusting questions of the greatest moment to the two hostile sections and in aiding in restoring them to peace & tranquility again. May their endeavors, aided by "wisdom from on high," soon lead to a more amicable arbitrament of our national troubles and strife than the sword has been able to accomplish.

Well, as William is ready to go with our letters to Mr. Norfleet, by whom we are going to send them, and as it is late in the evening for him to start, I am compelled to close, promising that I will soon write again to you. Meanwhile, I hope we will hear from you again & as often as you may find time to write.

32. The Democrats nominated General George McClellan for the presidency and Representative George Pendleton for the vice presidency. Knowing Pendleton's strong antiwar position and believing McClellan would negotiate a favorable peace settlement, Confederates hoped for a Democratic victory. "Ape and Hamblin" was a derogatory reference to Lincoln and his vice president, Hannibal Hamlin. By the time James wrote, however, Union success in the Battle of Mobile Bay, the fall of Atlanta, and Sheridan's continuing success in the Shenandoah Valley revived northern morale and support for the Lincoln administration's conduct of the war. See Weber, *Copperheads,* chap. 6.

33. We will see (French).

I have not made any attempts to get my furlough extended yet, but intend going, *Deo volente*,[34] on Monday next, to the Hospital at Marion & trying there. If I fail there, I will try the Board at Tuscaloosa, where Dr. Sawyer is. He, probably, may be able to help me get it extended.

Mama and all the children join me in warmest love to you. Mama commenced a letter to you yesterday but could not finish it as she was taken sick soon after.

The Dr desired me to give you his kind regards. Mr. Noch I've not seen for a long time, several days i.e. He always inquires kindly concerning you.

Believe me ever
Your affectionate brother,
James

P.S. Tell John how d'ye for us all. The servants all send you their kind remembrances including Daddy Simon, uncle George, etc. J.P.

———·◆·———

Richmond, Va.
Sept. 26th, 1864.

My dear Mama,

I am afraid you will have become uneasy at not having heard from me before this letter reaches you, but hope not, as Mr. Beck telegraphed to Greensboro the list of casualties in our Company in the battle of the 19th inst. at Winchester, and stated that I had received only a slight wound. However, you will no doubt, think that it strange that I have not written sooner as I always make it a rule to write immediately after a battle. It is just a week today since the fight occurred, but the first day or two afterwards our mail arrangements were disturbed, and since then I have been on the move, coming up the Valley to Staunton & thence to this place. So my letter had to be deferred till now. It was my intention to telegraph home immediately after my arrival here, but I was told that a letter would reach there equally as soon: however, when I go to mail my letter I think I'll dispatch anyhow, as I am

34. God being willing (Latin).

anxious to do all in my power to spare my dear Mama any anxiety on my account. I will now give you brief sketch of the battle and of my trip up the Valley and back to Richmond.

Early on the morning of the 19th inst., when in camp four miles south of Bunker's Hill & eight miles North of Winchester, our attention was attracted by cannonading in the distance, and 9 o'clock A.M. our Divis. started & marched to where the fighting was going on, which was about two or three miles Northeast of Winchester. While passing in rear of Gordon's Divis., which was then engaged, to get to the position which Gen. Rodes was to occupy, we found one of Gordon's Brigades (Evans') falling back in great confusion before the Yankees who were on the point of capturing one of our batteries. Just then Gen. Early ordered our Brigade to halt, front & charge—saying that if the enemy got that battery the day was lost. Most nobly did it obey, & with a loud yell rushed over the hill, met & hurled back the blue tide of the enemy—pouring in a fire which strowed the field with their dead & wounded, and in this manner pursued them for three quarters of a mile. Our Brig. then took its position in a piece of woods, from which the Yankees made several attempts to dislodge us but failed. They kept up a hot fire of musketry and part of the time of artillery, which cut up the timber terribly and killed & wounded a good many of our men. We succeeded in driving off the gunners & silencing the battery which was playing upon us—but every now & then they would run up & fire a round or two & then have to fall back again. Thus we held our position for several hours, until our Cavalry on the left was whipped & driven back, and the enemy about to get in our rear, when we were compelled beat a hasty retreat. The whole line had now given way & was falling back over the plain towards Winchester. Col. Carter, chief of artillery, stopped a battery & opened on the Yankees, while the gallant Gen. Gordon, with hat in hand (Gen. Rodes had previously been killed) galloped up to us & called upon the Alabamians to rally & hold the place. Four or five of our Co were together and stopped here, and after firing my last cartridge, I had got some more from Jim Webb and was in the act of loading again when I was struck in the side of my head with a fragment of a shell, I think, as it made such a large rent in my hat. It was a stunning blow, but thank God my life was spared and I received only a small cut in the scalp. Oh! Mama I am deeply impressed with a sense of gratitude & thankfulness to our most kind & merciful Heavenly Father for all His great blessings & especially for having shielded me & preserved my life so often in the midst of dangers; but know that I am not half as much so as I should be, and that I could never give thanks & praise unto Him sufficiently. At first I thought I was wounded pretty badly as it commenced bleeding pretty freely, but was happy to find that only the skin on my head was cut. The force of the missile was well spent I suppose, and then my hat, which was badly torn, helped to save my head. The death of the noble & gallant Genl. Rodes is a serious loss to the army, & is deeply regretted by all. He was beloved by his Div. which had the most implicit confidence in him & considered him one of the very best Maj. Genls in the Confederacy. Pick Moore was the nearest to him when he fell & brought him off the field on his horse. Gen. Battle then took command of our Divis. & Col. Pickens of our Brig. The Col tho' soon recd a painful wound thro' the right had & had to leave the field. By-the-way, he is an excellent officer & as gallant a little fellow as can be found anywhere. Our army continued to fall back to Fisher's Hill that night—21 miles south of Winchester. Besides marching 8 miles & fighting during the day, I walked that night 13 miles & then met with Joe Grigg who got in a wagon & insisted on my getting on his horse, which I did & rode the balance of the way—8 or 9 miles. We got to bed about 3 o'clock next morning, pretty much fatigued. Mr. Joe is always just as kind as he can be & will do anything in the world for me: he is one of my very best friends. The army took its old position behind the line of breastworks that we threw up a month or two ago at Fisher's Hill, and there I left it, and went with Col. P to a private house in the country.

I shall now have to stop with this narration now, and bring my letter to a close, in order that it may go by tomorrow morning's mail; but will try and write again in a day or two & will then give you an account of our trip the rest of the way to this city, etc., etc. Suffice it to say at present that we arrived here safely at dark last night and are in pleasant quarters. Col. P's hand has been very painful but is doing well, & I am perfectly well with only a little cut in the scalp which will be healed up in a few days. I telegraphed to you to-day & must beg you to excuse the brevity of the dispatch as it cost a dollar a word. Please remember me very kindly to all friends. Present my warmest

& best love to my dear sisters & brothers and accept the same, my beloved Mother, from

Your devoted son,
Saml Pickens

P.S. Many thanks to my dear Mama, Lou & Jamie for letters sent by Mr. Norfleet, & to Jamie for one also by Capt. Williams, which contained $400.00. The morning of the battle I had the pleasure of reading one from dear sister Mary also & am very much of obliged to her for it. S.P.

N.B. I will not be able to get a furlough on my wound, and have not heard from the application I made before the battle. I am afraid it will not be approved now since our reverses in the Valley; so I'll be doomed to another great disappointment. Jamie, I hope, will be able to get his furlough extended indefinitely. S.P. Sept. 27th, 1864.

———— • ————

Umbria, Ala.
Nov. 25th, 1864.

My beloved Son,

Your kind and affectionate letter written at Montgomery reached me and I was glad to hear that you had reached there in safety. Oh! my dear Sam, you cannot imagine how much I miss you—how much I have grieved at your absence. Your visit to us seems to me like a dream—one in which we enjoy all the happiness that can be found on Earth and from which we awaken to experience disappointment and sorrow. Your loved forever, your kind and affectionate love, your unremitted attention to me can never be forgot; nor can I ever feel happy without them. You are the life of my life, and my heart is bound up with yours. "Unfortunate and unhappy indeed is the condition of our country" which has called you away from me and from all who tenderly love you. But let us continue to put our whole trust in our Heavenly Father, who has mercifully watched over and preserved your life. You have passed through many and great dangers, and our continued gratitude is due to Him who has carried you safely through them. Thank God! may continue His loving kindnesses to us, and interpose between us and our cruel enemies, and put an end to this terrible war, is my unceasing prayer. I intended writing to you soon after you left us but my heart was so full of sorrow, I feared my letter would depress your spirits instead of bring a comfort to you. Five days after your departure from Umbria, Col. S.B. Pickens came and paid us a visit. He regretted exceedingly that you were not there, and that he had not come in time to have your furlough lengthened. He is much attached to you and spoke handsomely of you. We highly appreciated his visit which was a most agreeable one, for we found him a pleasant companion, genteel, lively and sociable. He stayed with us only 6 days and we were all sorry to part from him. His wound is still bad, yet he speaks of going to Va in two or three weeks. I think Jamie will go on with him. If Jamie must go, I trust he will accompany Col. P who will be a good friend to him.

Dr. Sawyer has lately paid us a visit: he has gone to Selma & Mobile, and will return this way on his route to Tuscaloosa. He wrote to me a day or two after you had gone, telling me of a house in Tuscaloosa to be rented. I would have given much if it had come before you went away, so that you could have determined the question whether to go or remain here. The children require schools and are crazy to go. But I cannot make a move without your advice on the subject. Dr. S says he can get corn for us in Tuscaloosa, which we can pay for by returning the same number of bushels at Drake's landing or at Newbern. He is anxious for us to go and is endeavoring to remove all difficulties in the way of our going. The house adjoins Mrs. Stafford's Seminary and rents at $1200 per year. Mary speaks of going the first of Jan whether I go or not. I know I shall feel great uneasiness at letting her go without me; but cannot put any impediment in the way of her completing her education for she is desirous of having a good one.

Dr. S was "truly sorry that he had not the pleasure of seeing Sammie." He enjoys good health in Tuscaloosa and looks better than he has looked for many years past. This section of country he says is too sickly for us to remain in any longer. You must, my dear Son, advise me what to do. I have implicit confidence in your judgment and will not consent to a move without your sanction. I have long since given up all thought of getting a private teacher—indeed I don't think the children would improve under one. Dr. S says many families in Tuscaloosa have plantations in the Canebrake from which they receive their supplies. Turkeys, butter etc., etc. We have not yet paid our visit to the Canebrake, because I don't like to leave Jamie who will soon be obliged to go away. I wish he could get some situation as a [*unclear*] quartermaster or something else to do that would suit his constitution. I have regretted not speaking to Col. Pickens about Jamie. Perhaps he could aid him in getting an office. We all liked the Col so much that we felt as though we had known him all our life.

Dr. Grigg has been here only once since you left us. He called when Col P was here and seemed glad to meet with him. All are well at the Dr's. I will go over and see them [*unclear.*]

The children are all well. My health has been very good since you left us. The weather has been intensely cold, but has moderated now. Mr. Willingham killed 23 hogs 3 or 4 days since, weighing upwards 3000 lbs. I wish you could be with us now to enjoy sausages etc. and all that pertains to hog-killing season. Mr. Lawless has commenced sowing wheat yesterday, and so did Mr. W. The weather has been so rainy, cold & disagreeable it could not be done sooner. We are getting on finely with ours having got 3 mules & 2 hands from Mr. W. Your friends Enoch is well. All the children unite with me in warmest & deepest love to you, my beloved Son. The prayer of your mother is that God! May bless & protect you. Remember us kindly to friends and to John.

NINE

---◆·◆·◆·◆---

The End

JANUARY–JUNE 1865

Sam returned to camp near New Market on November 27 after a long, arduous journey on crowded trains. He wrote in his diary that he was pleased to see the "boys" again and that they were doing "well." With Confederate reverses in the fall of 1864 and the reelection of Lincoln, morale in the army had suffered as men realized the war would not end soon. Yet, according to Sam, those who surrounded him had not succumbed to defeatism. Soldiers seeking some confirmation of their own confidence that the Confederate armies would recover rejected news of defeat as "Yankee" propaganda and willingly embraced misleading reports, including official ones, of Confederate successes. When reports of the destruction of the Army of Tennessee began circulating through camp, Sam wrote, the men dismissed them because they were "Yankee accounts" that "claimed victory" even though the Union Army retreated to Nashville, according to the Richmond papers. Such "victories" fostered hope that the West was not lost—that the Confederate Army might even force Sherman to surrender in Georgia.[1]

On December 13, 1864, Company D received orders to cook rations and be ready to leave camp at 8:00 on the morning of December 14. Struggling through snow, and eventually mud from the melting snow, the men marched

1. Diary of Samuel Pickens, November 27–December 6; Murray and Hsieh, *A Savage War*, 455–58.

toward Staunton, unaware of their destination. Lying on oil cloths on snow with few blankets, he and the others in his mess struggled to sleep, though exhausted from the day of hard marching.[2] Rumors spread around camp about where they were headed. Some soldiers thought they might be going to Tennessee or Georgia. According to Sam, all feared they might be sent to the trenches at Petersburg as they crowded into boxcars in Staunton. "We had heard so many terrible accounts of life in the trenches," Sam wrote, "that we had a dread & horror of having to leave the valley & come down into them—& from being sent during such a hard spell of weather—& marched rapidly thro the snow, we were confident Gen. Lee was apprehending an attack & that our destination was the trenches." The next day, the division arrived in Richmond, unloaded, and received the dreaded orders to march down to Petersburg.[3]

The Fifth arrived at the Petersburg line on a cold, rainy late December day.[4] It took a few days for the troops from the valley to adapt to life under siege. With the ranks of noncommissioned officers depleted, Sam rotated to the front to stand picket more often. While in the trenches, he and his men were exposed to the rain and cold, but, to Sam's surprise, little or no Union sniping or shelling. The only picket firing directed at Union lines, he reported, was directed at African American soldiers. On picket duty, Sam wrote, Confederate soldiers exchanged coffee and other items with their Union counterparts. Seemingly unaware of the irony, he explained that the only hostile engagements they had were with their own men who were fleeing to Union lines. Men faced with the conditions Sam described and hearing of the suffering of their families could no longer justify continuing to fight when a Union victory seemed to them to be just a matter of time, and they left in unprecedented numbers. So severe had the problem become that the Confederate command offered a thirty-day furlough to men who shot a deserter, according to Sam.[5] News of Sherman's capture of Savannah, the fall of Fort Fisher, and the collapse of the Army of Tennessee at Nashville further undermined the morale of civilians and soldiers. Yet, despite all the signs that the Confederate

2. Diary of Samuel Pickens, December 14–16, 1864.
3. Diary of Samuel Pickens, December 17–18, 1864.
4. Diary of Samuel Pickens, January 15, 1865.
5. Diary of Samuel Pickens, January 9, 1865.

war could not be sustained much longer, Sam still thought "that the tide of war will soon turn & I still confidently believe that a merciful God will bless us with ultimate success. 'The darkest hour precedes the dawn.' God grant that dawn soon appear on the horizon of our political sky now thickly overcast with murky & portentous clouds."[6]

In early February, rumors began to spread through camp about a conference to be held between the Union and Confederate governments to negotiate an end to the war. Like many soldiers and civilians in the Confederate states, Sam hoped the Confederate government might secure what they considered an honorable peace, but rumors were epidemic in camp, so he was skeptical about this one being true. And if a meeting did take place, as he had written to Mary, he doubted that anything would come of it. Nonetheless, he was hopeful when he read credible reports that Confederate emissaries would meet with U.S. officials. Alexander Stephens, Confederate vice president, Virginia senator R. M. T. Hunter, and Confederate assistant secretary of war John Archibald Campbell did meet with President Lincoln and Secretary of State William H. Seward at Hampton Roads, Virginia, for several hours on February 3, but the meeting ended when Lincoln refused to recognize the commissioners as representatives of a legitimate government and insisted upon unconditional Confederate surrender.[7]

For the Pickens family, failure of the peace negotiations, while disappointing, reinforced their commitment to Confederate independence. Mary Gaillard had opposed secession and war in 1861 because she feared the consequences of the Union's collapse for her family and her way of life. After the war began, she hoped that her sons could remain at home. But, when Confederate conscription laws forced Sam and James into the army, her commitment to the Confederate war effort deepened. She wrote Sam in early 1865 that only Confederate victory and independence would bring the reunification of her

6. Diary of Samuel Pickens, January 10, 17; February 9, 1865; Murray and Hsieh, *A Savage War*, 470–71; Glatthaar, *General Lee's Army*, 450–56; Power, *Lee's Miserables*, chap. 9. Fort Fisher was the key fort in a network of defenses defending the mouth of the Cape Fear River, the approach to the port of Wilmington, the single Confederate fort that remained open in late 1864 (McPherson, *Battle Cry of Freedom*, 819–24).

7. Diary of Samuel Pickens, January 30, 1865; McPherson, *Battle Cry of Freedom*, 821–24; Thomas, *The Confederate Nation*, 294–96.

family, and preservation of the lives enslaved people provided for her and her children. Defeat, Mary Gaillard suggested, would mean that all their sacrifice would have been in vain. The family knew that the war was not going well and that conditions for soldiers in the Petersburg trenches were abysmal.[8] Mary Gaillard's letters complained about Confederate impressment of crops and animals and how speculators exploited producers' desire to be paid directly rather than wait for government compensation they doubted would ever come. Yet she remained steadfast in her belief that the Confederacy would ultimately prevail and was reconciled to the likely departure of her younger son Willie for the army. Believing the war would continue until Confederate armies secured victory on the battlefield, Mary Gaillard planned to relocate the family to Tuscaloosa for the duration of the war.

As throughout the war, Sam's letters shaped his family's understanding of the prospects of the Confederacy. The surviving letters Sam wrote home in early 1865 mostly concealed from the family the misery of life under siege and the disintegration of the army he described in his diary. Only in a letter to Mary in January did he reveal, briefly, his doubts about the future of the Confederacy.

Camp Rodes
Chesterfield Co.,
Virginia
January 19th, 1865

My dear Sister,

As I have not yet written to thank you for two very affectionate and interesting epistles with which you have favored me since my return from home, I will make an attempt at doing so tonight, though it is very cold and I do not feel much like writing; but as Sergt. McCall of our Company is to

8. On class distinctions and the response of women to the collapsing Confederacy, see Faust, *Mothers of Invention*, 244–47. The experience of Sam and James reinforces Joseph Glatthaar's argument about the disproportionate number of men from wealthy families who served in the Confederate Army ("Everyman's War," 226–29, and *Soldiering in the Army of Northern Virginia*, chap. 11).

start to Greensboro on furlough in the morning, and three or four of the boys are seated around a box in my cabin writing letters home by the light of my wax paper, I'll try my hand too.[9] We don't like to lose our camp and was of the opinion that it would not be necessary for us to move, and here the matter was once more set at rest. But, alas our troubles are not to end here, it seems, for as Shakespeare says "sorrows come not single spies, but in battalions"[10] and "One woe doth tread upon another's heels so fast they follow."[11] So tonight the rumor is that our Brigade is to be sent to Wilmington, N.C. I don't believe a word of it though. The fact is you can't believe anything at all you hear now, and not half you see. Speaking of rumors, there are a thousand and one in circulation now—they pervade the atmosphere and even find their way into the newspapers. Especially has this been the case since Frank P. Blair and Gen'l Singleton (Yankees) have been on a visit to Richmond. Many of these rumors too are in relation to peace. Would that they could be satisfied! But I fear there is little hope of making an honorable peace with our enemies after the late success they have met with. I presume you have heard of the fall of Fort Fisher.[12]

I should like much to know if you are now in Tuscaloosa at school and if Mama has also gone with the rest of the family. If so, I trust you are all pleasantly situated & that you and the children will enjoy fine educational advantages and meet with no more interruptions. You must all write to me more frequently than you do. I have had only one letter in the last two weeks and that was very long and interesting one from Jamie. It reached me just after closing a letter to him. I was very glad to learn by it that you and Jamie were to receive the rite of confirmation. I must now make an end to this rather lengthy & [*sentence unclear.*] All the rest of my mess have long since been in bed and are snoring soundly. Give my warmest & best love to my

9. Sam was referring to W. A. McCall, who had enlisted in 1861 (CMSR Alabama, RG109).

10. From *Hamlet*, Act IV, Scene 5. King Claudius is speaking to Queen Gertrude.

11. From *Hamlet*, Act IV, Scene 7. Queen Gertrude tells Laertes that his sister has drowned.

12. Francis Preston Blair was engaged in discussions with Jefferson Davis about his proposal for what would be peace conference at Hampton Roads (McPherson, *Battle Cry of Freedom*, 821–22).

dearest Mama, Jamie, Louty and Icha, and accept also the same for yourself. Remember me very kindly to Dr. Grigg, Mr. Enoch and all enquiring friends. Howdy to all the servants. "A'dieu, le bon Dieu, je vous commende!"[13]

As ever, I remain
Your affectionate brother,
Samuel.

———•—•—

Trenches Dunn's Farm
Chesterfield Co., Va.
Feb. 11th, 1865

My dear Mama,

I have just been informed that an officer of our Brigade will start to Ala. this evening & have determined to pen you a few lines—tho' I will have but a very short time to write now. I mailed a letter to Lou a day or two since but as the Yankees have again cut the road there is no telling when it will reach home. I have had a sumptuous literary feast today in the form of a batch of dearly prized letters from home: one from you my dear Mama; one from Jamie; two from Mary & one from Louty. I don't know how to express my thanks to you all for these great favors, nor my deep regret that communication, now being near interrupted, I may be unable for some time to answer them, and also to receive more from you. I am truly sorry to hear that you have been suffering so from an attack of rheumatism or neuralgia, & hope you will be free from it in future. Jamie, I trust, will succeed in getting detailed for light duty. How I wish I could be with you to lend you my assistance in moving to Tuscaloosa. If you had not already shipped the box you spoke of sending me by Express do not send it, for I have no idea it would ever reach me. If an opportunity offers for sending them, I should like to have some socks. I hope you will be able to collect money enough to meet your wants by the time you are ready to move to T. I will write again

---

13. "To God, the good God, I commend you." Robert Burns often concluded his correspondence with this phrase. Burns's correspondence had been published by the 1850s. Pickens, it appears, had read at least some of it.

as soon as possible. That an all merciful God will bless you all and keep you under his special care and protection is the sincere and oft repeated prayer of

Your devoted son,
Sam.

———•———

Umbria Jan 5th '65

My beloved Son,

Your kind letter dated Nov 21st had been recd and I was rejoiced to find that letters could now be recd by mails. To be deprived of the comfort of having you with me, and cut off from communication with you is enough to crase[14] me. But thanks to a Merciful God! for the strong hope I have that you will be protected by His Almighty arm and return to me again. Another letter dated Dec. 11th containing apple seeds recd. I will attend to the planting of the seeds at the right time and hope you will enjoy the fruit with us.

We have just learned that your Division had been ordered to Petersburg. I was truly sorry because I thought you had probably gone into comfortable winter quarters in the Valley. I trust, however, that the campaign is over and that you will not have hardships to endure where you are. I hear from everyone that you make a fine soldier, and Major Seay, who dined with us a few days since, says he "learns you would not be at home now if you could." Mary, Lou, the Damers and Helen Withers who was spending the day with us, had much sport with Major Seay; but managed not to give offence by restraining their laughter until he spoke again, pretending then to enjoy his wit. They would have made him dance, but I prevented them from insisting upon his making a fool of himself. The Damers are staying with us & Dr. Grigg is attending the third & youngest daughter who is threatened with pneumonia. She is better today.

The children are pretty well. Jamie has had a return of his old disease lately and has been complaining: his appetite has not been good, and he does not look so well as he usually does. Mary has not been very well of late, tho' she is not sick: she looks thin and pale. Willie looks remarkably hearty

14. "Crase" means to break into pieces or crack.

again; but exposes himself to all kinds of weather. He was ordered to appear at Hollow Square last evening, but the weather was bad and Capt. Grigg was not there so the few who went came away without orders. Willie says he is in militia service, which he hates, but can soon get out of it by joining the Army: this I think he will soon do, as he is crazy on the subject. I would prefer sending him to school, but he will not listen to me when I commence telling him of the necessity of his being educated. He says when the war is over, he intends studying English, Latin & mathematics. Lou & Icha are well and in fine spirits. Lou is the life of the house: she is growing up very fast, and is almost as tall as Mary. Icha too is springing up, and should lose no time from his studies.

I wrote to you some time since to know your opinion about our going to Tuscaloosa to live. I have anxiously expected an answer, but have not yet recd it. Mary, Lou & Icha are all very anxious to go to school, and Willie declares he will never spend another summer here—indeed I am afraid to risk the children's health at this place. I have almost determined to go and take the house, which Dr. Sawyer wrote to me about. He says it is a comfortable three-story brick house with six large rooms, necessary out buildings, stable etc. etc. The rent of it is 1200 per year. Mr. Cowan wishes Umbria and promises to put it in good order, and to vacate it at any time we may wish to return, if we will give him two- or three-days notice. I was glad to hear of a tenant, as I would not like to leave the place unoccupied, for I know how soon it would go to ruin. So I told the Dr. I would let Mr. C have it if I go away. Mrs. Tuomey's school[15] is highly recommended, and Mary will go to it whether I move or not. I am aware that we shall have some difficulty in getting supplies but we must submit to some inconveniences in order to enjoy the benefit of school: I have a poor opinion of private tuition—indeed a male teacher cannot be got now and a female would only be an incumbrance. If you disapprove of our going, tell me so, and I will remain at home. I want a Counsellor and prize you above all others.

I have not collected one dollar on our corn accts and Mr. Briggs says he does not know when Government will pay. It is wrong to keep us out of money

15. Mrs. Tuomey was the wife of geologist Michael Tuomey. She opened the school during the war (Fleming, *Civil War and Reconstruction in Alabama*, 215).

for we don't know how to pay taxes, which will soon be collected. As to the money for our mules & horse impressed, I fear we shall never get it. I am unwilling to sell our corn on hand, but fear it will soon be impressed. A state agent called on me to purchase it and offered $3.50 per bushel payable on delivery or a little after. This agent said Mr. Kirksey of Eutaw would soon impress our corn etc. etc. and that I had better sell to him. Dr. G advised me not to do so. What say you about it. I want your opinion all the time about everything. Oh! What would I not give to have you at my side. God! Grant my prayer.

Well! We have at last got rid of the Lawless tribe, and glad am I to get rid of such dishonest people. Lawless carried off everything that was portable and money that he got from government on the exchange of a mule—$500 at least I suppose, so now he is independent of us having paid himself for his services. Jamie intends writing to him; but I doubt if he will reply. I hear that Mrs. Withers is going to employ Lawless. I regret to hear it, as he may be a troublesome neighbor. Mr. & Mrs. Cole seem to be very clever people—they are industrious and anxious to put the place in good order. I have no doubt they will suit us. The servants are being clad and their shoes will soon be finished. Robert is at the G.P. and Carey & Peter, I hear, are assisting him. Some of the hogs there have been killed & saved. Mr. Willingham has lost some of his second killing or rather some of them are touched, but the servants perhaps will eat them.

The servants are all well, make many inquiries about you & desire to be kindly remembered to you. Remember us to John—tell him Suky & their children are well. They stopped here 2 days since on their way to the Evans' place. Dr. G & family are well. The Dr said he would write to you. Mr. Enoch is still fond of you and often speaks affectionable of you. Poor fellow! He is often on a spree now & I fear will come to starvation with his family; some of them are here almost everyday.

On the 1st Sunday of this year, all of the family attended church in Greensboro, and Jamie & Mary were confirmed by Bishop Wilmer. I cannot tell you, my beloved Son, how ardently I desired that you were amongst the candidates but I feel assured that you have given your heart to your maker, and will soon unite yourself to some Christian church and I trust will be "an heir triumphant of Christs' church in Heaven." Platt Croom & his wife were confirmed and three others. We are much pleased with the Bishop.

Jamie wrote to Col. Pickens but has recd no reply. If he is with you, re-member us kindly to him and to all our friends. I have rheumatism in my hands so badly I can scarcely hold my pen, so I must beg that you will tear up my letters, so soon as they are read. I am anxiously expecting your likeness which I hope is a faithful representation of you. I thank you, my beloved Son, for attending to my request. All unite with me in warmest, deepest love to you.

May God! ever bless & protect you.

Yr Mother.

Pickens 1865
"On the front steps"
Sunday Evening Jan 8th '65

My beloved Brother,

I was delighted a few days ago on receiving one of your ever dear & welcome letters. Oh! Brother Sam we have missed you so much & besides the pain of separation we have for some time been denied the means of cor-respondence; but thank God it has again been opened & I trust we will never be troubled in the like manner again. It makes my heart ache to think of the suffering which has ensued from Sherman's unchecked course in Georgia. What a great pity it was that we had no force to resist him. I hate to think of Savannah, that beautiful city being occupied by the Yankees. I sincerely hope that Charleston will not be taken, I love that city because it was our dear Mother's birth place.

The weather is very changeable—this morning it was very cold & this evening is so mild that I find it pleasant on the gallery. It is cloudy & I fear we will have more rain in a few days.

We all passed a very dull Christmas. We attended church in Greensboro & went over terrible roads to get there. When we got to Mr. Hatcher's a shower of rain came up & before getting to town everyone was soaking. Our carriage leaks & we got the rain. The rain put a stop to many persons attending church. Jemmie & I expected to be confirmed, but the Bishop was quite sick & confirmation was postponed to the 1st of January. We attended

St. Paul's again last Sunday. Confirmation was administered & several were confirmed, amongst them Dr. P. Croom & his wife, Jemmie & myself. We so much wished for you my dear Brother, but I trust you will never let an opportunity pass for being confirmed. Mary Damer was also confirmed. I must stop writing till I get a candle as it is getting quite dark.

Jan. 9th

I did not finish this letter last night as I had to read. I never saw such weather. It has been raining hard all day, the roads are in a miserable condition. I don't suppose we will be able to ride out for a week or two. I suppose you have received letters from us telling of our anticipated move to Tuscaloosa. Yes, Mama has written to Dr. Sawyer to engage a house—the one he spoke of. It is a three story brick house with six large rooms & out house—stable, hen, house, coal house, & carriage house. I believe the house is a wing of Mrs. Stafford's residence, the lady who formerly kept the Presbyterian school in Tuscaloosa. The house is furnished partly. I wish Mama would go to T for she would be much happier with some friends to cheer her up. I expect to start for Tuscaloosa next week. I don't know whether I will be able to get off so soon. It is hard to leave dear old Umbria. Dr. Sawyer says Mama can buy corn in Tuscaloosa & her supplies can be sent up from the plantations. He says some families live in T and get their supplies from the Canebrake. Dr. Grigg called a few days ago to tell that Mr. Sam Cowin would be glad to get this place. He said he would put it in good repair. He has not been here yet, to make any proposition.

I suppose Willie has written all the news relative to the crop etc. The wheat is very good I think—not equal to Mr. Hatchers, however. We have employed Mr. Cole to take charge of the Goodrum place. The servants say the place looks differently already. He is a very industrious man & is making many improvements—building new cabins etc. Do you remember Green at the Canebrake? He was married to Missy, aunt Mary's daughter during Christmas week.[16]

16. Green and Missy were young enslaved people. As Mary wrote, Green was at the Canebrake and Mary was at Umbria with her mother. Green was approximately twenty-one and Mary about seventeen, based on their ages in the probate inventory of 1857.

Has cousin Sam reached Va yet—remember us kindly to him & tell him I am really going to Tuscaloosa, but have not gone yet. Ask him if he went to see Miss Julia Jones in Greensboro. Tell him he must not forget that he promised to make me his confidant.

Oh my the rain is pouring in torrents. When will the roads dry?

Mama received a very kind letter from cousin Israel P in answer to one she wrote him about some accounts, I believe. He offered to pay us very soon if Mama will accept the money. I hope she won't. Mr. Tood Cowin is at home. He intends leaving this week. I will try to find out what day he is going & will write by him.

I was glad to see by the paper that Genl. Joe Johnson had been reinstated. I hope we will soon hear better news from that army soon. John Dorroh has just come home on furlough. He was slightly wounded in the thumb. He represents the army as being in a completely demoralized condition. Gayle Dorroh was here a few nights ago to tea. He says the army is suffering for shoes & socks. You must write me word whether you have good gloves. I can get wool now & will not be able to get any later in the season. Have you lost your cap or is it wearing out? Answer all these questions.

I must close. I hope you are comfortably situated this gloomy day my dear Brother. I am in hopes you are comfortably fixed in winter quarters.

Write very soon. All join me in warmest & dearest love to you my beloved Brother.

However I remain your truly devoted
Sister

———◆———

"Umbria"
Jan 18th 1865

My beloved Brother.

I have been intending to write to you for several days, but the days pass so rapidly that I have not had a chance till this morning, or rather afternoon, for it is nearly dinner time.

I trust you are now snugly fixed in your new winter quarter, and I do most sincerely hope that you will be permitted to remain there all the winter.

Jemmie went to Tuscaloosa to report. He was quite sick last week & wrote or got me to write to Dr. Sawyer for him. William was sent with the note. Dr. S wrote to Jemmie telling him that he must report immediately.[17] He does not like the way in which Jemmie has acted—he thinks twas his duty to go to T much oftener. Mama wrote to Dr. Sawyer begging him to exert his influence with the board in trying to get a certificate of disability for Jemmie. With the certificate Mr. Enoch thinks that Jemmie will be able to get a contract in the Nitre Bureau—Mr. Melton (James) has just got a situation of that kind. I trust that dear Jemmie will be successful. He is not able to serve his country in the field when he is in other ways. Twill be such a comfort & relief to Mama to have Jemmie with her. I will write you what success J has met with when he returns tomorrow evening.

Well, I must tell you about our going to Tuscaloosa. William went to look at the home & was disgusted with the appearance of it. The plastering is in a dilapidated condition, the fire places are broken, the house is separated from Mr. Staffords only with a safe or press of some kind, the coal house is not secure, the garden is [*unclear*] Mr. Stafford & lastly there is no carriage house. I have given you William's unfavorable sentiment of the house & lot. Now it may be that William who is quite unwilling to go to Tuscaloosa [*rest of paragraph unreadable.*]

We are having beautiful and delightful spring weather. It cheers us up. Oh! how I wish you were here today dear brother Sam. We anticipate a pleasant ride on horseback this afternoon. 'Twould be such a happy ride were you to be our escort. I wish I could think that peace was not far distant. I wonder if the commissioners did any good by going North?[18]

---

17. W. T. Sawyer, assistant surgeon, Confederate Medical Department. He lived in the Hollow Square precinct near the Pickenses (U.S. Census, 1860). See Jones, *A Rebel War Clerk's Diary*, 35.

18. The commissioners Mary referred to here were Clement C. Clay of Alabama, James B. Holcombe of Virginia, and George N. Sanders. The three men, without government sanction, traveled to the Canada side of Niagara Falls, from where they sent notes to Horace Greeley, the editor of the New York *Tribune* proposing a peace conference. The Niagara "peace ne-

Mr. John Dorroh arrived at Eire a few weeks ago on furlough. He was slightly wounded in the thumb in the battle of Franklin, I believe. He represents the army of Tenn as being in a very deplorable condition. Our poor soldiers are barefooted having neither shoes nor socks. The army is also completely demoralized, declaring they will never fight under Hood again. I hope Johnson, whom you have heard ere this, has been reinstated, and take command of the army.

Our affairs indeed look gloomy but the darkest hour is just before day. I trust the dove of peace is about to dawn on our suffering and distressed country. I received a letter from Miss Minnie Tuomey telling me that there would be no vacancy in the school till the 15th of Feby. I hope I will be able to go to T then.

Dinner is ready. I must close. All join me in warmest and dearest love to you my dear good Brother. All friends including Mr. & Mrs. Enoch, the Dr. & family & Juliet beg to be very kindly remembered.

Your truly devoted
Sister Mary

As Mary revealed, James was already in Tuscaloosa, where he had been ordered to report for a physical examination to determine his fitness to return to the army. In the next two letters, he reported to his mother about his renewed appeal for a detail, hopefully to the Nitre or Tax in Kind Bureau, which would allow him to remain near home.

---

gotiation" was widely reported and criticized in both the Confederacy and the Union. See Richmond *Examiner*, July 26, 1864; Columbus (GA) *Daily Enquirer*, July 28, 1864; *Daily True Delta* (New Orleans), July 31, 1864; *Crisis* (Columbus, OH), July 27, 1864; New York *Herald*, July 27, 1864.

Tuscaloosa, Ala.
Jan. 21st, 1865

My dear Sam,

I have delayed to answer your last letter which I rec'd some time in Dec and partly answered but not as fully as I intended. I would have written by Capt. Williams, John Christian, or Henry Childress, but did not know that they would certainly leave when they said they would (they had said so often before that they intended to leave and did not at last do so). Lieut. Borden, tho, who was at our house on Monday last, told us he heard that they had certainly left the day before for Newbern & would take the cars. Mama also intended sending on a box to you by them, if they would have carried one, but was not aware of their intention to leave in time to pack it. I was very sorry that we could send neither letters nor a box by them, as the former would have been news from home & the latter a great treat to you. However, Mama intended, just before I left home, to pack and send to you a box of such provisions as would keep & as you would wish most.

As you will see by my letter, I write from Tuscaloosa, whither I was ordered by Dr. S on Sat last. I suppose he had grown tired of giving me weekly leaves of absence (as I had not reported to him since the day that John & I came up on 9th of Nov. However, I was too unwell the greater part of the time & the water between here and home was too high the other part, for me to attempt to come. So I wrote him word that I had been prevented, on this account, from coming, and sent William up on last Friday with the letter. The day before I sent William, I was taken with a severe attack of biliousness & was never sicker, for part of one night, in my life. William returned with a letter from the Dr to me saying that he had been very uneasy about me, that I had been the first one to whom he had been so lenient & that I would certainly be the last, and that I must report to him forthwith, when he hoped to make all things straight again. Oh, he actually threatened to send cavalry after me (or rather said that this would be done) if I did not come. But I remembered the Latin phrase "Is qui alium facit, facit per se"[19] and know that if the cavalry are sent that he could prevent it, and therefore, if he did not, he would be doing the same thing as send them himself. Suffice it to say, I

19. Legal term meaning "He who acts through another does the act himself."

came up as soon as I got able to take the ride, which was on last Wednesday morning. William & I left home rather late (about 10½) and got here at 9h. 45 min. P.M. The roads had been very bad indeed; washed dreadfully in some places, and in another a bridge had partially given way. However, they had dried very much & were getting almost as good as they were in Nov.; the places that were washed had been repaired, and we succeeded in reaching here very safely indeed.

Dr. S has been, apparently, very kind to me since my arrival here. He thinks I can get a detail in the Nitre bureau, and is kindly endeavoring to do this for me. I sincerely trust that he will succeed, as I do not think I could stand field service. He says he does not think I could either, but that no board would judge me unfit, as I look to be much stronger than I am. When I left home, all were very well indeed.

Mama received your letter telling her to use her judgment in deciding whether or not to come to this place & put the children at schools, not many days before I left home. She decided to come, if she could get a suitable house, and instructed me to look at Mrs. Stafford's rooms & if I thought they would suit to take them at once. I, immediately after my arrival here, went & looked at the rooms which Mrs. Stafford has rented and which I thought, with a little repair, would easily be made comfortable. So I engaged them for Mama. I did not like to advise Mama to come up here, as I know how hard it will be for her to obtain provisions and such conveniences as she would require if she left home. But, as she said, our place has become very unhealthy, and she dreads spending another summer there; and as she is anxious to have the children at school, I did not dissuade her from coming.

The weather, which has been very beautiful for several days past, (reminding one more of spring than winter) has again changed and last evening and this morning we had a great deal of rain. It is not yet settled, so I would not be surprised if we have another bad spell, and if the roads become very impracticable.

We were all glad to hear from you, indeed, as there had been so many interruptions to letters going & coming that we had despaired of receiving any by mail. We had, to the time I left home, rec'd two from you by mail from which fact, I hope, the mails will pass without interruption to & from Va. It is hard indeed to be denied the privilege of sending & receiving letters, as by means of them alone we can convey our thoughts, emotions & sentiments to each other when absent and apart.

I was sorry to hear that our Division had been recalled from the Valley, as I hoped they would be allowed to go into winter quarters there and have an easier & healthier time than in the trenches near Petersburg. Mr. Wynne, tho,' who heard from Jack just before I left, told me that the latter wrote him word that they are building quarters near Petersburg and would soon be ensconced for the Winter, if they are permitted to remain.

Well I must now close, as supper is almost ready and as I have extended my letter to such a length.

Your affectionate brother,
James.

———•———

Tuscaloosa, Ala.
Jan. 31st, 1865.

My dear Mother,

For the first time since my arrival here, I received letters from home on Saturday night last, being handed me by Andrew Pickens.[20] It seems that all my letters have been carried or sent by the Post Master, I presume, to the University, and I was denied the great privilege of hearing from home from you my dear Mama, & sisters & brothers, from the Wednesday on which I came up (the 18th) till last Saturday—ten days. I was greatly relieved on receiving them as I began to fear that something had occurred to prevent your writing. I was very sorry to hear that you were so unwell, but hope sincerely that you are now well again. We have had very cold, damp and disagreeable weather since I have been here and I expect you exposed yourself during that spell, which brought on your attack of rheumatism. Mama you ought to be very careful not to expose yourself to the damp & cold which we now have

20. Andrew Calhoun Pickens was another son of Joseph Pickens of Eutaw and grandson of Revolutionary War general Andrew Pickens of South Carolina. When James wrote this letter, Pickens was a student at the University of Alabama and a private in Company C, Alabama Corps of Cadets.

in such unvaried succession but which I trust will soon be followed by the mild and genial breath of spring.

Oh, Mama, you cannot imagine what a lonely time I have had since I left home. Although I did not think there would be much probability of my returning, on the day following my departure, yet I imagined I might do so. You can guess how disappointed I was when the buggy drove away and I was left alone. Dr. S has seemed very kind to me since I came up, but I am of the opinion that he might have continued my leaves of absence to remain at home until I found a situation in the Nitre or Tax in Kind departments. He endeavored to get for me a place in the Nitre department at this place, but as I found out that it was only for an overseer of hands and that the position would be a more arduous one than that of a soldier in the ranks, I immediately declined accepting it. It seems that the duty or office of clerk in this department has been filled, and I suppose it would be a hard matter to get a situation in the Nitre Bureau.

If Judge Lyon were at home I would try and get him to apply to Capt. Curry in the Tax in Kind Dept for a situation as clerk, as this would be the occupation which I would prefer. He is not at home tho' and I know of no one to whom I might apply. I would be very glad to get some place of the kind, as I am confident of my inability to perform field duty, and in this opinion Dr. Sawyer concurs with me. Moreover, if I had some place of the above kind, I could be more useful to the army than in rendering it the poor service which I have done since my enlistment. I fear such another spell of sickness as that I went through with last summer, & do not feel that I could survive half the exposure & fatigue to which I was then subject, if I had it to attempt again.

I sincerely and devotedly pray that some way may suggest itself whereby I may be permitted, with God's help, to return to you, my dear mother, & sisters & brothers & that soon we may be together again never to part while we live. God help me in the attempt. Mama I suppose I would not be giving you news if I mentioned the following facts, as your facilities for obtaining the latest items are much superior to those which are enjoyed by us up here. However, it is telegraphed that our Congress has appointed three commissioners who have been sent to Washington City to confer with the Northern Govt on the subject of a peace between the two sections. Vice Pres.

Stephens, Hon. R. M. T. Hunter of Va., & Judge Campbell of Ala. (who is the assistant Secretary of War) are the three gentlemen who, it is reported, have been appointed as Commissioners for peace. Oh, that our enemy may have their hearts changed towards us, and that, whereas they now seek our destruction, they may seek and endeavor to terminate this bloody war, and conclude with us for all generations, a speedy, just, an honorable and a lasting peace, and that our commissioners may soon return with the "glad tidings of great joy" & proclaim to this nation, as the heavenly chorister did on our Savior's birth, "peace on earth and goodwill towards men!" It is not well for us to be too elated; expecting that to happen which has so often deluded us; but I think that there are a great many here & elsewhere who will await the return of our Commissioners with no little degree of anxiety & interest. I sincerely trust that their endeavors may, if they fail to accomplish anything greater, lead to preliminaries which will result in the desired end, and bring us that peace which once we enjoyed, so unconsciously ignorant of its great worth & blessings. But it is all in God's hands, and when He seeth fit that we should again possess it, He will send it to us.

You no doubt read Cousin Sam's letter, which I was very glad to receive indeed. He had quite a fatiguing trip of it from Ala to So. Car but I am very glad he reached there in safety. I am sorry tho' that he intends returning to his command with his hand in the condition that he says it is, for he will find the army but a poor place to heal it.

Mama I mentioned that Andrew Pickens handed me the letters which I received last Sat. night. He knocked at the door on that night—and I was very much rejoiced to find that he had quite a considerable mail for me. I first saw Andrew that morning. He did not recognize me at first, but spoke to me as "Sam." He had grown so much that I would not have recollected him by height at all, as he was a boy a little larger than Icha when I saw him last. He came to see Dr. Sawyer, not imagining, he said, that I was here, in regard to Willie, who, he learned, was coming up to this place. He told me to say to Willie that a vacancy had occurred in the College & in his room, and that he hopes W would enter the Univ. and share it with him. He spoke of the many advantages attending one's first going to this institution prior to entering the service, with which advantages I was familiar, and said that he would insist on Willie's going there at any rate 'till the first of July, when he

& Willie leave. I wish Willie would avail himself of so good an opportunity of mental as well as physical culture. They go, at this institution, upon the old Roman principle, "mens sana in corpora sano"; or, "a sound mind in a sound body." I think Willie would like it very much after entering it. Mama please say to Mary & Louty that I am much obliged to them for their kind letters and will answer them very soon. Also to Mary that I delivered her note to Mrs Tuomey & received from her an answer which I enclose with this letter.

Dr. S requested me to go with him to Dr. Anderson's & form the acquaintance of his family. So on last Sunday evening we called there and spent an hour or two very pleasantly. Mr. Joe Davis, the President's brother lives with Dr. A., but I did not see him. He is quite an old man, upwards of 80 years, I believe. The Andersons are a very sociable, pleasant & hospitable family & altho' refugees of only a year's residence in this place are acquainted with a great many people here and like the place very much. A cousin of theirs, whom I saw the other evening whilst there, told me that the Methodist school was the best of the female schools. I have heard one or two others express the same opinion.

Oh, my dear mother, how glad I would be to get a leave of absence and go, for a short time at any rate, and be with you all again. If you think I could assist you when you are going to leave, please write me word and I will try and prevail on Dr. Sawyer to grant me the leave of absence.

I attended service at the Episcopal church on last Sunday and heard Mr. Nevins preach. His sermon was taken from the following text St. Luke, 4th chap., 21st verse. I do not think he is an interesting minister, his manner not being as animated as it should, to add to the delivery. The church is pretty well attended every Sunday.

As it is getting late, I must close my letter, promising to write to you again very soon & hoping soon to have the great pleasure of hearing from you.

Give my warmest love to Mary, Willie, Louty & Icha & accept, my dear mother, the same from your

Affectionate Son,
James

P.S. Remember me kindly to Mr. Enoch & his wife, Dr. Grigg & Mrs. G. and to all inquiring friends: and tell the servants all, howd'ye for me.

Please let me know Mama, when you hear from Sam, as I suppose it will be some time before he knows that I am here.

Dr. Sawyer requests me to send his kindest regards to you and the children.

Mama if there is enough wool at home, spun, to make me a pair of gloves, I would be glad of them as the cotton ones I have keep my hands cold, and are almost worn out. Miss Juliet will knit them for me, I suppose. If there be no spun wool at home and you could buy a pair from Aunt Edy McAlpine, I would be glad to have them. Also, please have a leather strap out about 3 ft. long and 1½ in. wide, and a buckle sewed on one end to strap the black bag with, in case I go away. After it is made, please put it with the black bag in the black trunk.

Your aff. son, James

———— •◆• ————

Umbria, Ala.
Jan. 23rd 1865

My beloved Son,

I had the pleasure of receiving a most affectionate and welcome letter from you ten days since and have been promising myself the pleasure of replying to it every day since; but a violent attack of rheumatism has prevented. I went to Wesley Chapel the day after your highly prized favor was rec'd, and took cold from sitting in the church, which you know is without a stove. I have never suffered so much in my life and think from the severity of the attack that it must have been neuralgia. Red pepper and mullein boiled together and used as a bath relieved me together with a bath of ley.[21] I mention the remedies used, so that you will know what to do for yourself and friends when similarly attacked. I am now well but afraid to go out, as the weather is cold and damp. We have had rainy weather for two months, and we have had roads that riding for pleasure is never thought of. I have

21. The combination of red pepper and mullein (a weed) was and is used to treat joint pain.

long wished to visit the Canebrake and Goodrum places, but cannot do so on account of the roads. I am afraid I shall go away without seeing the servants. Jamie left us on Wednesday last for Tuscaloosa where he will remain until the board of Physicians decides upon his case. I went to Dr. Sawyer to beg him to use his influence in getting a discharge for Jamie from field service, and told him that Hon. F.S. Lyons had promised to aid him in getting a detail. He promises to do so; but says Jamie looks so healthy that it will be difficult to get any board to give him a discharge. I am full of anxious care about Jamie. Knowing Dr. S to be a hard-hearted man, I look for no favors from him. I trust in God! that Jamie will be permitted to remain at home and engaged in making nitre. We miss Jamie more than I can express and I know he is sad at leaving us all to keep company with Dr. S. We must, however, look on the bright side of the picture, and hope that ere long we shall all be happily reunited. A merciful God will, I hope, deliver us out of the hands of our cruel enemies soon, scatter the clouds which surround us at present, and cause a bright day to open upon us. Then will our hearts rejoice when all fear is removed and we find ourselves a free and independent people. Oh! that we may all be made better by the trials and sufferings we have endured during our struggle for independence, and show our gratitude to Him, who has wonderfully and mercifully sustained us through all.

Finding it impossible to get a teacher for the children, and believing that private tuition would not do justice to their talents, I have determined to go to Tuscaloosa and am only waiting for the roads to improve. Jamie has engaged a part of Mrs. Stafford's house—6 rooms for us with kitchen & separate from hers. I am prepared to meet many difficulties in moving away and to be subject to many inconveniences, but have found the advantages of school accomplishments etc. etc. will make amends. I can quietly submit to almost anything, and will be abundantly satisfied if the climate proves healthy. Umbria has become so very sickly for several years past that I am really afraid to spend another summer here.

A few days since two letters came from the Office for Jamie. I recognized the hand writing of Col. S. B. Pickens and was so anxious to know his movements that I took the liberty of opening his letter. I was confident that Jamie would not object to my doing so. The letter was dated Jan 3rd and he said he would leave home in a few days for Va., so I suppose he is now with you. Remember us all kindly to him, and tell him I hope his hand is well. I have not yet rec'd any money for corn, but hope Capt. Curry will pay us the next time he comes to Greensboro. I can't go away until I am paid, as we are without funds. I have sent to Cap May for the rent of the Eubank place, but he has paid no attention to my note. Jamie kindly drew off all my papers for court before he left, and I am to send them to Mr. Wm. Webb to arrange for a settlement with Judge Oliver. Mr. Webb says if the roads are too bad in March for me to go to Eutaw to sign the papers, I can defer doing so to the next term. As I am going to Tuscaloosa, I would prefer signing them before I leave Greene.

Everything is going on as usual. The children are well and enjoy themselves with the Damers (three in number) who have been staying with us since the day after Christmas. Jamie is engaged to Juliet: he never said one word to me on the subject, but wrote to tell me of it, as soon as he reached Tuscaloosa. He is devotedly attached to her, and never left her side when he was at home. I trust they will live happily together. I don't know Jamie's plans, but sincerely hope he will complete his avocation before he marries. I think it would be advisable to complete Juliet's education and if I were Jamie, I would induce her to go to school for two years. But of this they are better judges than I, and will act for themselves. The children are delighted at the thought of going to school and Mary was so bent on going, that she wrote to Mrs. Tuomey & engaged a place in her school. I hope they will all be remarkably studious and make up for lost time. Willie protests against going to school until the war is over. I regret that he [*Rest of sentence is unclear.*]

I hope to hear that you are in comfortable Winter quarters, and are getting on well. Oh! my beloved son, how anxiously & constantly do I think of you, and how earnestly do I pray that we may soon meet. Words are inadequate to express how much I love you—how much I miss you. Oh! that my prayer may be heard & answered. I intend sending you a box by express this week, and will put in it only such things as will keep so that if the box be delayed sometime on the road, the things in it will be good. Willie is going to give in our tithe tax this morning & is waiting for our letters, so I must close. I am sorry I did not send you some socks by Capt. Williams. We intended writing, but the roads & weather were too bad to send a servant out.

I will write to you soon & tell John about Suky and her family. Remember us kindly to him. Your friends are all well and send much love to you always. All unite with me in warmest love to you, my ever dear, good son. May God! almighty bless you.

Mother

Umbria
February 28th

My beloved Son,

I sent a long letter to the office today for you, but as the mails are so uncertain now I will avail myself of a private opportunity which now offers to send you a few lines. Lieut. Webb has just called to say that he will take any commands for us. He will start in a few minutes, so I have only time to say we are all well. We heard from James today. He was well & had written to Hon. F. S. Lyon about a detail. I don't know whether we should go to Tuscaloosa or not: raids are spoken of but Mary says go on. All unite with me in deepest love to you my ever dear, good Son. God bless & protect you. $500 dollars sent.

Your Mother

While the Pickenses prepared for their move to Tuscaloosa, General James Wilson planned to strike south from Lauderdale County to eliminate the problem of Nathan Bedford Forrest, destroy the large munitions factory at Selma, and occupy Montgomery. As Wilson advanced south, he ordered Union Brigadier General John Thomas Croxton's brigade to Tuscaloosa, where Union forces burned down facilities supporting the Confederate war. A few days later, Wilson's troops entered Selma and destroyed the Confederate munitions works there before proceeding to Montgomery. The *Alabama Beacon* warned that Union troops could occupy Greensboro any day and advised citizens that their property would be safer if they did not flee.[22]

22. Murray and Hsieh, *A Savage War*, 486–88; McIlwain, *Civil War Alabama*, 254–59; *Alabama Beacon*, March 31, 1865.

Under the circumstances, Mary Gaillard cancelled the move to Tuscaloosa. The family remained at Umbria, waiting for news from Sam.

Sam's last battle began on the night of April 1. Division commander Bryan Grimes had assigned the Alabama Brigade to defend a section of the Confederate line that crossed the Jerusalem Plank Road. The Fifth Alabama's position was southwest of the road, facing the western end of the Union line held by Brigadier General Robert B. Potter's Second Division of John G. Parke's Ninth Corps. On the afternoon of the 1st, Parke received orders from General Meade to begin an assault on the Confederate line at 4:00 the next morning. According to Parke, Meade telegraphed an order around 10:00 that night to initiate an artillery barrage to be followed by the assault if the barrage created an opening in the Confederate line. Parke, however, reported that the Confederate front remained "well manned and alert," so he prepared to launch the assault at 4:00 am April 2 as General Meade had originally ordered.[23] At 4:30, the Union attack began and quickly overran the position of the Fifth, capturing hundreds of Confederate soldiers, including Sam.[24]

Union troops marched the Confederate prisoners to transports that sailed down the James River, around Fortress Monroe in Hampton Roads near Old Point Comfort, and up the Chesapeake to the U.S. prison camp at Point Lookout, Maryland. The camp had been established in 1863, after the Battle of Gettysburg, at the tip of a peninsula between the Potomac River and the bay. Sam entered the prison on April 4. A facility designed for ten thousand prisoners held double that number at the time. The conditions Sam described in his diary were miserable, and, he believed, unnecessary, because the Union government had the resources to provide adequate food, shelter, and sanitation. Yet, he complained, Confederate prisoners were forced to endure near starvation, exposure to the weather, and limited access to clean water. Such conditions were designed to humiliate and punish Confederates, Sam thought. Indulging in a common myth of southern prisoners of war and southerners generally, Sam wrote that the Confederacy treated Union prisoners better.[25]

23. Parke Report, *OR*, ser. 1, vol. 46, pt. 1: 1015–17; Greene, *The Final Battles of the Petersburg Campaign*, 334–38.

24. Greene, *The Final Battles of the Petersburg Campaign*, 334–38; Diary of Samuel Pickens, April 2, 1865.

25. Diary of Samuel Pickens, April 5, 1865.

What the Confederates learned about the war during the first week was based on rumors that circulated through the camp. By April 7, Confederate prisoners were hearing stories that the Army of Northern Virginia had regrouped south of the Dan River and captured two "Yankee corps." In North Carolina, they heard, Johnston "whipped Sherman. Sheridan killed." Two days later, the news was that Lee was trapped and would be forced to "fight or surrender." Then, Sam awoke to the firing of "200 guns. . . . to celebrate surrender of Gen. Lee & army." The next day Union troops fired another two-hundred-gun salute to announce the surrender of Johnston. Having heard so many rumors, the men in the camp refused to believe that what Sam referred to as the "Horror of horrors" had actually happened. On April 11, he wrote, one of the prisoners reported that another "dispatch recd contradicting report of Johnston's surrender" and others that Johnston was "fighting like thunder." Despite what he described as "official" reports about the surrender of the Army of Northern Virginia, Sam and his comrades desperately grasped any rumor that the struggle might not be over. "We can't realize the truth of the astounding events that are transpiring so rapidly—crowding on us: & we can't believe it either." Even after learning of Lee's surrender at Appomattox, Sam held out hope that, with divine intervention, a way could be found to extend the fighting and establish an independent Confederate state. He refused to accept the increasingly undeniable reality that "after all the sacrifices made—immolation of so many noble heroes—it is not to end in our favor—that we are to lose our independence & be in subjection to the Yankees! God forbid!" If the Confederacy could not secure its independence on the battlefield—or by "conquering a peace" as Sam put it—he prayed that God would yet "deliver us out of the hands of our too powerful enemies & bless us with Independence & Peace." Rumors of pockets of continued Confederate resistance circulated through the camp for the rest of the month.[26]

While Sam was in prison, U.S. officials offered a glimpse of a future southerners imagined and feared if somehow the Confederacy did not miraculously recover. A few weeks after Sam entered Point Lookout, the Union Army replaced camp guards with African American troops and, on one occasion, sent armed African American policemen into the camp to main-

26. Diary of Samuel Pickens, April 12, 15–19, 1865.

tain order. Sam wrote that "it is humiliating to think of being under such a guard," though he admitted he found them "about as respectable as Yankees." He was less sanguine, and even more humiliated, after his encounter with the African American policemen later. On May 26, he wrote "Negro police came in last night . . . halted every one on street—cursed ordered them back to their tents." The men, whom Sam described as "ignorant wretches," were armed with pistols and one fired at a man, missed him, but wounded another lying in his tent. The wounded man had to have his leg amputated, Sam heard. Sam wanted to hold an "indignation meeting" to demand the removal of the policemen. Authorities at the camp assured the Confederates that those responsible for the incident would be punished.

Imagining lives of such daily humiliation at the hands of men they had enslaved and controlled, many Confederate prisoners were reluctant to take an oath of allegiance to the United States as a condition of their release as long as Confederate armies remained in the field and a glimmer of hope remained. Their assumption when they first arrived at Point Lookout was that, as long as hostilities continued, they would be paroled until exchanged, as had been the practice through most of the war. After the surrender of the Army of Northern Virginia, Sam and his comrades thought they would be offered at least the same terms of parole as Confederate soldiers at Appomattox. But U.S. officials considered the paroles for surrendering troops a term of the surrender not to be extended to soldiers who had been captured during combat. With Confederate armies still fighting, Sam and most of his company viewed such an oath as treason. Sam also suspected that U.S. officials would use Confederates swearing allegiance to reinforce the narrative that southern soldiers had been manipulated by nefarious political leaders into joining the rebellion and now, by taking the oath, were acknowledging how wrong they had been. On May 1, Sam wrote "I believe Yankees prefer all to go on & take it [the oath] as they have been doing & then will publish to the World that they took oath voluntarily—going to prove that the poor deluded, ignorant creatures were duped, misguided & forced into this war & are only glad of opportunity to return to Glorious Union." Though he and the rest of the men from his company thought they would eventually have to take the oath, they delayed, hoping, it seems, for something to change on the battlefield. But, by May 3, many of the men concluded that hopes for continued Confederate resistance were, to say the least, unreasonable, if not delusional, and decided the oath was "an evil that can't be avoided." That day and the next, Sam and his comrades registered for the oath so they could finally go home.[27]

27. Diary of Samuel Pickens, May 1, 2, 3, 1865.

Epilogue

While they awaited news from Sam that spring of 1865, the Pickenses and their neighbors confronted the meaning of Confederate defeat, living in fear of the dismal future they thought was a certainty. Only a month before the old order collapsed, Mary Gaillard Pickens knew that the war for Confederate independence, the defense of the world as she had known it, was not going well, but seemed cautiously optimistic that, with God's help, her family would be reunited in the victorious Confederacy and life would go on much as it had before the war. She certainly did not appear to believe that everything would come crashing down as quickly as it did. We have no record of her thoughts as she witnessed the collapse of the Confederacy, but her neighbor, Augustus Benners, recorded in his diary how quickly the system of slavery collapsed after the surrender of Confederate forces in the Department of Alabama and the depression that set in among former enslavers as they contemplated what was in store for them. Lieutenant General Richard Taylor surrendered on May 4 near Mobile. On May 12, Benners wrote, "There is a great gloom hanging over the people by reason of the destruction of the labor system of the countryside—no one knows what to depend upon or what to do." A neighbor told him that the formerly enslaved "are leaving from the Plantations and going to Selma—They are working slowly." Two days later he added that, while none of the "negroes" on his plantation were leaving, "they are leaving other plantations in squads." U.S. government authorities issued orders requiring landowners to hire the men and women they had held as slaves. Benners and the press reported that freed people were reluctant to return to the plantations; to them freedom meant something other than labor for their enslaver. By late 1865 and through 1866, however, freed people had few alternatives.[1]

After his return, Mary Gaillard turned over management of the plantations to Sam. During the fall of 1865, Sam began the necessary, and humbling, process of negotiating contracts for the three plantations with people his family once enslaved. The contracts stipulated the "wage" laborers were to receive for the year. With cash in short supply, Sam paid laborers at the end of the year with shares of the crop they produced. He then had to negotiate new contracts for the next year. Sam complained to his mother in early 1867 that freedmen understood their leverage in a competitive labor market and drove hard bargains, driving up labor costs. Increased labor costs were in addition to increased prices of mules and other supplies. With cotton prices depressed, the Pickenses took on more debt than Sam wanted to cover operational expenses. But it could be worse, Sam wrote Mary Gaillard; they were doing better than most in the county, many of whom struggled just to feed themselves.[2]

While economic conditions in the county remained challenging, Andrew Johnson's plan for Reconstruction restored white economic and political domination of the former Confederacy. Alabama's Presidential Reconstruction legislature quickly acted to establish African Americans as second-class citizens with no right to vote and limited civil rights. Freedmen never accepted those terms, of course, and by the end of 1866 began to organize and demand full political and civil equality with the support of local, state, and national Republicans. In Washington, Republicans in Congress observed the implementation of Johnson's Reconstruction policy with dismay. They

1. Not surprisingly, the "problem" of labor was a constant source of anxiety, speculation, and rumor during the period. The Freedmen's Bureau instructed planters and freedmen to enter into contract arrangements and provided guidelines to be followed by both parties. See Hubbs, *Guarding Greensboro*, 208–10, and *Alabama Beacon*, June 23, 1865; September 8, 15, 22, 1865.

2. Sam Pickens to "Mama," January 2, 1867. A detailed examination of Reconstruction in Greene/Hale County is beyond the scope of this work but is addressed in Hubbs, *Guarding Greensboro*, chap. 10. On the broader context of Reconstruction, see Fitzgerald, *Reconstruction in Alabama*, and Rogers, *Reconstruction Politics*.

too viewed the restoration of southern governments under Johnson's plan as a victory for the same forces of reaction that had carried the nation into the bloody Civil War. During the fall of 1865 and into 1866, Republicans in Congress acted to protect the rights of freed people first by refusing to seat congressional delegations from former Confederate states and then creating the Joint Committee on Reconstruction to investigate conditions in the South. Congress passed a civil rights bill in March 1866 and, after President Johnson vetoed it, overrode his veto. The Civil Rights Act of 1866 guaranteed federal protection of fundamental civil rights of all Americans regardless of race or previous condition of servitude. A few months later, Congress approved the Fourteenth Amendment, potentially strengthening federal protection of Blacks' civil rights. Former Confederate states reacted to Republicans' intervention with defiance. In response to their refusal to approve the Fourteenth Amendment and their clear intent to disregard federal law, Congress passed the Reconstruction Acts of 1867, which divided the former Confederate states into military districts and required them to craft constitutions guaranteeing Black rights, including the right of Black men to vote.

To Sam Pickens and his former comrades in the Fifth Alabama, the actions of Congress violated the terms of surrender as they understood them. Confederate soldiers grudgingly accepted the emancipation of the enslaved but otherwise expected to rebuild a social order in which African Americans would continue to be subordinate to white people. Sam and other veterans resented what they viewed as a congressional plan to impose "negro rule" by extending to Blacks "the right to vote."[3] This inversion of the social order, Sam wrote to his mother, was a dangerous humiliation of men who had acted in good faith since the end of the war. As a Democrat, he supported the political resistance to the Republican governments elected after approval of the state constitution of 1868. Whether he was complicit in Klan and other violence against Republicans is unclear. In a letter to his mother in the summer of 1867, he blamed the killing of Alex Webb, a freedman and

3. On the southern understanding of the terms of surrender at Appomattox and sense of betrayal when congressional Republicans challenged the racial order that the former Confederate states sought to construct under Johnson's plan of Reconstruction, see Varon, *Appomattox*, chap. 9.

Republican activist in Greensboro, on Republican intervention and sharply criticized Blacks who protested the killing. Furthermore, he certainly knew men who did engage in acts of terrorism against Black voters. However, while he clearly supported the strategic goal of the Klan, it was not necessarily in his or other planters' interest to embrace their tactics. Planters depended on Black labor. Enabling, publicly endorsing, or participating in Klan or other intimidation of Blacks further complicated planters' contract negotiations. A careful manager of the family business, Sam was acutely aware of the need to maintain a working relationship with the men and women who worked the Pickenses' land as laborers and later as sharecroppers. But his relationships with Black laborers and sharecroppers remained tense, to say the least.

Life at Umbria in 1866–67 deepened Sam's "gloom" over business and political affairs. To his mind, the social order was descending into chaos and his "home" offered no respite from the misery. The house was not a home, Sam wrote his mother. It was full of the relatives of Juliet Damer, James's wife, none of whom he knew well or at all. When Mary Gaillard and the children left, he wrote, he "knew that home would no longer be like itself . . . but could not realize how very disagreeable I would find it under existing circumstances. At home, it is true, but what sort of home is it now! A numerous household, but of whom does it consist! Of strangers, yes of strangers—but who nevertheless, feel much more independent than I do. They even seem to regard me as an intruder. A crowd always around me, but no congeniality. I am actually lonely a great portion of my time."[4] Nonetheless, Sam lived in crowded Umbria for the rest of his life, managing his portion of his inheritance and, it appears, advising James about the management of his land. He never married. Suffering from declining health, Sam traveled to Waukesha, Wisconsin, in 1890 for the spring water believed to possess medicinal properties. He died there soon after arriving.[5]

Mary Gaillard Pickens returned to Raleigh after the war ended, where her daughters Mary and Louty resumed their education at St. Mary's. Though she had turned the management of the plantations over to Sam, she continued to offer advice about business matters. She, for example, urged

4. Sam to "Mama," April 9, 1867.
5. *Alabama Beacon,* September 16, 1890.

Sam to support the building of the Selma, Marion, and Memphis Railroad, which would pass through Greensboro and, she believed, revive the town's and the region's economy. She died in 1873.[6]

James married Juliet Damer the day before Union soldiers captured Sam on April 2.[7] James and Juliet, and some of her relatives, lived at Umbria. When Sam returned home and met his in-laws for the first time, he wondered why James was so taken with Juliet and the Damers. In Sam's judgment, Juliet "saddled" James "with a burden—a most unfortunate one. His wife will carry him away to Virginia or Maryland, or else be miserable, and make him so too." She made expensive plans for travel every summer, Sam informed his mother, and James went along to make her happy, going into debt to pay for his wife's lavish taste. Sam feared James's willingness to fund Juliet's whims would mean a life of "monetary difficulties" for him.[8] James did struggle financially, as Sam predicted, though his management of his portion of his father's estate was likely more to blame than his wife. In his will, Sam left most of his estate to James so he could pay his debts.[9]

What happened to John immediately after the war is uncertain. Sam did not mention him after being captured, and the Pickens correspondence after the war is silent as well. However, census records suggest that John moved to Greensboro after the war with Suky and his two children, Laura and John. According to the 1870 census, there was one John Pickens in Hale (formerly Greene) County with a wife named Suky and two children. This John Pickens was fifty-nine and worked as a domestic servant. Suky identified her occupation as "keeping house." Women and men working outside the home identified their occupations as "domestic servant," so it appears that Suky stayed home to take care of her children. In 1880, John identified his occupation as "house servant" and Suky still identified hers as "keeps house." Young John was sixteen when the census taker arrived, and Laura no longer lived in the household, having married Charles Owens, a farm laborer. Laura and Charles lived near Greensboro. The last record of John Pickens Sr. in Greensboro was a notice in 1894 in the *Greensboro Watchman* announcing

6. *Alabama Beacon*, February 23, 1878.

7. Alabama County Marriages, 1809–1950.

8. Sam to "Mama," April 9, 1867, Pickens Family Papers.

9. Will Records, 1867–1928: Alabama Probate Court, Hale (formerly Greene) County.

his death. The announcement described John as a "respected colored man."[10] Only seventy-eight-year-old Suky appears in the 1900 census, and she was living with her cousin in Greensboro.[11]

Mary Pickens returned to school at St. Mary's soon after the war ended. She continued to suffer from poor health and the depression she described in her letters after the death of Tom Biscoe. She married Robert Withers, a longtime family friend, in April 1876 and died two years later of unknown causes.[12]

William C. Pickens completed his education at the Green Springs Academy. When he reached the age of twenty-one, he inherited his portion of his father's estate, which included Canebrake Plantation. Like the rest of the white plantation owners in the county, William struggled to find adequate labor as freed people exerted their power in a competitive labor market to find better situations each year. He married Helen Withers, the sister of Robert, in 1872 and died just two years later.[13] Helen retained ownership of Canebrake and other property while residing at Governor Israel Pickens's home in Greensboro, Greenwood, which the Withers family had purchased. She died in June 1912.[14]

Louisa "Louty" Pickens married Francis D. Pickens, the brother of Col-

10. *Greensboro Watchman*, March 29, 1894.

11. All of this is necessarily speculative, since this John Pickens could obviously be some-one else. However, the circumstantial evidence is compelling. First, many slaves took the last name of their enslavers after the war. Second, this John Pickens was the only one in Hale County married to a Suky. Third, we know from a letter that Mary Gaillard wrote in July 1863 that John and Suky had two children, one named John Jr., who was born in early 1863. It seems unlikely these are all coincidences.

12. *Alabama Beacon*, April 19, 1876; February 23, 1878. Alabama County Marriages, 1809–1950.

13. Samuel to James, January 20, 1873; James to Sam, February 4, 1872; "Lou" to James, February 17, 1873; Miles Pickens to Sam, February 23, 1873, all in Pickens Family Papers. Alabama County Marriages, 1809–1950. Michael Fitzgerald has suggested that a frustrated William was involved in Klan activity during this period. I have not seen any direct evidence of William's ties to the Klan, other than being related by marriage to Eyre Damer, the author of a 1912 book about the Klan in the region during Reconstruction. See Damer, *When the Ku Klux Rode;* Fitzgerald, *Reconstruction in Alabama,* 190.

14. Will Records, 1867–1928: Alabama Probate Court, Hale County; U.S. Census, 1900, 1910.

onel Samuel Bonneau Pickens. She and her husband left Hale County for Birmingham, Alabama, where Francis worked as a bookkeeper for the rest of his life.[15]

Israel "Icha" Pickens managed his portion of his father's estate after the war. He married Mary Gaillard Sawyer, and they had two children. Israel died in 1889 of pneumonia.[16] Mary G. Pickens was active in the Greensboro chapter of the United Daughters of the Confederacy. She chaired the committee that commissioned the monument to Confederate soldiers dedicated in Greensboro in 1904. Mary and Israel's daughter participated in a tableau as "the South" at the ceremony dedicating the monument. Eleven other young women represented the Confederate states.[17]

15. Alabama County Marriages, 1809–1950.

16. *Greensboro Watchman*, November 28, 1889. In the 1880 census, Israel identified his occupation as "farmer" (U.S. Census, 1880).

17. *Confederate Veteran* 12 (October 1904): 476.

ACKNOWLEDGMENTS

About fifteen years ago, the late Clarence Mohr, then the chair of my department at the University of South Alabama, called me into his office to tell me about a call he had received from a Mobile attorney, John McCall, asking if we might be interested in acquiring for the university archives a collection of nineteenth-century historical documents his family possessed. Mr. McCall's grandfather, Doy Leale McCall, had been an amateur archivist who traveled the state, gathering whatever historical documents he could find. The McCall family wanted to move the collection from their Montgomery home to an archive where they would be preserved. Professor Mohr and I agreed to travel to Montgomery to see the collection. What we saw in Montgomery was a remarkably complete documentary record of the family of Samuel Pickens Jr., a younger brother of Governor Israel Pickens. Recognizing the importance of the Pickens papers, Professor Mohr and I returned to Mobile to report to the university provost, David Johnson. We recommended that the university enter negotiations with the McCall family to acquire the collection so that it would be preserved for future generations. With the support of Dr. Johnson, along with the late Gordon V. Moulton, university president, and James Yance, a member of the board of trustees, the university reached an agreement with the McCall family to place their collections in the newly established McCall Rare Book and Manuscript Library.

The letters included in this book are part of the much larger Pickens Papers Collection. Michael Parrish, who appraised the McCall Collection for the University of South Alabama, suggested that I edit the Civil War letters for publication. As an accomplished historian of the Civil War, Professor Parrish knew that the Pickens correspondence offered a unique view of the integration of home front and battlefront. Over the last decade or so, Professor Parrish has always responded to my many questions about the editing process and Civil War historiography. In the final stages of the project, he read a much longer version of the manuscript and offered suggestions for revisions that greatly improved the final product. Professor Parrish and my editor at Louisiana State University Press, Rand Dotson, have been unfailingly supportive. Thanks as well to the anonymous reviewer for LSU Press whose extensive comments on the initial draft of the manuscript helped me immensely as I edited and revised what would be the final draft.

Over the years, a number of people, sometimes unknowingly, helped me think through the meaning of the Pickens letters. The members of the Pensacola Civil War Roundtable patiently listened to yearly presentations based on the correspondence and asked questions that identified areas that needed clarification. My thanks to Larry Garrett for the invitations to speak to the group. Without the assistance of University of South Alabama students who rotated through the university archive, we could not have processed the Pickens Papers in just two years. The students knew about my project and remained alert to any documents that would help. If I try to name individuals, I will surely leave someone out, so thanks to everyone who contributed. As I completed the final draft, Jada Jones at the McCall Rare Book and Manuscript Library expedited the reproduction of letters and documents I needed to complete the pre–Civil War story of the Pickenses. Thanks to Ms. Jones for the assistance. Without the support of the late Clarence Mohr and his successor as department chair, David Messenger, for my yearly requests for reassignment from some teaching duties, I might never have completed this book.

There were times when I considered dropping this project. My wife, Julie, as always, reassured me and encouraged me to continue. This one is dedicated to her and our son, Tucker.

BIBLIOGRAPHY

MANUSCRIPT SOURCES

Alabama Department of Archives and History

    Alabama Census of Confederate Soldiers, 1907 and 1921.

    Alabama County Marriages, 1809–1950.

    C. C. Clay Papers.

    Confederate Regimental History Files.

    Muster Rolls of Alabama Civil War Units, SG025006–25100.

    12th Alabama Infantry.

Atlanta History Center Collection

    Memoirs of Henry Beck, 1864–65.

Greene County Probate Court

    Inventory of the Estate of Samuel Pickens Jr.

    Last Will and Testament of Samuel Pickens III.

    Will Records, www.ancestry.com/search/categories/clp_wills/ (accessed
        September 12, 2023).

Doy Leale McCall Rare Book and Manuscript Library, University of South Alabama

    Diary of James Pickens.

    Diary of Samuel Pickens.

    Pickens Family Papers.

National Archives

    Compiled Service Records of Confederate Soldiers Who Served in
        Organizations from the State of Alabama (CMSR).

    Confederate Amnesty Papers, 1865–67.

    Confederate Papers Relating to Citizens or Business Firms.

    United States Confederate Officers Card Index, 1861–65.

Southern Historical Collection, University of North Carolina, Chapel Hill

    Lenoir Family Papers.

Texas Board of Health

University of Alabama Libraries Digital Collections.

    Greene Springs School Records. cdm17336.contentdm.oclc.org/digital
    /collection/u0003_0000592/search.

U.S. BUREAU OF THE CENSUS

Population Schedule of the Seventh Census of the U.S., 1850.
Population Schedule of the Eighth Census of the U.S., 1860.
Population Schedule of the Ninth Census of the U.S., 1870.
Population Schedule of the Tenth Census of the U.S., 1880.

NEWSPAPERS

Alabama Beacon (Greensboro).
Baltimore Sun.
Charleston Mercury.
Commercial Register (Mobile).
Crisis (Columbus, OH).
Daily Dispatch (Richmond).
Daily Enquirer (Columbus, GA).
Daily Reporter (Selma).
Daily Richmond Enquirer.
Daily True Delta (New Orleans).
The Democrat (Huntsville).
Eufaula Democrat.
Examiner (Richmond).
The Farmer's Register.
Franklin Repository (PA).
The Greensboro Watchman.
Independent Monitor (Tuscaloosa).
Mobile Advertiser and Register.
New York Herald.
North Alabamian (Tuscumbia).
Southern Republic.

PRINTED PRIMARY SOURCES

Acts of the called session, 1862 and of the Regular Session of the General Assembly of Alabama.
    1862.
Alabama Senate Journal. 1826.
Bartholow, Robert. "The Various Influences Affecting the Physical Endurance, the
    Power of Resisting Disease Etc., of the Men Composing the Volunteer Armies of
    the United States." In Flint, ed., *Contributions relating to the causation and prevention*
    of disease, 3–41.

Bloom, John Porter, and Clarence Edwin Carter, eds. *The Territorial Papers of the United States: Alabama Territory.* Washington, DC: Government Printing Office, 1952.

Confederate Veteran 12 (October 1904): 476.

Davis, William C., and Sue Heth Bell, eds. *The Whartons' War: The Civil War Correspondence of General Gabriel C. Wharton and Anne Radford Wharton, 1863–1865.* Chapel Hill: University of North Carolina Press, 2022.

Flint, Austin, ed., *Contributions Relating to the Causation and Prevention of Disease, and to Camp Diseases.* New York: Hurd and Houghton for the U.S. Sanitary Commission, 1867.

Jones, John Beauchamp. *A Rebel War Clerk's Diary at the Confederate States Capital.* New York: J. B. Lippincott, 1866.

Jones, Terry L., ed. *The Civil War Memoirs of Captain William J. Seymour: Reminiscences of a Louisiana Tiger.* El Dorado Hills, CA: Savas Beatie, 2020.

Journal of the Alabama House of Representatives. 1821.

Park, R. E., "Diary of Captain R. E. Park." *Southern Historical Society Papers* 1 (June–July 1876).

Pate, James P., ed. *When This Evil War Is Over: The Correspondence of the Francis Family.* Tuscaloosa: University of Alabama Press, 2006.

Peters, DeWitt C. "Remarks on the Evils of Youthful Enlistments and Nostalgia." *American Medical Times* 7 (February 14, 1868).

Snedecor, V. Gayle. *Hand drawn maps of the Precincts of Greene County, 1858.* alabamamaps.ua.edu/index.html.

———. *1963 reprint of Snedecor's 1855–56 directory of Greene County, Alabama.* Eutaw, AL, 1963.

Twenty-Fifth Annual Convention of the Protestant Episcopal Church in the Diocese of Alabama. Mobile: Farrow, Stokes, & Dennett, 1856.

War of the Rebellion: A Compilation of the Official Records of the Union and Confederate Armies. 128 vols. Washington, DC: Government Printing Office, 1880–1901.

SECONDARY SOURCES

Abernethy, Thomas Perkins. *The Formative Period in Alabama, 1815–1828.* Montgomery: Brown Printing Co., 1922.

Alabama County Marriages. Family Search. Database with images. familysearch.org /ark:/61903/1:1:QKZ3-HHZ1 (accessed February 19, 2021).

Anderson, David. "Dying of Nostalgia: Homesickness in the Union Army during the Civil War." *Civil War History* 56 (September 2010): 247–82.

Anderson, Donald Lee, and Godfrey Tryggve Anderson. "Nostalgia and Malingering in the Civil War." *Perspectives in Biology and Medicine* 28 (Autumn 1984): 156–66.

"Andrew Pickens, Jr. 16th Governor of the State of South Carolina, 1816–1818." www
.carolana.com/SC/Governors/apickens.html.

Ayers, Edward L. *The Thin Light of Freedom*. New York: W. W. Norton, 2017.

Bailey, Hugh C. "Israel Pickens, People's Politician." *Alabama Review*, April 1964, 83–85.

Baptist, Edward. *The Half Has Never Been Told: Slavery and the Making of American Capitalism*. New York: Basic Books, 2014.

Barney, William L. *The Making of a Confederate: Walter Lenoir's Civil War*. New York: Oxford University Press, 2008.

Bergeron, Arthur W. *Confederate Mobile*. Baton Rouge: Louisiana State University Press, 2000.

Beringer, Richard E., et al. *Why the South Lost the Civil War*. Athens: University of Georgia Press, 1996.

Blair, William. *Virginia's Private War: Feeding Body and Soul in the Confederacy*. New York: Oxford University Press, 1998.

Bonner, Robert E. *The Soldier's Pen: Firsthand Impressions of the Civil War*. New York: Hill and Wang, 1972.

Brannon, Rebecca. *From Revolution to Reunion: The Reintegration of the South Carolina Loyalists*. Columbia: University of South Carolina Press, 2016.

Brantley, William H. *Banking in Alabama, 1816–1860*. Birmingham, AL: Oxmoor Press, 1967.

Broadus, John A. *A Memorial of Gessner Harrison, July 2, 1873*. Charlottesville, VA: Chronicle Steam Printing House, 1874.

Brown, Kent Masterson. *Retreat from Gettysburg: Lee, Logistics, and the Pennsylvania Campaign*. Chapel Hill: University of North Carolina Press, 2005.

Browning, Andrew H. *The Panic of 1819: The First Great Depression*. Cambridge, MA: Harvard University Press, 2005.

Carmichael, Peter S. *The Last Generation: Young Virginians in Peace, War, and Reunion*. Chapel Hill: University of North Carolina Press, 2005.

———. *The War for the Common Soldier: How Men Thought, Fought, and Survived in Civil War America*. Chapel Hill: University of North Carolina Press, 2018.

Carroll, Dillon J. "'The God who Shielded Me Before, Yet Watches over us All': Confederate Soldiers, Mental Illness, and Religion." *Civil War History* 61 (September 2015): 252–80.

"Charles Minnigerode (1814–1894)." *Encyclopedia of Virginia*. encyclopediavirginia.org /entries/minnigerode-charles-1814-1894/.

Clarke, Frances. "So Lonesome I Could Die: Nostalgia and Debates over Emotional Control in the Civil War North." *Journal of Social History* 41 (Winter 2007): 253–82.

Clarke County Genealogy and History Network. alabama.msghn.org/clarke/.

Collins, Darrell L. *Major General Robert E. Rodes of the Army of Northern Virginia: A Biography.* New York: Savas Beatie, 2008.

Cooper, William J. *We Have the War upon Us: The Onset of the Civil War, November 1860–April 1861.* New York: Alfred A. Knopf, 2012.

Damer, Eyre. "The Vanished Plantation System." *New Country Life,* May 1918, 90–94.

———. *When the Ku Klux Rode.* New York: Neale Publishing Co., 1912.

Daniel, Larry J. *Conquered: Why the Army of the Tennessee Failed.* Chapel Hill: University of North Carolina Press, 2019.

Dean, Eric T., Jr. *Shook over Hell: Post-Traumatic Stress, Vietnam, and the Civil War.* Cambridge, MA: Harvard University Press, 1997.

"Descendants of Theodore Gaillard, Esquire." www.genealogy.com/forum/surnames /topics/gaillard/72/.

Doyle, Patrick J. "Replacement Rebels: Confederate Substitution and the Issue of Citizenship." *Journal of the Civil War Era* 8 (March 2018): 3–31.

Dupre, Daniel. "Israel Pickens." In Samuel L. Webb and Margaret E. Armbrester, eds., *Alabama Governors: A Political History of the State,* 821–25. Tuscaloosa: University of Alabama Press, 2001.

Durrill, Wayne K. *War of Another Kind: A Southern Community in the Great Rebellion.* New York: Oxford University Press, 1990.

Edwards, Laura F. *Scarlett Doesn't Live Here Anymore: Southern Women in the Civil War Era.* Urbana: University of Illinois Press, 2000.

Eicher, David J. *The Longest Night: A Military History of the Civil War.* New York: Touchstone, 2001.

Faust, Drew Gilpin. "Altars of Sacrifice: Confederate Women and the Narratives of War." *Journal of American History* 76, no. 4 (March 1990): 1272–73.

———. "Christian Soldiers: The Meaning of Revivalism in the Confederate Army." *Journal of Southern History* 53, no. 1 (February 1987): 63–90.

———. *Mothers of Invention: Women of the Slaveholding South in the American Civil War.* Chapel Hill: University of North Carolina Press, 1996.

———. *This Republic of Suffering: Death and the American Civil War.* New York: Alfred A. Knopf, 2008.

Fitts, Alston, III. *Selma: A Bicentennial History.* Tuscaloosa: University of Alabama Press, 2016.

Fitzgerald, Michael W. *Reconstruction in Alabama: From Civil War to Redemption in the Cotton South.* Baton Rouge: Louisiana University Press, 2017.

Fitzhugh, George. *Cannibals All or, Slaves without Masters.* Richmond, VA: A. Morris, 1857.

Fleming, Walter Lynwood. *Civil War and Reconstruction in Alabama*. New York: Columbia University Press, 1905.

Ford, Lacy K. *Deliver Us from Evil: The Slavery Question in the Old South*. New York: Oxford University Press, 2009.

Fox-Genovese, Elizabeth. *Within the Plantation Household: Black and White Women of the Old South*. Chapel Hill: University of North Carolina Press, 1988.

Freehling, William W. *The Road to Disunion: Secessionists Triumphant, 1854–1861*. Oxford, UK: Oxford University Press, 2007.

Fussell, Paul. *The Great War and Modern Memory*. New York: Oxford University Press, 1973.

Galhunter, J. M. "History of St. Paul's Episcopal Church Greensboro, Alabama." stpaulsgreensboro.dioala.org/About/galhunters-history-of-st-pauls.html (accessed September 14, 2023).

Gallagher, Gary W. *The Confederate War*. Cambridge, MA: Harvard University Press, 1999.

———. *Lee and His Army in Confederate History*. Chapel Hill: University of North Carolina Press, 2001.

Garrett, William. *Reminiscences of Public Men in Alabama for Thirty Years*. Atlanta: Plantation Publishing, 1879.

Genovese, Eugene D. *Roll, Jordan, Roll: The World the Slaves Made*. New York: Pantheon Books, 1972.

Genovese, Eugene D., and Elizabeth Fox-Genovese. *Fatal Self Deception: Slaveholding Paternalism in the Old South*. New York: Cambridge University Press, 2011.

Glatthaar, Joseph. T. "Everyman's War: A Rich and a Poor Man's Fight in Lee's Army." *Civil War History* 54 (September 2008): 229–46.

———. *General Lee's Army: From Victory to Collapse*. New York: Free Press, 2009.

———. *Soldiering in the Army of Northern Virginia: A Statistical Portrait of the Troops Who Served under Robert E. Lee*. Chapel Hill: University of North Carolina Press, 2011.

Glymph, Thavolia. *Out of the House of Bondage: The Transformation of the Plantation Household*. Cambridge, UK: Cambridge University Press, 2008.

Greene, A. Wilson. *The Final Battles of the Petersburg Campaign: Breaking the Backbone of the Rebellion*. Knoxville: University of Tennessee Press, 2008.

Gudmestad, Robert H. *A Troublesome Commerce: The Transformation of the Interstate Slave Trade*. Baton Rouge: Louisiana State University Press, 2003.

Guelzo, Allen C. *Fateful Lightning: A New History of the Civil War and Reconstruction*. Oxford, UK: Oxford University Press, 2012.

———. *Gettysburg: The Last Invasion*. New York: Alfred A. Knopf, 2013.

Hager, Christopher. *I Remain Yours: Common Lives in Civil War Letters.* Cambridge, MA: Harvard University Press, 2018.

Hanna, Martha. "A Republic of Letters: The Epistolary Tradition in France during World War I." *American Historical Review* 108 (December 2003): 1338–61.

———. *Your Death Would Be Mine: Paul and Marie Pireaud in the Great War.* Cambridge, MA: Harvard University Press, 2006.

Hesseltine, William B. *Civil War Prisons: A Study in War Psychology.* Columbus: Ohio State University Press, 1930.

Hirschhorn, N., R. G. Feldman, and I. A. Greaves. "Abraham Lincoln's Blue Pills: Did Our 16th President Suffer from Mercury Poisoning?" *Perspectives in Biology and Medicine* 44, no. 3 (Summer 2001): 315–32. doi: 10.1353/pbm.2001.0048.

Holt, Michael F. *The Fate of Their Country: Politicians, Slavery Extension, and the Coming of the Civil War.* New York: Hill and Wang, 2004.

———. *The Rise and Fall of the American Whig Party: Jacksonian Politics and the Onset of the Civil War.* New York: Oxford University Press, 1999.

"Howard's Grove Hospital." *Civil War Richmond.* www.civilwarrichmond.com/hospitals/howard-s-grove-hospital (accessed September 26, 2023).

Howe, Daniel Walker. *What Hath God Wrought: The Transformation of America, 1815–1848.* New York: Oxford University Press, 2007.

Hubbs, G. Ward. *Guarding Greensboro: A Confederate Company in the Making of a Southern Community.* Athens: University of Georgia Press, 2003.

———, ed. *Voices from Company D: Diaries by the Greensboro Guards, Fifth Alabama Infantry Regiment, Army of Northern Virginia.* Athens: University of Georgia Press, 2003.

Hurt, R. Douglas. *Agriculture and the Confederacy: Policy, Productivity, and Power in the Civil War South.* Chapel Hill: University of North Carolina Press, 2015.

Jabour, Anya. *Scarlett's Sisters: Young Women in the Old South.* Chapel Hill: University of North Carolina Press, 2007.

Jones-Rogers, Stephanie E. *They Were Her Property: White Women as Slave Owners in the American South.* New Haven, CT: Yale University Press, 2019.

Keegan, John. *The Face of Battle: A Study of Agincourt, Waterloo, and the Somme.* New York: Penguin Books, 1976.

Kolchin, Peter. *American Slavery: 1619–1877.* New York: Hill and Wang, 2003.

Kramer, Lloyd S. *Nationalism in Europe and America: Politics, Cultures, and Identities since 1775.* Chapel Hill: University of North Carolina Press, 2011.

Laird, Matthew R. "Archaeological Data Recovery Investigation of the Lumpkin's Jail Site, Richmond, Virginia." *Encyclopedia of Virginia,* August 2010. encyclopediavirginia.org/entries/lumpkins-jail/.

Lambert, Robert Stansbury. *South Carolina Loyalists in the American Revolution.* Clemson, SC: Clemson University Digital Press, 2010.

Lande, Gregory. *Psychological Consequences of the American Civil War.* Jefferson, NC: McFarland & Co., 2017.

Laskin, Elisabeth Lauterbach. "Good Old Rebels: Soldiering in the Army of Northern Virginia, 1862–1865." PhD diss., Harvard University, 2003.

Lebergott, Stanley. "Why the South Lost: Commercial Purpose in the Confederacy, 1861–65." *Journal of American History* 70 (June 1983): 58–74.

Lebsock, Suzanne. *The Free Women of Petersburg: Status and Culture in a Southern Town, 1784–1860.* New York: W. W. Norton & Co., 1985.

Lepler, Jessica. *The Many Panics of 1837: People, Politics and the Creation of a Transatlantic Financial Crisis.* New York: Cambridge University Press, 2013.

Levine, Bruce. *Confederate Emancipation: Southern Plans to Free and Arm Slaves during the Civil War.* New York: Oxford University Press, 2006.

———. *The Fall of the House of Dixie: The Civil War and the Social Revolution That Transformed the South.* New York: Random House, 2013.

Linden, Glenn M., and Virginia Linden. *Disunion: War, Defeat, and Recovery in Alabama: The Journal of Augustus Benners, 1850–1885.* Macon, GA: Mercer University Press, 2007.

Linderman, Gerald. *Embattled Courage: The Experience of Combat in the American Civil War.* New York: Free Press, 1987.

Link, William A. *Roots of Secession: Slavery and Politics in Antebellum Virginia.* Chapel Hill: University of North Carolina Press, 2003.

"LYON, Francis Strother, 1800–1882." *Biographical Directory of the United States Congress.* bioguide.congress.gov/scripts/biodisplay.pl?index=L000542.

Martinez, Jaime Amanda. *Confederate Slave Impressment in the Upper South.* Chapel Hill: University of North Carolina Press, 2013.

Mathisen, Erik. *The Loyal Republic: Traitors, Slaves, and the Remaking of Citizenship in Civil War America.* Chapel Hill: University of North Carolina Press, 2018.

Matrana, Marc R. *Lost Plantations of the South.* Jackson: University Press of Mississippi, 2009.

Matt, Susan J. *Homesickness: An American History.* New York: Oxford University Press, 2011.

Mays, Ashley. "'If Heart Speaks Not to Heart': Condolence Letters and Confederate Widows' Grief." *Journal of the Civil War Era* 7 (September 2017): 377–400.

McIlwain, Christopher Lyle. *Civil War Alabama.* Tuscaloosa: University of Alabama Press, 2015.

McKiven, Henry M. "Thomas H. Watts, 1863–May 1865." In Samuel L. Webb and

Margaret E. Armbrester, eds., *Alabama Governors: A Political History of the State*, 73–75. Tuscaloosa: University of Alabama Press, 2001.

McPherson, James M. *Battle Cry of Freedom: The Civil War Era*. Oxford, UK: Oxford University Press, 1988.

———. *For Cause and Comrades: Why Men Fought in the Civil War*. New York: Oxford University Press, 1997.

———. *War on the Waters: The Union and Confederate Navies, 1861–1865*. Chapel Hill: University of North Carolina Press, 2012.

McPherson, James M., and James K. Hogue. *Ordeal by Fire: The Civil War and Reconstruction*. New York: McGraw Hill, 2010.

Mitchell, Reid. *Civil War Soldiers: Their Expectations and Their Experiences*. New York: Simon and Schuster, 1988.

Moore, Albert Burton. *Conscription and Conflict in the Confederacy*. New York: Macmillan Co., 1924.

Murphy, Sharon Ann. *Other People's Money: How Banking Worked in the Early American Republic*. Baltimore: Johns Hopkins University Press, 2017.

Murray, Williamson, and Wayne Wei-siang Hsieh. *A Savage War: A Military History of the Civil War*. Princeton, NJ: Princeton University Press, 2016.

National Institute of Neurological Disorders and Stroke. "Trigeminal Neuralgia Fact Sheet." www.ninds.nih.gov/Disorders/Patient-Caregiver-Education/Fact-Sheets/Trigeminal-Neuralgia-Fact-Sheet (accessed August 10, 2021).

National Park Service. *Civil War Soldiers and Sailors System*. www.itd.nps.gov/cwss/ (accessed August 31, 2023).

Noe, Kenneth W. *Reluctant Rebels: The Confederates Who Joined the Army after 1861*. Chapel Hill: University of North Carolina Press, 2010.

O'Brien, Michael. *Conjectures of Order: Intellectual Life and the American South, 1810–1860, Vol. 1*. Chapel Hill: University of North Carolina Press, 2004.

O'Sullivan, Lisa. "The Time and Place of Nostalgia: Re-Situating a French Disease." *Journal of the History of Medicine and Allied Sciences* 67 (October 2012): 626–49.

Ott, Victoria E. *Confederate Daughters: Coming of Age during the Civil War*. Carbondale: Southern Illinois University Press, 2008.

Owens, Thomas McAdory, and Marie Bankhead Owens. *History of Alabama and Dictionary of Alabama Biography*. Chicago: S. J. Clarke, 1921.

Park, Robert Emory. *Sketch of the Twelfth Alabama Infantry of Battle's Brigade, Rodes' Division, Early's Corps of the Army of Northern Virginia*. Richmond: Wm. Ellis Jones, 1906.

Patchan, Scott C. *The Last Battle of Winchester: Phil Sheridan, Jubal Early, and the Shenandoah Valley*. El Dorado Hills, CA: Savas Beatie, 2013.

———. *Shenandoah Summer: The 1864 Valley Campaign.* Lincoln: University of Nebraska Press, 2007.

Pfanz, Harry W. *Gettysburg: Culp's Hill and Cemetery Hill.* Chapel Hill: University of North Carolina Press, 1993.

Phillips, Jason. *Diehard Rebels: The Confederate Culture of Invincibility.* Athens: University of Georgia Press, 2010.

Potter, David M. "The Historian's Use of Nationalism and Vice Versa." *American Historical Review* 67 (July 1962): 924–50.

———. *The Impending Crisis: America Before the Civil War, 1848–1861.* New York: HarperCollins, 1976.

Power, J. Tracy. *Lee's Miserables: Life in the Army of Northern Virginia from the Wilderness to Appomattox.* Chapel Hill: University of North Carolina Press, 2002.

Quigley, Paul. *Shifting Grounds: Nationalism and the American South.* New York: Oxford University Press, 2012.

Rable, George C. *Civil Wars: Women and the Crisis of Southern Nationalism.* Champaign: University of Illinois Press, 1989.

———. *Fredericksburg! Fredericksburg!* Chapel Hill: University of North Carolina Press, 2002.

———. *God's Almost Chosen Peoples: A Religious History of the American Civil War.* Chapel Hill: University of North Carolina Press, 2010.

Rhea, Gordon C. *The Battles for Spotsylvania Court House and the Road to Yellow Tavern, May 7–12.* Baton Rouge: Louisiana State University Press, 1997.

Roberts, Alisdair. *America's First Great Depression: Economic Crisis and Political Disorder after the Panic of 1837.* Ithaca, NY: Cornell University Press, 2013.

Rogers, William Warren, Jr. *Reconstruction Politics in a Deep South State.* Tuscaloosa: University of Alabama Press, 2021.

Roper, Michael. "Nostalgia as an Emotional Experience in the Great War." *Historical Journal* 54, no. 2 (June 2011): 421–51.

Rothbard, Murray. *The Panic of 1819: Reactions and Policies.* Auburn: Ludwig von Mises Institute, 2007.

Rothman, Adam. *Slave Country: American Expansion and the Origins of the Deep South.* Cambridge, MA: Harvard University Press, 2005.

Rubin, Anne Sarah. *A Shattered Nation: The Rise and Fall of the Confederacy.* Chapel Hill: University of North Carolina Press, 2005.

Sacher, John M. *Confederate Conscription and the Struggle for Southern Soldiers.* Baton Rouge: Louisiana State University Press, 2021.

———. "The Loyal Draft Dodger? A Reexamination of Confederate Substitution." *Civil War History* 57 (June 2011): 152–78.

Salmon, John S. "Morton's Ford." *The Official Virginia Civil War Battlefield Guide.* Mechanicsburg, PA: Stackpole Books, 2001.

Saunders, Robert, Jr. *John Archibald Campbell: Southern Moderate, 1811–1889.* Tuscaloosa: University of Alabama Press, 1997.

Schantz, Mark S. *Awaiting the Heavenly Country: The Civil War and America's Culture of Death.* Ithaca: Cornell University Press, 2008.

Scott, Josephine. "The Wilson School." *State Normal Magazine* 8 (June 1904): 215–18.

Sears, Stephen W. *Chancellorsville.* Boston: Houghton Mifflin Co., 1996.

Severance, Ben H. *A War State All Over: Alabama Politics and the Confederate Cause.* Tuscaloosa: University of Alabama Press, 2020.

Sheehan-Dean, Aaron. *Why Confederates Fought: Family and Nation in Civil War Virginia.* Chapel Hill: University of North Carolina Press, 2007.

Sommerville, Diane Miller. *Aberration of Mind: Suicide and Suffering in the Civil War–Era South.* Chapel Hill: University of North Carolina Press, 2018.

———. "'A Burden Too Heavy to Bear': War Trauma, Suicide, and Confederate Soldiers." *Civil War History* 59 (October 2018): 23–48.

Starobinski, Jean. "The Idea of Nostalgia." *Diogenes* 14 (June 1966): 81–103.

Stevenson, Brenda. *Life in Black and White: Family and Community in the Slave South.* New York: Oxford University Press, 1996.

Stoker, Donald. *The Grand Design: Strategy and the U.S. Civil War.* New York: Oxford University Press, 2010.

Stoops, Martha. "Saint Mary's School." In *Encyclopedia of North Carolina,* ed. William S. Powell. Chapel Hill: University of North Carolina Press, 2006.

Taylor, Alan. *American Republics: A Continental History of the United States.* New York: W. W. Norton & Co. 2021.

Thomas, Emory M. *The Confederate Nation: 1861–1865.* New York: Harper & Row, 1979.

Thornton, J. Mills, III. *Politics and Power in a Slave Society: Alabama, 1800–1860.* Baton Rouge: Louisiana State University Press, 1978.

Todd, Richard C. "The Produce Loans: A Means of Financing the Confederacy." *North Carolina Historical Review* 27 (January 1950): 46–74.

Tracy, Susan J. *In the Master's Eye; Representations of Women, Blacks, and Poor Whites in Antebellum Southern Literature.* Amherst: University of Massachusetts Press, 1995.

Varon, Elizabeth R. *Appomattox: Victory, Defeat, and Freedom at the End of the Civil War.* New York: Oxford University Press, 2013.

Walsh, Chris. "'Cowardice Weakness or Infirmity, Whichever It May Be Termed': A Shadow History of the Civil War." *Civil War History* 59 (December 2013): 492–526.

Walther, Eric H. *William Lowndes Yancey and the Coming of the Civil War.* Chapel Hill: University of North Carolina Press, 2006.

Watson, Samuel J. "Religion and Combat Motivation in the Confederate Armies." *Journal of Military History* 58, no. 1 (January 1994): 29–55.

Weber, Jennifer L. *Copperheads: The Rise and Fall of Lincoln's Opponents in the North.* New York: Oxford University Press, 2006.

Weiner, Marli F. *Mistresses and Slaves: Plantation Women in South Carolina, 1830–1880.* Urbana: University of Illinois Press, 1998.

Wert, Jeffrey D. *From Winchester to Cedar Creek: The Shenandoah Campaign of 1864.* Mechanicsburg, PA: Stackpole Books, 1997.

Whitaker, Walter C. *Richard Hooker Wilmer, Second Bishop of Alabama: A Biography.* Philadelphia: George W. Jacobs & Co., 1907.

White, Jonathan W. *Midnight in America: Darkness, Sleep, and Dreams during the Civil War.* Chapel Hill: University of North Carolina Press, 2017.

Wilentz, Sean. *The Rise of American Democracy: Jefferson to Lincoln.* New York: W. W. Norton, 2005.

Wollaston, John. *Ann Gibbes (Mrs. Edward Thomas).* 1767. www.worcesterart.org /collection/Early_American/Artists/wollaston/ann/discussion.html.

Wood, Kirsten. *Masterful Women: Slaveholding Widows from the American Revolution through the Civil War.* Chapel Hill: University of North Carolina Press, 2004.

Woodward, Colin Edward. *Marching Masters: Slavery, Race, and the Confederate Army during the Civil War.* Charlottesville: University of Virginia Press, 2014.

Woodworth, Steven E. *While God Is Marching On: The Religious World of Civil War Soldiers.* Lawrence: University Press of Kansas, 2001.

Wright, John D. *The Language of the Civil War.* Westport, CT: Greenwood Press, 2001.

Wyatt, Susan. "Re: John Gaillard M. Judith Peyre, SC." www.genealogy.com/forum /surnames/topics/gaillard/72/.

Yerby, William Edward Wadsworth. *History of Greensboro, Alabama from Its Earliest Settlement.* Montgomery: Paragon Press, 1908.

INDEX

www.ingramcontent.com/pod-product-compliance
Lightning Source LLC
Chambersburg PA
CBHW021608130325
23451CB00002B/62